The REAL Jerry Lewis Story

Welcome to
The REAL Jerry Lewis Story
written by
Rick Saphire with Sheila Saphire

To Sheila & Rick —
Two of the NICEST
people I know —
love
Jerry

The REAL Jerry Lewis Story

The REAL Jerry Lewis Story

The cover picture is from the
the Joseph Lewis collection and was
photographed during the farewell appearance of
Dean Martin & Jerry Lewis at New York's
Copacabana nightclub on July 25, 1956

The REAL Jerry Lewis Story

Copyright 2024 by Rick Saphire

All rights reserved.
This eBook or any portion of it may not be reproduced or used in any manner whatsoever without the express written permission of the publisher except in the case of brief quotations in critical articles or book reviews.

Written and Designed by York Publications in the United States of America.

For more information, or to book an event, contact:
Admin@YorkPublications.com
Website: http://www.JerryLewis.com
Book design by Rick Saphire
Second Printing: September 4, 2024

Table of Contents

Table of Contents	6
Dedication	8
About the Author	9
Foreword by Gary Lewis	12
Preface: The Day the Clown Died	14
Family Matters	21
The Name Game	50
Friends & Lovers	73
The Pasqualina DiPalma Story	75
Patti & Jerry Lewis	87
The Judy Scott Story	104
Taking the Pledge	113
Let's Go to the Tote Board	139
Dean Martin & Jerry Lewis	165
Martin & Lewis: Un-vestigation	185
Jerry and Me on Network TV	205
The Catskills: My Alma-Matzoh	223
Essen, Fressen, and Take a Lesson	235
Jerry's Future "Lies" in the Catskills	240
I've Heard That Song Before	264
Relatively Speaking	267

The Suzan Lewis Story	288
Imitation, the Highest Form of Effrontery	303
The Real Gary Lewis Story	317
The Real Joseph Lewis Story: Think Pink Baby	342
Rick and Jerry Together Again	351
Show Business Is Like No Business	359
Marketing Jerry Lewis	371
A Capitol Idea	389
Germany Revisited	398
Bits & Pieces	417
Epilog: Jerry Lewis in a Nutshell	431
Acknowledgments	433

Dedication

To Gary Lewis,
a friend,
a theatrical client,
a talented superstar,
a good guy,
and a survivor.

About the Author

Author Rick Saphire was born in 1947, and his journey into the world of show business began at a remarkably young age. At five years old, he was already performing as a singer and dancer on stage in Newark, New Jersey, and at the bungalow colonies in the Catskill Mountains in upstate New York. His aunt's gift of a magic set for his 5th birthday sparked a lifelong hobby and became a central part of his early performances.

Rick Saphire as Jerry Lewis' protégé in 1965

When Rick Saphire was 15, he achieved the distinction of being the youngest professional comedian to date to appear on NBC's *Tonight Show* with guest host Jerry Lewis, who proudly dubbed Rick his protégé. Jerry Lewis was instrumental in securing a position for Rick on the social staff at Brown's Hotel in the Catskills for the 1963 summer season, which became a pivotal turning point in Rick's career as it provided him with valuable experience in the hospitality and entertainment industries. That was only the start, and Rick's association with the Brown family lasted longer than many marriages.

Working in the Catskill hotels, Rick quickly learned about the resort business and rose through the ranks to become a social director, comedy master of ceremonies, entertainment director, and respected comedian at prestigious East Coast hotels. Rick Saphire, a highly talented entertainer, is renowned for his quick wit, impeccable timing, and boundless creativity. He captivates audiences as a comedian, master of ceremonies, and guest speaker.

Rick Saphire, a man of many skills, followed in the footsteps of his uncle, Ernest D. Glucksman, who managed the legendary Jerry Lewis for over a decade. Rick has represented a long list of celebrities like entertainer Jerry Lewis, actress Margot Kidder, legendary actress Hayley Mills, comedian Rip Taylor, famous child-actor George "Spanky" McFarland, *Passions* star Juliet Mills, comedian Charlie Callas, rock 'n' roll icon Gary Lewis of Gary Lewis & the Playboys, superstar Mickey Rooney, actor Sir John Mills, and many others. Not content with just rubbing elbows with the stars, Rick also dabbled in radio, hosting both local and international programs. For years, Rick performed nostalgic shows for various audiences, including college campuses, theaters, and senior citizen organizations. In addition to his entertainment career, Rick was a businessman who owned and operated magic shops in Pennsylvania and New Jersey for 40 years.

Rick Saphire as Jerry Lewis' manager in 2005

Rick Saphire, who represented A-list celebrities for many years, often turned down requests for personal meetings with the stars, advising fans, "Admire your heroes and appreciate them for their work rather than for who you think they are because you will likely be disappointed."

When asked why he decided to write this book, Rick Saphire quipped, "I wasn't busy that day."

Foreword by Gary Lewis

Since the mid-1960s, I've been the proud leader and vocalist of the rock 'n' roll group Gary Lewis & the Playboys. Back in 1965, my music heroes were The Beatles. I was a dedicated fan, yet I didn't feel the slightest bit of remorse when I knocked them out of first place on *Billboard*'s Top 10 music charts with my first record release, "This Diamond Ring."

Between 1965 and 1966, my group had seven Top 10 songs. Success was a team effort. I had help from my producer and arranger and from Dick Biondi, who hosted a nationally syndicated radio program out of Pasadena, California. Biondi was not only instrumental in popularizing Gary Lewis & the Playboys, but he was a great guy. I would bring him promotional copies of my group's new singles, and he would immediately play them on the air, creating a demand for our music. Thanks to disk jockeys like Cousin Brucie (Bruce Morrow) of WABC Radio in New York City, our popularity grew from Coast to Coast.

What is interesting about my entertainment career is that I am just one member of a family show business dynasty that began in the 1920s. The Roaring Twenties had prohibition, gangsters, flappers, burlesque, and vaudeville. My grandparents, Daniel and Rachel Levitch, were entertainers on the vaudeville circuit, performing their "songs and snappy patter" under the stage names of Danny and Rae Lewis. My grandparents were married just over a year when their only child, my father, Jerome Levitch, was born. My dad would ultimately become known as Jerry Lewis.

While just a teenager, my father started his show business career as a record mime. During his 15-minute act, he lip-synced to popular records of the day while wearing outrageous costumes and contorting his face into numerous funny expressions. In 1944, while performing as an intermission act under the name of Jerry Lewis, my dad met a beautiful and talented big band singer named Esther Calonico, known professionally as Patti Palmer. My parents married the following year, and I was born and named Cary Harold Lee. At the age of two, my parents renamed me Gary, and eventually, I followed my unique path into the family's show business tradition.

The story of how the five of us became successful show business troupers and the scores of people whose lives we impacted and who impacted our lives is documented as never before in the pages ahead. Some of the facts in this book will seem like a fantasy, something that could only happen in the movies. However, author Rick Saphire proves, "Truth is often stranger than fiction." So, please fasten your seat belts and join me for the ride through *The REAL Jerry Lewis Story*.

Yours truly,
Gary Lewis

Preface: The Day the Clown Died

**Jerry Lewis picture personalized
to Ricky Saphire in 1957**

Show business was not on my mind on August 20, 2017. I was attending my friend's 60th birthday celebration at a lavish restaurant in my adopted hometown of Cherry Hill, New Jersey, along with my family, and all was right with the world. Hearing the tone on my cellphone that told me I had a text message, I checked it. It read: "Rick, I'm so sorry to hear about the death of your friend Jerry Lewis."

Like a flashback scene from a 1940s movie, I sat there in a fog while the voices and festive music surrounding me seemed very distant. My mind replayed a scene from 1953 when my mom, dad, sister Joanie and I vacationed in New York's Catskill Mountains. We met up with my Uncle Ernie, who invited us to go with him to the famous Grossinger's Hotel. Uncle Ernie escorted Joanie and me into the opulent dining room to meet his business associate. As we approached the table, I saw Jerry Lewis sitting there having lunch. He stood up to greet us, trying desperately to hold his prunes in his mouth while he wiped his hands on the fancy cloth napkin. I was six, and Jerry Lewis was my idol. As he stood up, he seemed to get taller and taller and taller. He seemed like a giant to me. After exchanging a few polite niceties, we left him to finish his prunes.

Who would have imagined back then that one day I might assume my uncle's role as Jerry Lewis' personal manager and travel the globe with him? The answer to that question is, "I did," and I did.

My flashback was interrupted when my wife asked me what was wrong. I must have looked pretty grim during the 30 seconds or so that I was thrust back into the past. I replied, "Jerry died."

I didn't want to cause a scene at Mark Haltzman's affair, but he came over to ask if I was okay. He then announced to his family and guests that Jerry Lewis, Rick's long-time friend and client, had just passed away. The room was in stunned silence for about 6 seconds, and then the party resumed without further interruption.

While a few people approached me to offer condolences, some attendees admitted they didn't realize Jerry Lewis was still alive.

Several days after the passing of the 91-year-old Jerry Lewis, I decided that this would be the right time to publish my memoirs about our relationship and his life and career.

From the time I was a child, my uncle, Ernest D. Glucksman, treated me like a son, always inviting me to join him when he was on the East Coast with his famous clients. Uncle Ernie knew I wanted to be in show business as I was fascinated with the entertainment industry. He also knew Jerry Lewis was my comedy hero. My parents were very supportive, especially my mother, who also had a background in the field of entertainment.

Starting at six years old, I was the proverbial "fly on the wall," present at many of the Martin & Lewis comedy performances onstage and privy to the Martin and Lewis drama backstage. When Dean and Jerry dissolved their act, Uncle Ernie became Jerry's personal manager and producer. As the years went by, both my uncle and Jerry were very helpful to me regarding my entertainment career. The newspapers referred to me as Jerry Lewis' protégé. When I was a 15-year-old comedy-magician, Jerry Lewis invited me to be his guest on *The Tonight Show* on July 6, 1962, B.C. (before Carson). Around that time, Uncle Ernie also became my personal manager. He often shared insider information and insights with me, as if he were dictating his own memoirs. I learned early on that there is a separation between an entertainer's theatrical persona and an entertainer's personal life. Based on the talks with my uncle and others involved in Jerry Lewis and his world, including Jerry himself, I learned quickly that significant disparities exist between the publicly circulated fabrications and the real Jerry Lewis story.

When people ask me why the world needs another book about Jerry Lewis, the answer is quite simple: *The REAL Jerry Lewis Story* contains a myriad of factual information regarding his life and career, much of which has never before surfaced in print. Previously published accounts about Jerry Lewis's rise to fame are urban legends created and disseminated by Jerry, his agents, and his publicists in order to provide him with an interesting theatrical past and to hide his personal past.

The details I share with the reader are based on private conversations, personal observations, and first-hand knowledge. Because of my relationship with Jerry Lewis, people often shared their Jerry Lewis stories with me. Some of these were funny, and some were disturbing. Many of the stories were the release of pent-up frustrations with this show business icon.

Due to our close family connections and our friendship, Jerry Lewis was often candid in his conversations with me. He talked about his childhood, his parents, his personal relationships, his opinions about other performers, and his varied business dealings, sharing intriguing excerpts of his life and his perspectives. Lots of his stories turned out to be mere babble, while many unbelievable things he shared were actually factual.

While conducting my research, I discovered evidence from historical documents, media broadcasts, archived newspaper and magazine articles, interviews, video clips, and photographs, dating back to the 1920s that prove truth is stranger than fiction. Much of my information comes from my direct conversations with Jerry. While managing an appearance for Jerry in Germany in 2005, I asked him about his highly publicized affair with Marilyn Monroe. His thoughtful answer was serious and cryptic, but he knew I would understand.

It has been widely reported that in the early 1940s, Jerry Lewis began his career working in the Catskill Mountains at Brown's Hotel in Loch Sheldrake, New York. Most accounts claim that Jerry worked there as both a busboy and social director. Legend has it that Brown's Hotel in New York was where Jerry Lewis created his record lip-sync act that launched his comedy career. The real story is far more compelling.

I am proud to share this captivating narrative as a tribute to one of history's greatest entertainers and, at the same time, in my opinion, the most contentious, exasperating, mean-spirited, angry, self-absorbed, frustrated, over-sensitive, fearful, creative, funny, and talented people I have ever known.

I fully understand people wondering why I, an ordinary person, would write an intense book about Jerry Lewis' life and career. Jerry Lewis played a crucial role in influencing my decision to enter the entertainment industry when I was a child. He significantly contributed to my career from my early years until just before his passing. Moreover, he had a close association with many members of my family. During Jerry's latter years, I was able to pay back some of his kindnesses by providing him with quality appearances that generated fees for him commensurate with Jerry's status as an international superstar. I will delve into these details in the upcoming pages.

I am profoundly grateful to Jerry Lewis. At 16, I worked at Brown's Hotel in the Catskills, where I met Sheila, my future wife. Years later, we were blessed with our devoted daughter, a healthcare professional, her accomplished husband, and our exceptional grandchildren.

I deeply believe that Jerry Lewis would have wanted someone to reveal the aspects of his life that shaped him, including the positive and negative elements. This book is not about painting a perfect picture but about presenting a true and honest composite of a complex individual. Without these uniquenesses, the character that Jerry portrayed on screen and in nightclubs from the mid-1940s to the early 1970s would not have emerged. Thus, I trust that Jerry's devoted fans will continue to hold him in high regard even after reading my candid depiction of his life.

Jerry Lewis' legacy of laughter will undoubtedly continue to bring joy to people from all walks of life for decades and even centuries to come. His body of work will have a lasting influence on new entertainers, who will also bring laughter and smiles to people worldwide. Jerry was truly one of the most gifted and entertaining individuals to have ever lived, leaving an indelible mark on the world. His impact is not just a fleeting moment of laughter but a lasting imprint on the field of entertainment.

The REAL Jerry Lewis Story

Family Matters

Four members of the Lewis family musical dynasty

Everything in life is a matter of...timing. And so it was with Jerry Lewis, that awkward kid from Newark, New Jersey, whose unprecedented rise to fame made him an internationally revered yet often reviled celebrity.

Because Jerry Lewis was such a dominant figure in the 20th century, little attention was paid to the other talented members of his family, such as his parents who were known professionally as singer Danny Lewis and his musical accompanist, pianist Rae Lewis. Jerry's wife was big band vocalist Patti Palmer. In the 1960s, Jerry's oldest son became the rock 'n' roll icon, Gary Lewis of Gary Lewis & the Playboys. Jerry Lewis was an entertainer, producer, and fundraiser, which brings the longevity of this talented dynasty to over 100 years. Honorary mention should go to others such as orchestra leader, dancer, and vocalist James DiPalma, whose stage name was Jimmy Palmer. Like the stars in the universe, all these talented luminaries aligned to create a constellation of enduring entertainment. Jerry Lewis did not become famous on his own. Family and fate paved the way for his rise to fame.

In the Beginning

The early 1920s marked the end of World War I, and the United States entered the Jazz Age with flappers, gangsters, and Prohibition. As the country's focus switched from the war abroad to the US economy, interest in records, spectator sports, and talking pictures grew. Radio, magazines, and newspapers turned sports figures, politicians, and entertainers into national celebrities.

Born in 1902, Daniel Levitch began earning a living as a crooner known as Danny Lewis. On January 25, 1925, Danny married Rachel Brodsky, a pianist from Russia, and 14 months later, on March 16, 1926, Danny and Rae became the parents of a baby boy, Jerome Levitch, who later became known as Jerry Lewis, the "King of Comedy."

My family's connection to Jerry Lewis began even before Jerry was born. In the 1920s, my mother, Rose Sober, known to her friends as Rosie, started her career in New York City as a stenographer and secretary for Leo Feist, Inc. This company controlled more than 80 percent of the music industry back then. As Feist's personal secretary, she established connections in the field and developed relationships with professional composers, writers, actors, musicians, singers, and theatre critics.

One of Rosie's close friends was a sports writer, turned entertainment columnist, Ed Sullivan, who had become a giant in the newspaper industry as a syndicated reporter in the days before TV. In 1948, he not only created but hosted his famous television variety program, *The Ed Sullivan Show* until 1971. Rosie and Ed Sullivan often had lunch together and enjoyed the camaraderie of the other show business professionals who joined them. Interested in helping Rosie get a better-paying job, Sullivan arranged for her to meet his friend, publisher and songwriter Irving Berlin.

Mother of author, Rick Saphire

My mother told me that Berlin lamented to her that he had written a song he couldn't publish because he needed a closing line. Admitting he occasionally suffered from writer's block, Berlin proceeded to sing the lyrics he had written: "Remember, we found a lonely spot, and after I learned to care a lot, you promised that you'd forget me not…"

"…But you forgot to remember," Rosie chimed in.

Although my mother rarely talked about her show business connections, she enjoyed telling me this story. Berlin must have liked her contribution because he kept it as the song's closing line. Published in 1925, Berlin's song "Remember" is still a popular standard.

Rosie's friendship with Irving Berlin grew. In 1927, she left Leo Feist and went to work for the Irving Berlin Music Company in Manhattan. As a key member of his secretarial staff, she was a stenographer, office manager, typist, switchboard operator, and Berlin's official "forger." Covers of Berlin's published sheet music often featured a picture of the artists associated with the particular songs and a facsimile of their signatures. Because the performers were not usually around when the sheet music originals were ready for printing, Rosie used her artistic skills to replicate the artists' autographs on the master page. Sheet music collectors worldwide probably have my mother's handiwork in their collections.

As Irving Berlin's "gal Friday," Rosie knew everyone: A-list entertainers, composers, lyricists, producers, and hopefuls looking for a lucky break, including Danny Lewis, a nice-looking young man with a smooth singing style. While Danny performed in supper clubs, resorts, nightclubs, and other venues as a singer, accompanied on the piano by his wife, Rae, he also maintained a day job, working at Newark, New Jersey's Broad and Market Music Store as a salesman, where he sold sheet music and records, often singing the tunes for the customers and pitching titles to retailers.

During the Roaring Twenties, sheet music was a coveted, trendy item. Along with the musical notes and lyrics, there were illustrations for ukulele chords, which eliminated the need to read music. Because the ukulele was affordable and easy to play, it was found in millions of homes and prevalent on college campuses.

After the Levitches became parents, they embarked on yet another career. Beginning in April 1926, Danny and Rae Lewis starred on a local radio program broadcast in the densely populated New York metropolitan area. Their radio show was heard on various stations for the next several years. An asset to Berlin's business, this now-seasoned singer could promote Berlin standards and introduce new Berlin tunes on his radio program, in his act, and in the music stores. At the same time, Danny had access to fresh Berlin material for his act. A picture of

Danny Lewis, "Newark's Own Songbird," appeared on Berlin's "When You and I Were Seventeen" East Coast sheet music cover. Through her job with Irving Berlin, Rosie knew Danny, who would bring his son to her office, and she saw the boy grow up. By the time Rosie left her job with Irving Berlin to raise a family, she  had witnessed Jerome Levitch transform into the young man the world would know as Jerry Lewis.

By 1933, Danny Lewis' radio career had ended, and he took to the road, performing at various hotels in the mountains and vacation resorts. Billed as the "Silver-Voiced Baritone," Danny Lewis appeared in vaudeville and burlesque houses from Baltimore to Buffalo throughout the 1930s. Vaudeville and burlesque simultaneously gained popularity in America after World War I. Whereas Vaudeville was "clean" in its artistic presentation of social class and behaviors, burlesque was "naughty," focusing on parody displayed by rowdy clowns, low-brow comedians, and scantily clad female dancers and singers. During the Great Depression, a 1933 dinner special consisting of soup, entrée of fish or meat, salad, dessert, and a beverage could be had at Hans Jaeger's Restaurant on Lexington Avenue in New

York City for $1.00. In those days, it cost $.25 to $.40 per ticket to see the strippers, laugh at the comics, and hear the singers, like Danny Lewis.

During the school year, when Danny and Rae were performing away from home, Jerry stayed with Rae's mother, Sarah, with whom he was close. After Grandma Sarah died in 1937, Jerry stayed with relatives. When his parents went to work as staff entertainers for the winter season of 1938-39 at the Hotel Arthur, run by Charles and Lillian Brown, in Lakewood, New Jersey, Jerry stayed in Newark with an aunt.

Danny Lewis had a polished style and could sing in different languages, including Yiddish, which appealed to Lakewood's Jewish clientele. In the evenings, Danny was the show's host who sang a few songs each night, as Rae provided the musical accompaniment. Danny charmed audiences with his snappy patter and his musical repertoire, which he could portion out throughout the week. In his role as the Master of Ceremonies, Danny would tell jokes, promote the activity schedule for the next day, and introduce other entertainers performing that evening. While not all of the guests had contact with the hotel owners, everyone knew the emcee, the hotel's goodwill ambassador. I understand the importance of Danny's position as a show host because, years later, I was the comedy emcee for several prominent hotels in the Catskills, including Brown's Hotel in Loch Sheldrake, New York.

Although Jerry's parents accepted work at the Hotel Arthur for the 1939-40 season, they were concerned about leaving their 13-year-old son home again with relatives as he was having problems at school. During his winter break, Jerry joined his parents in Lakewood. The Browns, who became friends with Danny and Rae, suggested that Jerry move to Lakewood and attend school with their daughter, Lonnie, who was a year his senior. Jerry and Lonnie had instantly become friends, like siblings, and for three seasons, they enjoyed the mild Lakewood winters together. Both of them were "hotel kids," and their friendship lasted a lifetime.

During the 1940-41 season, 14-year-old Jerry rekindled his friendship with Lonnie, who often played records in her hotel room to keep herself entertained by singing, dancing, and lip-syncing to popular tunes of the day. One day, Jerry happened to walk by her room, heard the music, knocked on her door, and entered. Lonnie continued her one-woman show unfazed. Jerry joined in the fun by mimicking her with exaggerated gestures and funny facial expressions. Within minutes, they were laughing uncontrollably as they saw themselves in the mirror, miming to the records. Little did they know that this was how comedian Jerry Lewis would get his start.

Danny and Rae were hired once again as the house act at the Hotel Arthur for the winter season of 1941-42. As part of their deal, the hotel provided room and meals for their 15-year-old son. Although Jerry was too young to be salaried, the Browns gave him a job working for tips as a tea boy, which suited his talents for clowning. Every late afternoon and evening, Jerry would serve tea and cookies to the guests in the lobby and dish out laughs with his zany antics. According to Lonnie Brown, nobody missed "teatime" because it was the best show in town.

The Hotel Arthur in Lakewood, New Jersey, where Jerry Lewis really got his start in show business

The following winter season, 16-year-old Jerry Lewis briefly worked as a soda jerk at Gottlieb's Drug Store in Lakewood. In those days, many pharmacies had counter service where the drugstore assistant would mix a flavored syrup with carbonated water and add a scoop or two of ice cream. Popular from the 1920s through the 1960s, the term soda jerk got its name because the handle of the soda fountain spigot had to be "jerked" down to dispense the soda water. Always looking for a laugh, Jerry found a way to make an ice cream soda the vehicle for comedy. Like a scene from a Charlie Chaplin movie, he took a scoop of ice cream intended for the soda glass, and with a flick of his wrist, he sent the creamy ball hurling toward the ceiling. On its descent, Jerry would catch the ice cream in the glass… sometimes. While some found his fun-loving silliness charming, the pharmacy owner was not amused. Had this been part of a Jerry Lewis movie, it would have been hilarious, but this was Jerome Levitch, and the humor escaped his boss. So, after the laughter died down, Jerry had to look for a new job.

During a conversation with Richard B. Wolpin, a Lakewood historian, I learned that Jerry was friends with Arnold Mohel, a Lakewood native. One day, while visiting Arnold's house, Jerry got himself into trouble. Despite being young, Jerry stood six feet tall and looked older than his years. It must have been quite a sight when Mrs. Mohel entered her living room to find Jerome Levitch jumping up and down on the couch, looking like a wild ape, a persona that later contributed to Jerry Lewis' stardom. Mrs. Mohel was not pleased and spoke to her son, banning the "meshugana" (Yiddish for crazy person) from ever coming into their house again. On the other hand, Jerry's hosts, the Browns, tolerated his antics as his clowning entertained their guests.

During the summer of 1942, the Browns and their staff went to the Catskills to manage the Hotel Ambassador, a summer resort owned by the Merl family in Fallsburg, New York. Danny and Rae Lewis joined them there. This season, Danny and Rae's deal included room and meals for their son, who had dropped out of school. As a favor to his parents, the Browns offered the 16-year-old a job as a busboy. This position was short-lived because Jerry was more interested in clowning with the guests and staff than assisting his waiter by serving beverages, appetizers, soup, and desserts, and carrying trays of dishes to and from the kitchen. Jerry's several hours as a busboy may have inspired his early interactions with Dean Martin, especially when he dressed up as a server and wreaked havoc with the audience. Unsuccessful as a busboy at the Hotel Ambassador, Jerry needed something else to do to keep him out of trouble, so the Browns offered him a position on the athletic staff. Within days of starting his new job, Jerry broke his arm playing baseball and could not perform his duties for the rest of the season.

In his first radio interview in 1948, Jerry Lewis boasted how he had been hired in 1942 to work at Brown's Hotel in Loch Sheldrake, New York, as a busboy, waiter, athletic director, social director, and entertainer, all at the same time. That was an impossibility. At 16, Jerry had no prior hotel experience and was never hired to be a waiter, social director, athletic director, and entertainer all at the same time, as he often claimed. His job at the Hotel Ambassador was a political appointment, not a job of merit. Jerry performed as a record mime in a few places in Lakewood, but he only worked as a busboy at the Hotel Ambassador in the Catskills for a few days.

As if attesting to an alibi, Jerry repeatedly stated he got his showbiz start at Brown's Hotel in the early 1940s, but this could not have been true since Charles and Lillian Brown did not open the doors to Brown's Hotel in Loch Sheldrake until the summer of 1944, and that summer, Jerry was on the road with his pantomime act and met Patti Palmer in Detroit.

Record Mime Jerry Lewis' first professional photograph signed to the girl who invented Jerry's record mime act

Irving Kaye, nicknamed Googs, worked as a bellhop for the Browns in Lakewood and was a local comedian. When Irving saw Jerry's record act, he saw his chance to become a theatrical agent. Kaye, a family friend, took a liking to young Jerry and eventually became his traveling assistant and companion.

Although Lonnie enjoyed performing the record pantomime act with Jerry, she really wanted to be a singer, but her parents did not want her to be involved in show business or with Jerry. Jerry's parents did not want him to pursue a career in show business either. However, Jerry had a mind of his own. With the help of the Browns and Googs, Danny and Rae acquiesced, agreeing to let Jerry pursue his dream. With time on his hands and support from family and friends, Jerry was free to contact agents and seek club dates, and Irving Kaye was eager to assist him.

Despite their best efforts, Jerry's club dates were few and far between. His pantomime act, like acrobats or animal acts, was called "a dumb act" because there was no dialogue. Lip-syncing and mugging to three recordings for 12-15 minutes, Jerry was often the middle act in a three-act show and paid $3 to $5 per performance. Record acts were so common they were considered "a dime a dozen."

Jerry was known to use his father's fame and name to gain access to the offices of booking agents in New York. Eventually, Jerry's father relented and introduced him to a powerful producer and promoter named Abner J. Greshler. Initially, Greshler auditioned Jerry as a favor, but he soon realized that he could use him to replace an act he was losing. Greshler decided to groom Jerry to take the place of comic Dick Wesson of the Wesson Brothers while he searched for a straight man to replace the other half of the comedy duo, Gene Wesson.

Over the Years

After my mother passed away, her youngest sister Selma, also known as Judy, disclosed some family secrets to me. Aunt Judy revealed that before my parents got married, Rosie and Ed Sullivan briefly had a more-than-casual relationship. According to Aunt Judy, Rosie and Irving Berlin also had a relationship, adding that when my mother left the Berlin office, he was melancholy and unproductive for some time.

My mother never name-dropped despite knowing many established artists who frequented Irving Berlin's office. However, she occasionally came face-to-face with people from her past. During a flight from Newark to Miami in 1960, my mother asked me to find out if a man seated a few rows in the back was Lanny Ross. When I spoke to him, he seemed surprised that a 13-year-old boy would know who he was. Instead of giving me a direct answer, he smiled, reached into his carry-on satchel, and pulled out a leather sheet music binder with "Lanny Ross" embossed in gold letters. I reported my findings to my mother, who got up from her seat to greet the man. "Hi, Lanny," she said. "I haven't seen you since the Berlin days."

Staring at her for a second, he responded, "Rosie." My mother took the empty seat next to Lanny and spoke to him for 15 minutes while I returned to my seat to think about how scared I was to fly. From their conversation, I discovered that Lanny Ross was not only a singer but also a songwriter and pianist.

One day in 1962, my mother and I attended a taping of Jackie Gleason's American Scene Magazine while it was still at the CBS studio in Manhattan. My mother's eyes lit up when Gleason announced his comedy star was Henny Youngman. After the show, she suggested we go to the stage door, which was out of character for her. As the stage door opened, several musicians walked out, holding their instrument cases. Then, a man walked out carrying a violin case. "Hi, Henny," Mom said. "How's your brother?"

"Lester? Oh, he's fine. Do we know you?" he asked.

My mother answered, "Yes, from the Berlin office."

They had not seen each other in over 20 years, and her reply sparked a memory synapse. Looking at her for a second, he squealed, "Rosie. How've you been?"

After introducing me to her old friend, she and Henny Youngman spoke with each other for a few minutes. On the bus ride home, I asked my mother how she knew Henny and his brother. "I knew him from the Irving Berlin office," she replied, "but I never really liked him. I did like his brother, Lester." Lester had been Henny's manager for 35 years. This was one of the few times my mother opened up and told me about the show business personalities she had known. As my mother described it, the Berlin office resembled an annex to the Friar's Club, an organization frequented by the "who's who" in show business. Though my mother mentioned that she knew Al Jolson, Milton Berle, Bing Crosby, and Eddie Cantor, she offered only a few details. She never mentioned any involvement with either Ed Sullivan or Irving Berlin, as Aunt Judy had claimed. Perhaps she forgot to remember.

After my mother left her job at the Berlin offices, she frequently traveled to Manhattan with my sister, Joanie, to visit Irving Berlin. Joanie fondly recalled "Uncle Irving," who would give her hugs and kisses and toss her about, letting her play his famous transposing piano. Mom, who had been acquainted with just about every big star in the industry, rarely spoke of the olden days. Every time I

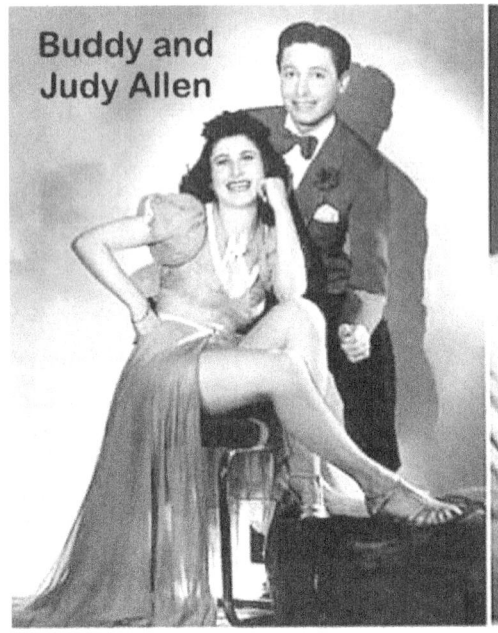
Buddy and Judy Allen

went into the City with my mother, we deliberately passed the building where she had worked with Irving Berlin for so many years. I often asked her if we could drop in on him, but we never did. She would gaze up wistfully at the building with a tear in her eye.

When my mother's youngest sister, Selma Sober, became a professional dancer, she changed her name to Judy. From the 1930s through the 1940s, she and Saul Browamik were dancing partners, performing as Buddy and Judy Allen. In 1935, they were hired by Ernest D. Glucksman, the entertainment director at the Flagler Hotel in the Catskills, to perform as a dance team. In those days, the duties of the director of entertainment ranged from hiring all of the athletic staff to producing theatrical extravaganzas for the hotel guests to enjoy. Some of these shows could compete with Broadway, and a few made it to the Great White Way.

On August 3, 1940, Judy and Buddy had a small Jewish wedding in South Fallsburg, New York, witnessed by Pearl and Murray Janofsky. If you don't recognize the name, Murray Janofsky, you might recognize his stage name, Jan Murray. Murray, a bright, popular young comedian, worked in nightclubs in New York City and at the hotels in the Catskills. When World War II ended, television started to light up its 8-inch, black-and-white screens, creating a demand for good-looking, well-spoken, polished hosts for variety and game shows, and Jan Murray was perfectly suited for this role.

Jan Murray's second wife, Toni Mann, was the beautiful lead chorus dancer at the Copacabana in Manhattan. Her looks were so striking that an artist drew a picture of her wearing a costume worthy of Carmen Miranda, and she became the iconic logo for that famous night spot. When 19-year-old Gary Lewis went to the Copa with Jan Murray's son, Howard, Gary met Toni. Unaware that Toni was his friend's mother, Gary politely flirted with her. Toni patted young Gary on the head and said he was very cute. I have no idea whether Gary remembers this story because I didn't run it by him, but he'll likely be surprised when he reads it in this book.

Howard Murray's father took him, his girlfriend, and his two sisters to see Jerry Lewis in a show. Afterward, they all went backstage. Jerry greeted them smoking a cigarette and wearing his robe with a towel around his neck. Howard was thrilled because Jerry remembered his sisters and him, which impressed his girlfriend. Going into another room for a few seconds, Jerry returned and presented Howard and the three girls with a wad of money totaling $10,000 in cash.

Jan Murray and Jerry Lewis

Incredulously, Jan Murray asserted, "What? Are you out of your fuckin' mind, Jerry? What are you doing?" Jerry matter-of-factly replied, "It's okay. I'll just gamble it away later."

Jan was startled at Jerry's bizarre generosity, and the kids were disappointed because they could not keep the money.

After the end of World War II, Buddy and Judy Allen decided to end their partnership, on stage and off. Uncle Buddy, who became a successful New York booking agent, once told me he may have divorced Judy, but he did not divorce the family. For several years, Uncle Buddy was my theatrical manager. Aunt Judy retired from dancing around 1950 and remarried a few years later to...guess who?... Ernest D. Glucksman.

Always interested in expanding his show business horizons, Ernest D. Glucksman accepted an offer in 1950 from an executive of the fledgling National Broadcasting Company's television division in New York to produce a show starring a good-looking singer from Ohio and a monkey-like character from Newark. Once a month, he would direct and produce *The Colgate Comedy Hour*, starring Martin & Lewis.

In 1952, my Aunt Judy married Uncle Ernie. Their marriage lasted till his death in 1979. Asked to be the Maid of Honor, Aunt Esther, the eldest of my mother's two sisters, was sent four airplane tickets so she, her husband, and their two children could fly from New York to California to attend this gala event. Theirs was a true Hollywood-style wedding with singer Carol Richards and actor and song-and-dance man Donald O'Connor as part

The REAL Jerry Lewis Story

[Photo labeled: Esther Cooper, Jerry Lewis, Judy & Ernie Glucksman, Donald O'Connor, Carol Richards]

of the wedding party. My cousin Joseph and his younger sister Bonnie were the only children in attendance, and they were bedazzled by the grandeur of this affair.

There were real diamonds at the wedding as far as the eye could see...and as far as the eye could see, they were real diamonds. The men looked debonair in their tuxedos, while the ladies in their exquisite gowns looked like princesses and smelled like flowers. After the ceremony, held in a beautiful small room, everyone moved to a larger reception area. Like a scene from a fairytale, there were lots of lovely people listening to the music and singers singing while the guests danced. The multi-layered wedding cake seemed to reach beyond the chandeliers. Cousin Joseph, who recognized many of the guests as celebrities he had seen in the movies and on television, sat next to comedic actor Ben Blue. When my five-year-old cousin Bonnie accepted an invitation to sit on the lap of one of the guests, he remarked to her, "You're cute."

To the surprise of everyone, she slapped him. "Don't speak to me that way," my little cousin cautioned the man. Everyone chuckled at her reaction to his compliment. Years later, Bonnie learned the man she reprimanded was television and movie star Tony Curtis.

Jerry Lewis attended the event with his wife, Patti. Despite having a cold, Jerry was determined not to miss the special occasion, especially since he was Best Man.

In 1953, when I was six years old, my Uncle Ernie, who was Jerry's executive producer, arranged for my sister Joanie and me to meet my idol, Jerry Lewis. As usual, my family was vacationing at a bungalow colony in the Mountains during the summer. What was unusual was that Uncle Ernie and Aunt Judy were also there, staying nearby at Brown's Hotel. Even more unusual was that Jerry was there, too, lunching at Grossinger's, one of Brown's competitors, and Dean Martin was nowhere in sight. My mother told me that, due to the dress code, she could not go into the dining room in shorts, at least, that was her excuse for staying outside with my father while Uncle Ernie escorted Joanie and me into the lavish hotel dining room.

Jerry Lewis
PACIFIC PALISADES
CALIFORNIA

June 11, 1957

Joan and Ricky Saphire
8 Tower Road
Livingston, New Jersey

Dear Joan and Ricky:

Thank you both for your very nice notes of June 3. I was happy to hear that the pictures arrived.

I am really looking forward to being with both of you in July, and will definitely plan on that informal get-together.

Patti, the children, Uncle Ernie, and Aunt Judy join me in sending our love to you.

Hoping to hear from you real soon, I am

Always,

Jerry

JL/jt

Photo labels: Judy Glucksman, Patti Palmer Lewis, Joanie Saphire
Photo by Herbert Saphire

Jerry Lewis was sitting by himself at a table. As he tried to keep some prunes from slipping out of his mouth, the movie star stood up to shake my hand. There was Jerry Lewis, looking as if he were 12 feet tall. That was our first meeting of the many times Jerry and I would be together.

As a child, I had the opportunity to watch Martin & Lewis perform live on countless occasions, unlike other kids who had to be satisfied loving the zany antics of Martin & Lewis from afar. I was present at many of their TV shows and club dates, and I was often backstage. Watching Martin & Lewis on TV's *The Colgate Comedy Hour* became a family tradition. Even though my uncle was the producer of scores of TV spectaculars, the *Colgate* show was our favorite. Now and then, we caught a glimpse of Uncle Ernie in a TV sketch or Aunt Judy dancing in the chorus. Of course, we always looked forward to seeing

Jerry, Joanie & Herb Saphire

"Produced and Directed by Ernest D. Glucksman" on the opening or closing credits.

Uncle Ernie often invited our family to Jerry's shows in New York. When we attended one of Jerry's appearances in 1953, my sister Joanie was introduced to his wife, Patti, who was sitting in the audience. Before meeting Jerry, Patti had been a well-known big band singer who performed under her professional name, Patti Palmer. After becoming pregnant with Jerry's child, she left the entertainment industry to focus on being a devoted wife and mother. Patti was one of those genuinely charming people whom everyone instantly liked.

In the summer of 1954, Joan and our father went to California to visit Uncle Ernie and Aunt Judy, and my sister spent a lot of time with Jerry and Patti. When Joan, who was 12 years old at the time, addressed Patti as Mrs. Lewis, Patti replied, "Please, Joanie, if you don't want me to call you Miss Saphire, don't call me Mrs. Lewis. Call me Patti." She then extended her arms to my sister and hugged her warmly.

Patti was firm but fair when disciplining the boys. When Gary did some risky flips off the diving board to impress my sister, Patti softly admonished him by saying he had been told to wait to do those dives until he had instructions on his form. As a typical ten-year-old boy, Gary Lewis made a face and responded with a long, drawn-out, "Oh, Mom."

Jerry and Patti were very close to my family in many ways. Jerry was not only a business associate but also a good friend of my Uncle Ernie. For years, Patti and my Aunt Judy were also close. Jerry used to send personally autographed pictures and personal letters to my sister Joanie and me. In June 1957, he wrote, "I am really looking forward to being with both of you in July and will definitely plan on that informal get-together." When Jerry heard that my sister was ill, he called her. I thought the world of Jerry back then. No entertainer could have had a more dedicated fan than I was. When Joanie visited the Glucksmans in Beverly Hills for the summer of 1958, she was included in the social events with the Lewis family.

I often wondered why Jerry Lewis paid me so much attention. Although I was a funny kid who sang, danced, and performed magic tricks, I was not more talented than other showbiz kids. Despite what my business card claimed, I was not really "The World's Greatest Magician." Furthermore, my uncle Ernie would never have asked Jerry to favor me, yet Jerry still helped me in many ways.

On one of my trips to my elementary school principal's office for clowning in class, he reprimanded me, saying, "You don't have to be the class clown just because you're Jerry Lewis' cousin." As I left Mr. Broomall's office, I was both relieved and confused: Relieved because I didn't really get into trouble, and confused because I really didn't know Jerry Lewis was my cousin.

Throughout the years, people from various walks of life have asked me if I was related to Jerry. When I visited Uncle Buddy at his New York booking agency, he wanted to know if I had been in touch with Jerry Lewis. When I told him I hadn't spoken to Jerry in a year, he responded, "Oh, I'm surprised, considering your relationship to him." For the moment, I thought I was sitting in my principal's office again.

Uncle Buddy became quite serious and inquired, "Rick, don't know how you're related to Jerry?"

"Uncle Buddy," I answered, "I really don't know what you're talking about."

My response surprised him. Sounding as if he had divulged something he should not have, he replied, "Rick, if you don't know how you're related to Jerry, it isn't my place to tell you. I don't want to change your opinion of your father." I found his response unsettling, but he quickly changed the subject to discuss my upcoming bookings at the Lambs Club and the New York Playboy Club. However, this was my second indication that there was more to these family matters than rumors.

The last time I saw my Aunt Judy in the early 2000s, I was representing Jerry Lewis, and he had asked me to extend an invitation to her to come to the telethon. She declined, saying, "Oh, no, I don't want to start that again." I understood her reaction because Aunt Judy and Uncle Ernie had tolerated Jerry's erratic behavior for years, and the dissolution of Ernie's business relationship with Jerry had been contentious and final. During a rare moment of introspection, Jerry admitted he regretted how things turned out with Ernie, and I shared this with my aunt. Acting impulsively on misinformation, Jerry accused my uncle of wrongdoing and refused to listen to the facts. After Uncle Ernie died, Jerry realized the truth, but Aunt Judy still preferred to keep her distance.

An incident occurred between Jerry and my father several years earlier at Brown's Hotel, which left a few scars and unanswered questions. I took the opportunity to ask my aunt if she knew anything about the argument. "Yes, I know all about it," she said, "and so does Jerry. He's talked about it for years." She added that Jerry would have done more for me, but as he put it, "If I take Ricky, I have to take Herb [my father]." I wanted to know what did happen between Jerry and my father, but all she was willing to offer was, "I can't tell you. It's not my place to change your opinion of your father."

People often remark that some of my gestures and facial expressions resemble Jerry Lewis. As a child, I always thought we were simply friends, but as I grew older, it became apparent that Jerry Lewis' involvement in my life was more than that. We met when I was a six-year-old boy, yet Jerry stayed in touch for years after that meeting, sending me letters and autographed mementos. He put me on network television with him when I was a relatively inexperienced teenage performer, stating on *The Tonight Show*, "Fifteen years old. I see myself all over again." Jerry Lewis and Uncle Ernie arranged for me to work at Brown's Hotel in Loch Sheldrake during the 1963 summer season, which became my career for quite a few years. In several newspapers highlighting my career, I was identified as "Jerry Lewis' protégé." Publicity articles in teenage fan magazines always connected me with Jerry Lewis. As per Jerry's instructions, Uncle Ernie set up an interview for me with Bessie Little, editor of Sterling Publications. Friendly and cordial, she told me how happy she was to meet me and that Jerry thinks the world of me, and had given her a quote to include in her article for *Teen Life Magazine*: "'Rick's a born comic...Right now, he's knocking 'em dead at Brown's Hotel in Loch Sheldrake in upstate New York, the place where I started my career. Rick's one of the most versatile entertainers I know. He's got a funny line of chatter as he does his magic tricks. And what poise...' America's Nutty Professor told us."

When Jerry asked me to become his theatrical representative, I gladly accepted, jokingly adding, "We'll keep it in the family." And Jerry agreed. Our relationship was much more than business. In addition to discussing bookings and traveling together across the United States and Europe, Jerry and I often called to tell each other jokes and funny stories. We also shared anecdotes about our mutual friends and individual family members.

When I finally asked Jerry, point-blank, how the two of us were related, he stopped dead in his tracks. As cryptic as the others had been, Jerry only said, "I'd rather not discuss it. It's not my place to change your opinion of your father," and then he changed the subject. Subsequently, my wife asked Jerry the same question and received the same reply.

My mother started working for composer and lyricist Irving Berlin in the 1920s, long before she met my father, Herb Saphire. She knew singer Danny Lewis and his son Jerome. In 1962, when my mother and I were with Jerry in New York City, awaiting his *Tonight Show* appearances, Jerry mentioned that his father would be joining us at NBC. Suddenly my mother remembered she had something pressing to do and left. It was strange that she wanted to avoid seeing Danny.

When Jerome Levitch began calling himself Jerry Lewis, he rustled the branches on his family tree, changing the surname of his heirs to Lewis; however, his ancestors remained Levitch. Today, as science and history have reached across time, a DNA test indicates that I am related to the Levitches and to the Lewises. When Jerry stated he did not want to tell me how we were related because he did not want to change my opinion of my father, was he talking about Herb or Danny or someone else?

The REAL Jerry Lewis Story

The Name Game

```
STATE DEPARTMENT OF HEALTH   297   BUREAU OF VITAL STATISTICS
PLACE OF BIRTH                                    334   2408
County  Essex                    State  NEW JERSEY   Registered No.
Township_____ or Borough_____ or
City  Newark     No. Clinton Private Hospital St. _____ Ward
        (If birth occurred in a hospital or institution, give its NAME instead of street and number.)
FULL NAME OF CHILD    Jerome Levitch
Sex of   | Twin,         | Number    | Legitimate? | Date of  6th
Child    | triplet,      | in order  | "Yes" or "No"| birth  16   Mar.   Tues, 19 26
Male     | or other?     | of birth  | Yes         |       (Month) (Day)      (Year)
         | (To be answered only in event of plural births.)
```

Jerome Levitch, the son of Daniel and Rachel Levitch, is known worldwide as Jerry Lewis, a professional entertainer and fundraiser. Jerry's original birth name was often disavowed even before he became a celebrity. The mystery surrounding Jerry Lewis' true identity and the origins of his showbiz career have long been a source of fascination for fans and critics alike. But the truth is even more intriguing than any fictional account. My research has unearthed unsettling details about Jerry Lewis' early life. However, this is *The REAL Jerry Lewis Story,* and it depicts a man with faults and attributes, aliases and alibis, all contributing to the entertainment legacy that this superstar brought to the world.

There are differing descriptions of Jerry Lewis' childhood activities. Jerry's parents were professional entertainers, performing under the stage names Danny and Rae Lewis. While Danny was a charming master of ceremonies and vocalist, Rae, an accomplished pianist, was his accompanist. In some interviews about his youth, Jerry claimed he traveled extensively with his parents and saw their act often. However, Jerry's parents were local performers who worked close to home at numerous

© 2024 Rick Saphire

Manhattan, Brooklyn, and Newark radio stations, vaudeville theatres, and nightclubs. From the late 1920s into the mid-1930s, Danny and Rae had their own radio show in New York City.

Jerry's living arrangements during the school year were somewhat ambiguous. On occasion, he mentioned living with his grandmother and other family members while his parents were on tour. However, he later expressed frustration over being transferred from school to school as he traveled with his parents, which seemingly contradicted his previous statement. Danny and Rae were primarily an East Coast act with occasional short-term work in upstate New York and Canada. When Danny performed at burlesque houses, Rae was not on the bill, and Jerry would not have been permitted to attend those shows. Burlesque houses in the 1930s and 40s often featured explicit content, in which the MC and comedians had to perform "blue" material (dirty jokes) or risk being booed off stage, making it unlikely that young Jerry would have been present. During several winter seasons, Danny and Rae were the house act at the Hotel Arthur in Lakewood, New Jersey, and during the summer season, they appeared at hotels in the Catskill Mountains. Whenever Jerry accompanied them on these occasions, it was during winter break or summer vacation, and Jerry remained enrolled in his hometown school.

Jerry said that while growing up, he was closest to his mother's mother, Sarah, crediting her with being the only family member who understood and accepted his unorthodox behavior and mannerisms. In memory of her deceased husband, Joseph Brodsky, Grandma Sarah nicknamed her grandson Joey, which is what some friends and family called him. Jerry often spoke about living with his loving grandmother while his parents were on the road, but he rarely mentioned that Grandma Sarah had remarried, and he was also supervised by his step-grandfather, whom he feared.

So, how did Jerome "Joey" Levitch become Jerry Lewis? Several media accounts of Jerry's early attempt at show business suggest he initially called his record pantomime act "Joey Levitch and His Hollywood Friends." However, those aftermarket reports were likely generated from the same source: Jerry Lewis. If he ever used the name "Joey Levitch," it must have been when he performed for a local fundraiser, a school assembly, or a private function because there is no indication that Jerry ever used the name "Joey" professionally.

In several interviews, Jerry mentioned attending from seven to more than a dozen schools due to his parents' need to travel with their vaudeville act, but the exact number differed in each interview. Mathematically, he would have had to change schools at least once a year, and there is no corroborating evidence to support his claim. Since he was able to stay with his grandmother or other relatives, there was also no need for him to switch schools. School records indicate that Jerome attended Union Avenue Grammar School in his Newark neighborhood. Despite Jerry's claim that he was left back when he was 11 years old, he finished his primary schooling on time, along with his peers, and was promoted. After completing eighth grade in June 1940, he began ninth grade in September 1940 at the highly-rated Weequahic High School in Newark, New Jersey. However, there is more to Jerry's educational background than meets the eye. As a result of his delinquent behavior, Jerome Levitch transferred schools locally.

Within the pages of forgotten history lies an enigmatic tale of a teenage boy, who attended several different schools. Although he claimed to have transferred schools because of his parents' work, that was not the case. Jerry repeatedly got himself into trouble. At the tender age of 14, Jerome Levitch was expelled from Weequahic High School in ninth grade. Using a relative's address, Daniel Levitch enrolled his son in the Boys' Vocational School in the nearby city of Irvington on September 9, 1940. This was a short-lived arrangement, lasting only 13 days due to Jerome Levitch's misconduct. On September 26, 1940, Daniel Levitch moved his son Jerome out of the vocational school. The next day, on September 27, 1940, he registered his son, Jerome Levitch, under the alias of Jerry Lewis. Jerry's tenure at Irvington High School was doomed. Six months after transferring there the 15-year-old was expelled.

As an adult, Jerry admitted to his disruptive behavior and expulsions as a student, but he distorted the facts. In retrospect, he portrayed himself as a type of antihero who defended the honor of his ancestors against antisemitism.

Although Jerry expressed a dislike for school, he received passing grades for most of his first term at

Irvington High School: English 70, Science 62, History 70, Algebra 70, Physical Training 83, and Print Shop 72. In Jerry's own words, he said, "I was an average student, verging on stupid."

What led to Jerry's dropping out of school? What secrets was he hiding? Until now, there have been many unanswered questions, conflicting sordid details, and contradictions about the early life of comedian and actor Jerry Lewis, leaving fans and historians alike wondering about the truth behind his youth. In November 1940, the socially insecure 14-year-old Jerome Levitch, who at the time had no act, no agent, no prospects, and no need for a stage name, applied for and received a Social Security Card using the fake name of Jerry Lewis. However, just as Superman and Clark Kent were the same under the cloak, Jerry Lewis and Jerome Levitch were one and the same.

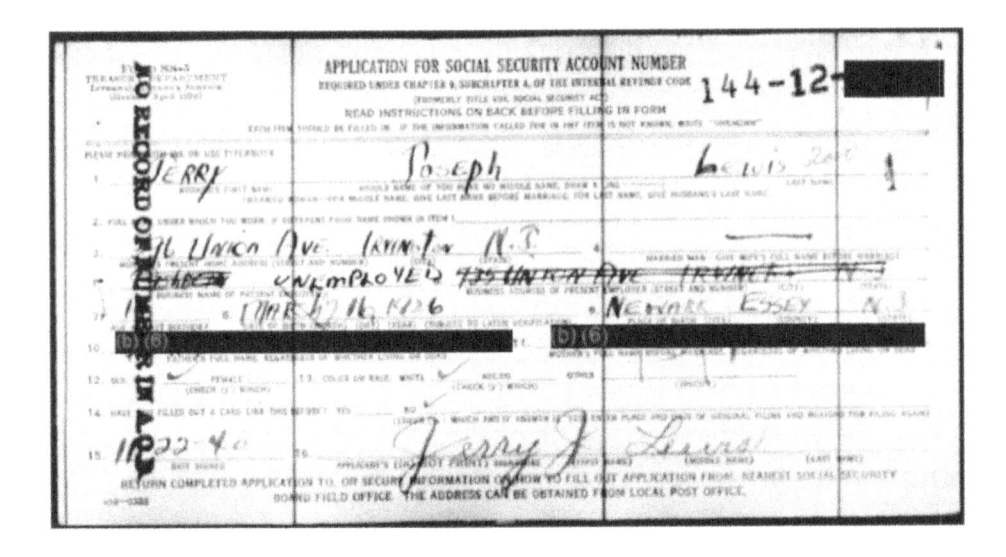

Despite using the aliases of "Joseph Levitch" and "Joseph Lewis" to cover his tracks, "Jerry Lewis" was always Jerome Levitch. His Social Security Card application might have been the first time Jerome intentionally hid his identity on an official document, but it was not the last. In January 2000, he filled out an FBI fingerprint document, containing an entry that stated Jerry Lewis was known as Joseph Levitch. The use of fake names and aliases adds to the intrigue surrounding his life.

It's not that he hated school; it was just the principal of the thing

By the 1980s, Jerry Lewis' health and career were on the decline, and he shifted his focus from being funny to being controversial. According to Jerry, his expulsion from Irvington High School on March 21, 1941, was a dramatic one. Reminiscent of Julius Kelp in *The Nutty Professor*, Jerome Levitch caused an explosion in the chemistry lab. Jerry's science teacher then marched him into the principal's office.

In the 1980s, Jerry gave interviews in which he vividly recounted how his principal had made an ethnic slur, and in a fit of rage, Jerry retaliated by punching the man in the mouth. Jerry bragged that the force of the blow caused the administrator to stumble and crash backward through a large plate-glass window, as he fell to the ground below. Jerry admitted he was expelled because he broke his principal's jaw and/or collarbone, depending upon the interview.

Feeling confident he would not be prosecuted for an assault he committed 40 years earlier as a minor, he talked about this incident to get publicity for himself. Reveling in the attention he received every time he openly confessed to his wrongdoing, Jerry usually embellished his story. Although there is no statute of limitations on involuntary manslaughter, Jerry told his tale as a preemptive defense in case he was ever questioned about it.

Jerry Lewis was seemingly proud of his assault. On October 23, 1982, Christian Williams of *The Washington Post* quoted Jerry Lewis as saying, "I did it and was expelled for it. It wasn't meant to be that violent, but it really did some damage. And it was wonderful." Around this same time, Jerry was videotaped in another interview, boasting, "I hit him [Principal Haertter] and knocked him through the back bay window. He could have been killed, and I could have been one of the first young Jews to go to the chair in New Jersey." For the man, known as a comedian and a humanitarian, this was a bizarre admission, and he exhibited no remorse for what may have been a fatal attack. During a video interview with Robin Leach in November of 1986, Jerry justified this 1941 assault by accusing his principal of being "a part of the Nazi Bund Party."

The REAL Jerry Lewis Story

Jerry Lewis often changed the details of his attack on Edward D. Haertter, although some aspects remained constant. Jerome Levitch was a troubled kid and a troublemaker. Like the cartoon character Bart Simpson, nothing was ever Jerry's fault. Jerry was adept at turning a story around so he became the victim, if not the hero. After causing physical harm to Principal Haertter and damaging school property, Jerome Levitch was expelled from Irvington High School. Despite justifying his assault on the principal as a reaction to an antisemitic comment, Jerry's anger must have been brewing beneath the surface for a while to erupt into such physical violence.

After his expulsion from high school, Jerry was slated to attend a vocational school, one step away from a reformatory. However, this is where the trail of his schooling goes cold. There is a 1941 class picture from Lakewood High School in New Jersey, suggesting Jerry's parents accepted Charles and Lillian Brown's offer to have their son live with them and go to school with Mrs. Brown's daughter, Lonnie. He apparently completed ninth grade in Lakewood, began tenth grade there, and then dropped out of school as soon as he turned 16, which is likely when he became a soda jerk.

Once out of school, Jerry had little contact with anybody from Irvington High School and focused his attention on developing a career in show business as a record mime. Being a pantomimist meant Jerome Levitch could travel, change his name, and hide his real identity under wigs and hats while using props and lip-syncing to records.

Years later, Jerry explained he was comfortable being a mime since he was uncomfortable speaking to crowds. I never believed that, but doing a "dumb act" was a way for Jerry, who had a very piercing, distinctive voice, to remain incognito. He wanted to keep Jerome Levitch, alias Joseph Levitch, out of the public eye and ear. In my opinion, after learning that his principal had died the year following the assault, Jerry's paranoia took over, and he worried that his attack might have caused or at the least contributed to Mr. Haertter's demise. He did not feel remorse because he may have killed a man, but he did feel fear because he might be implicated in Principal Haertter's death.

Jerry Lewis had been my hero. Unearthing this information was unsettling to me, but this is *The REAL Jerry Lewis Story*.

Edward Daum Haertter, who was a United States veteran of World War I, had been the principal of Irvington High School since 1922. According to the New Jersey State Archives in Trenton, the doctor, who, for a year, treated

Mr. Haertter for stomach sarcoma, signed his death certificate on April 20, 1942. Although my research was intended to exonerate Jerry, the findings are inconclusive. While Jerry's attack on his principal, who was already suffering from terminal disease, may or may not have contributed to Haertter's death, Jerry believed it did.

When Patti and Jerry's first son was born in 1945, they lived in Newark, New Jersey. To distance himself from the Haertter incident, 19-year-old Jerry named his son Cary Lewis, cutting his family off from the branches of the Levitch family tree.

On October 27, 2000, nearly 60 years after the altercation, Jerry Lewis felt emboldened and expounded on the attack, seemingly taking pleasure in recounting the assault as if it were justified, arguing that his principal made an antisemitic comment that "hit a nerve." Jerry Lewis retold this anecdote to screenwriter, and producer Sam Denoff in a video interview for the Academy of Television Arts & Sciences. Masking the severity of the situation with comedy, Jerry assumed a German accent, misstating his principal as Alfred Hurder. In this interview, six decades after the event, Jerry recapped how he punched the man in his mouth, and notched it up by adding, "Haertter has great-grandchildren that I'm trying to find. I want to deck a few of them, too." Jerry confessed to his involvement without fear of prosecution, but not without fear of persecution.

Ironically, on a 1955 program, Jerry Lewis addressed his own guilt as he wrote and recorded his own special material:

This is Jerry Lewis. I don't suppose there is any one of us who can't look back to our childhood and remember at least one time when we did something wrong and got away with it. Maybe it wasn't a very serious thing, sneaking into a movie or stealing an apple off a fruit stand. And yet, after we'd done it, we were left with a funny sense of guilt. Even though we hadn't been caught or even suspected of any wrongdoing, there wasn't going to be any punishment: No allowance cut off the next month. No big speech and then go to bed without your dinner. Nothing.

We got away with it. And yet, that was the day when we learned once and for all, that nobody gets away with anything. Not really. Because no matter how many people don't know when we've done something wrong, WE always do, and our conscience won't let us forget it.

In my opinion, Jerry was thinking about his assault on the principal, and in this case, his conscience would not let him forget it.

Name Changes

Jerry Lewis was known to fabricate stories about his background to amuse himself, entertain others, and distract from the truth. In 1942, Jerome Levitch performed a record mime act as Jerry Lewis for $3 to $5 a show at some small venues in Lakewood, New Jersey.

Years later, Jerry claimed he originally wanted to use the name Joe Lewis or Joey Lewis. He felt he could not use the name Joe Lewis because it sounded like the 1937-1949 Heavyweight Champion of the World. And, if he called himself Joey Lewis, he thought he might be mistaken for veteran comedian Joe E. Lewis, who added an "E" to his name to avoid being confused with the boxing champ. Of course, Jerry Lewis wouldn't have been confused with anyone if he used the name on his birth certificate: Jerome Levitch.

During the next two years, Jerry crafted his mime act, working wherever he could. Abner J. Greshler, a theatrical agent and promoter, was in need of a new act to replace the Wesson Brothers, who had been a mainstay of his corporate productions. After Jerry auditioned, Greshler decided to groom him as his replacement for comedian Dick Wesson. As a successful talent manager and show producer, Abby Greshler was a hard-working, creative representative who looked out for his singers, dancers, novelty acts, musicians, comedians- and for himself. Greshler's forte was producing variety shows for private business organizations. Some of the venues paid him $100,000 or more for these entertainment extravaganzas. The buyers did not know how much the individual performers were being paid for their services, and the salaried performers did not know how much Greshler was paid for these entertainment packages. The corporate shows were not advertised to the public, and often, the acts were paid in cash, which left no paper trail.

President Roosevelt signed the Selective Service Training and Service Act of 1940, which was the first peacetime conscription in the history of the United States. It required all men between 21-35 to sign up for the peacetime draft. When Dean Martin registered for the draft, he provided his professional name, Dean Martin, as well as his legal name, Dino Paul Crocetti, on his registration application to make himself available should he be called to active duty. On October 16, 1941, shortly before the United States officially entered World War II, Crocetti, age 23, filed his draft registration application in Dayton, Ohio, and listed his mother, Angela, as "the person who will always know his address." Identifying his employer as Sammy Watkins Orchestra, he provided his address as the Hollenden Hotel in Cleveland, Ohio, where he was staying.

After the December 7, 1941, attack on Pearl Harbor, Congress passed legislation requiring all men between the ages of 18 and 64 to register for the military. Millions of Americans were drafted or volunteered for service in the armed forces and served their country with pride. Hollywood celebrities were no exception and enlisted for active duty. Actor Peter Falk, best known as the star of TV's *Columbo*, joined the Merchant Navy and served as a cook and busboy despite having one glass eye. Because actor Paul Newman was colorblind, he was unable to enlist as a pilot but served as a radioman and gunner instead.

Jerry Lewis claimed exemption from military service due to a punctured eardrum and a heart murmur, but he contradicted himself in a 1993 interview with Sally Jesse

Raphael. When asked about having had his first heart attack at age 30, Jerry Lewis replied, "I had a heart murmur. That's when they suspected that I might have had a problem, but it was nothing of any consequence." A punctured eardrum was not a military exemption in 1944. The real issue is that Jerome Levitch did not enlist for military service, making it impossible to examine his medical records.

In 1944, during wartime, conspiring to generate a false and misleading draft registration to evade serving in the military was a serious violation of federal laws and a risky gamble taken by Jerome Levitch and Abner J. Greshler, who did not want to risk losing an important entertainer to the draft.

By 1944, America was fully entrenched in World War II, and Jerome Levitch, age 18, was required, by law, to register with the Selective Service. The young record pantomimist was just the right age to be called up for active duty. A scheme was hatched to hide the talented teenager from the World War II draft. The plan was for Jerome Levitch to use the false name of Jerry Lewis on his Selective Service Application, just as he had previously done on his transfer record out of Irvington High School and on his Social Security Card. Greshler booked Jerry into the Warner Brothers' Earle Theatre in Washington, D.C., where he appeared with other performers at the opening of Frank Sinatra's movie, *Higher and Higher.*

Step 1- Jerry went to his official Selective Service office, Local Board No. 21 at 1 East 44th Street in New York and picked up his pre-stamped, blank draft registration card.

Step 2- Although Jerry had 30 days from his 18th birthday to register with the Selective Service, he brought the blank New York draft registration card to Washington, D.C., where it was filled out on March 18, 1944, two days after his 18th birthday. He presumably did not want to fill out the application in Manhattan where somebody might recognize him as Jerome Levitch. On the draft document, Jerry listed his residence as the Hotel Holland on West 42nd Street in Manhattan and Greshler's office at the RKO Building, Radio City, New York, as his place of employment. However, an agent's office is not typically where a performer works. He also named Abner J. Greshler as the person who would always know his whereabouts. By not listing his parents, Daniel and Rachel Levitch as contacts, Jerry eliminated any connection to his real family name on his draft registration card.

Step 3- Next, Jerome Levitch, using the alias of Jerry Lewis, submitted his draft application in person to the draft board in Washington, D.C., and signed it "Jerry Lewis." Because Jerry's draft application was from New York, the registrar in Washington could not countersign it, so this essential line was left blank. When the D.C. office sent the resulting draft card to Abby Greshler's Manhattan business address, Jerry Lewis received what appeared to be a legitimate draft card to carry in his wallet as required by law, but this card could not be legitimate if issued to a fake name, Jerry Lewis.

Federal law mandated that local draft boards be notified of any changes in the status of military registrants. However, neither the draft board in Washington, D.C., nor his local draft board in New York was informed when Jerome Levitch got married and moved to New Jersey because, by design, there was no such person in the military named Jerome Levitch.

Following the end of World War II, all men in the United States were required to re-register for the draft, even if they had served or were previously turned down by the Selective Service. When Jerome Levitch signed up this time, he listed Mrs. Jerry Lewis, 10 Lehigh Avenue, in Newark, New Jersey, as his contact and Hal Wallis at Paramount Pictures in Hollywood, California, as his employer. This second Selective Service System

Registration Card indicates that "Jerry Lewis" was rejected from serving in the armed forces back on May 8, 1944, yet there were no records indicating that "Jerry Lewis" suffered from any disqualifying disabilities, and there were no records of Jerome Levitch at all. To put it in simple terms, the whole thing appears to have been a fraud.

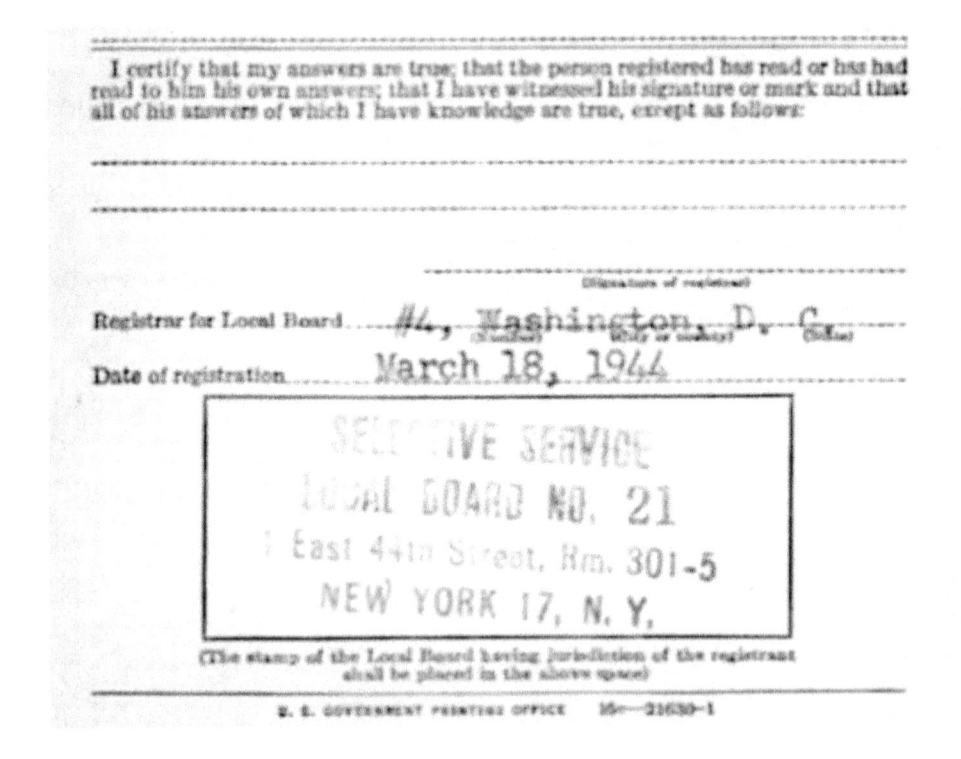

```
I certify that my answers are true; that the person registered has read or has had
read to him his own answers; that I have witnessed his signature or mark and that
all of his answers of which I have knowledge are true, except as follows:
```

Registrar for Local Board #4, Washington, D. C.

Date of registration March 18, 1944

SELECTIVE SERVICE
LOCAL BOARD NO. 21
East 44th Street, Rm. 301-5
NEW YORK 17, N. Y.

(The stamp of the Local Board having jurisdiction of the registrant shall be placed in the above space)

Bogus Names

Controversies over Jerry Lewis' real name date back to his teens when he was a fledgling entertainer in New

York. Abner "Abby" J. Greshler, a theatrical agent and employer, was not only involved with Jerry's career, but he profoundly influenced Jerry's life. Continuing to use his assumed name on government documents and disavowing his real name, Jerry sought to be known as Joseph Levitch. In sketches, Jerry often referred to his partner Dean Martin, born Dino Paul Crocetti, as Pauly. In return, Dean Martin publicly and frequently teased Jerry Lewis about his name, calling him "Germ." Dean's moniker for Jerry went unquestioned since they always made up names for each other. In reality, though, this nickname was a verbal contraction of Jerome's legal name: Jer'm, which Dean pronounced as "germ." For the rest of his life, Jerome Levitch's mission was to convince the world that his given name was Joseph.

In TV comedy sketches, in his movies, and on the radio in the 1950s, Jerry sometimes referred to himself as Gerald Lewis or Joseph Levitch. During an early comedy bit on TV, Dean and Jerry are in a flashback, telling how they met as children. In this routine, they introduce themselves as Paul Crocetti and Jerome Levitch. This was the only time I recall Jerry using his real name. Jerry then quips, "I can one day see our names up in lights: Martin & Lewis." In the 1960 film *The Bellboy*, Jerry plays an inept bellhop and also makes a cameo appearance as himself, an egotistical, arrogant celebrity. The scene was funny except to people who knew Jerry Lewis as an egotistical, arrogant celebrity. The closing credits include "Joe Levitch," as if an actor with that name played the real Jerry Lewis. It was an inside joke. The star toyed with his name in the 1961 movie *The Errand Boy*, produced by Ernest D. Glucksman and written by Bill

Richmond and Jerry Lewis. As another inside joke, "Joseph Levitch" subtly and briefly appears on a billboard in a scene. Jerry played different roles in *Hardly Working*, and in the closing credits, the character of the little old lady portrayed by Jerry Lewis is attributed to Joseph Levitch. The media described this as Jerry's joke because that supposedly was his real name. However, the joke was on the media since Jerry's name at birth was Jerome Levitch.

It is common for entertainers to legalize their professional stage names. In the case of Joseph Levitch, however, who later became known as Jerry Lewis, it was unclear how "Joseph" could legally change his name as his legal name was Jerome Levitch. On March 5, 1948, Hofmann & Katz, a New York law firm, filed a petition with the New York City Court on behalf of Mr. and Mrs. J. Levitch, based on misinformation, to legally change Joseph Levitch's and Esther Levitch's names to Jerry Lewis and Patti Lewis, respectively. The Court was also asked to change Levitch's two-year-old son's name from Cary Levitch to Gary Lewis, but the child was not named Cary Levitch.

Knowingly and willfully making false, fictitious, or fraudulent statements or misrepresentations while under oath may be a felony under the Federal Criminal False Statement Act. Purposely providing wrong and misleading information to a judge under oath is, at minimum, contempt of court. In this instance, the court was being asked to change one fake name for another.

```
                        AT a Special Term, Part II of the
                        City Court of the City of New York,
                        Held in and for the County of New
                        York, at the Courthouse, located
                        at 52 Chambers Street, in the
                        Borough of Manhattan, City of New
                        York, on the /5 day of March,
                        1948.

P R E S E N T:
            HON.  Henry S. Schimmel
                         Justice

- - - - - - - - - - - - - - - - - - - - - - - -

In the Matter of the Application of

JOSEPH LEVITCH and ESTHER LEVITCH, his wife,
and CARY LEVITCH, an infant, by

JOSEPH LEVITCH and ESTHER LEVITCH, his natural      140/48
guardians,

for leave to change their names to

JERRY LEWIS, PATTI LEWIS and GARY LEWIS,
respectively

- - - - - - - - - - - - - - - - - - - - - - - -
```

On April 24, 1948, based on false information, Jerry's attorneys and the court changed his fake name from Joseph Levitch to Jerry Lewis. There are no court orders indicating that Jerome's legal name at birth was ever changed to Joseph. This means that Jerry Lewis' legal name from his birth in 1926 until his passing in 2017 remained Jerome Levitch. In the end, Jerome Levitch signed his will with a name that was never legally his.

Many published reports state that the first child of Jerome and Esther was named Cary Levitch because his mother was enamored with actor Cary Grant, but later his first name was changed to Gary. These reports are inaccurate. On July 31, 1945, the future rock 'n' roll star was born. The next day, the New York Department of

Health generated his birth certificate, stating the baby boy was named Cary Harold Lee Lewis. Yes, Lewis, not Levitch. Was Jerry trying to give his son a stage name for a birthday present? In my opinion, Jerome wanted to disassociate himself, his wife, and his son from the Levitch family name because he feared involvement in the death of his principal. Whatever his motive, inconsistencies exist.

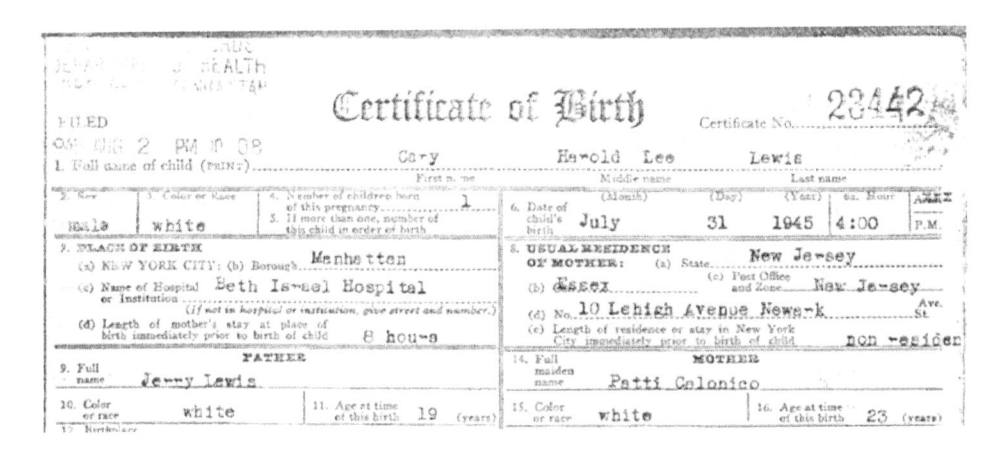

From the Bureau of Records, Department of Health City of New York, Cary Lewis' Certificate of Birth states:

- The baby's birth certificate names him as Cary Harold Lee Lewis, thus eliminating any record of the child's connection to his paternal ancestors, who were all named Levitch.
- The baby's father's real name was entered as Jerry Lewis, but his real name was Jerome Levitch.
- The New York Bureau of Records lists the baby's mother's maiden name as Patti Calonico, but her real name was Esther Calonico, not Patti.

- The parents entered the date of their marriage as November 2, 1944, but their New York Marriage Certificate proves they were married on April 30, 1945.

Jerome Levitch often skirted the law as he sought to disassociate himself from his real identity, especially after his attack on his high school principal. Starting as a teen, he lived a lifetime of duplicity. Skilled at playing the name game, Jerome Levitch veiled himself in secrecy:
- Jerry Lewis was named Jerome Levitch at birth, no middle name.
- Fourteen-year-old Jerome Levitch misrepresented himself as Jerry Lewis on his Social Security Card.
- Fifteen-year-old Jerome Levitch was misrepresented as Jerry Lewis on his school records.
- Eighteen-year-old Jerome Levitch misrepresented himself as Jerry Lewis on his World War II Draft Card.
- Nineteen-year-old Jerome Levitch added the middle name of "Joseph" on his marriage documents.
- Nineteen-year-old Jerome Levitch misrepresented his son's birth name as Cary Lewis, not Levitch.
- Jerome Levitch petitioned the Court to change his fake name of Joseph Levitch to the fake name of Jerry Lewis.
- Jerome Levitch signed his fictitious name on many legal documents, including his will.

Jerome Levitch hid his real identity by using a stage name. However, one person found Levitch's assumed name troublesome as it interfered with his own life and career. I take you back to the early 1950s when Jerry Lewis was an aspiring performer with the potential to influence the world of show business. In this case, I am not referring to Jerome Levitch but to the entertainer whose first and last name at birth was legally Jerry Lewis. When this "Mr. Lewis" started making a name for himself in the music world, and it came time for him to register himself with the various theatrical unions and organizations, he was prevented from doing so. Comedian Jerry Lewis had registered it as his stage name. After some failed legal wrangling, the pioneer rock 'n' roll icon had only one option. In order to use his birth name, he added his middle name, Lee, which fit comfortably between Jerry and Lewis. Described as rock 'n' roll's wild man and "The Killer," Jerry Lee Lewis, the pianist, singer, and songwriter, rose to fame using a name he didn't want, while comedian Jerry Lewis rose to fame using a name he didn't own.

Friends & Lovers

In the mid-1940s, an aspiring comedian named Jerome Levitch befriended a talented Italian singer. The young Levitch admired his new theatrical friend, who was several years older than he was and who had already sung on radio, vocalized with various bands, and was an up-and-coming recording artist. Eventually, these two entertainers would appear together on nightclub stages and network television and record together for Capitol Records.

To the chagrin of some people, Jerome and his Italian partner became lovers. The idea of their lurid affair reviled members of both of their families. During the mid-1940s, this kind of relationship was often frowned upon. Against all odds and without family approval, Jerome and his lover announced their union. After a long and sometimes rocky relationship, and to the surprise of millions, this seemingly inseparable team ended their partnership and went their separate ways.

In writing *The REAL Jerry Lewis Story,* I have included many details about entertainer Jerry Lewis' life and career. This book serves as an addendum to every publication written about comedy legend Jerry Lewis with one significant difference: It contains interesting and surprising facts never before revealed.

The truth can often be misleading, but here are the facts: The team of Dean Martin & Jerry Lewis was NOT the partnership described above. The story actually refers to

Jerome Levitch, of Jewish heritage, and Esther Calonico, of Italian Catholic heritage. This famous show business couple was known to the world as comedian Jerry Lewis and his wife, the popular big band vocalist Patti Palmer Lewis.

What were YOU thinking?

The Pasqualina DiPalma Story

The Wedding

Pasqualina Grace Esther "Patti" Calonico DiPalma Palmer Levitch Lewis was Jerry Lewis' first wife, who gave up her career as a performer to marry Jerry and raise their family.

A local newspaper reported: "On a joyful Tuesday in January, Esther Calonico, daughter of Mr. and Mrs. Angelo Calonico of Detroit, Michigan, was married at St. Anthony's Church, officiated by the Reverend Father Domenic. Esther, a professional entertainer, wore a flattering chocolate brown dress with dark green accessories and carried orchids. The handsomely attired groom, also an entertainer, appeared in many major theaters, conventions, and nightclubs. Following the ceremony, a reception was held at the Nelson Hotel. Later in the evening, the popular Bobby Byrne Orchestra played at a party for the couple, the groom interacting with the band to the guests' delight. The bride and groom received numerous telegrams of congratulations and beautiful gifts from friends and acquaintances."

What Jerry Lewis wore on this wedding day is unknown because the 15-year-old was not invited. Esther Calonico, who later became Mrs. Patti Lewis, would not meet the yet-to-be-crowned "King of Comedy" for another 2½ years. One of Hollywood's best-kept secrets is that Patti married Jimmy Palmer on January 13, 1942, but their marriage was short-lived. Patti's marriage to Jerry

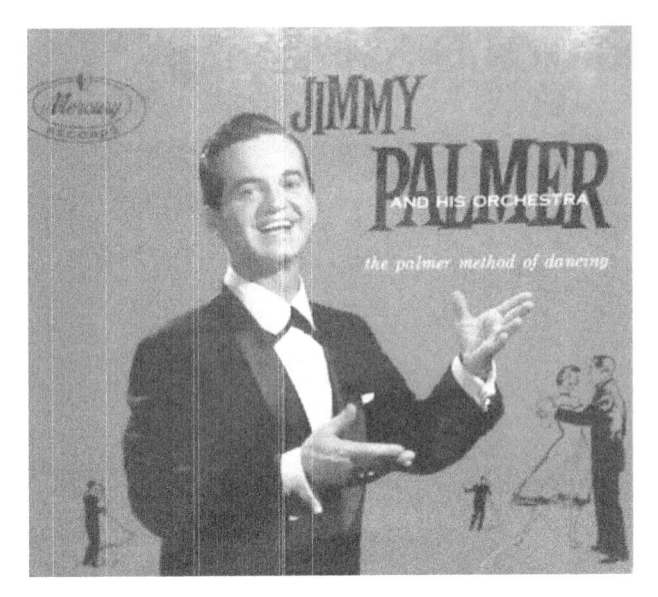

Lewis lasted for 36 years, although he was unfaithful from the start. As one of her sons commented, "The bigger the diamond, the worse Dad's offense." Patti told Joseph, her youngest son, that she always knew which starlet Jerry was having an affair by the number of close-ups the actress got in his movies. In 1980, Patti Lewis filed for legal separation from Jerry Lewis, claiming divorce was against her Catholic beliefs. Despite her religion, Patti divorced two husbands.

In 1983, Patti Lewis wrote an autobiography titled *I Laffed Till I Cried: Thirty-six Years of Marriage to Jerry Lewis*. It did not garner much attention because the reviewers and other media sources were primarily interested in finding salacious details about Jerry Lewis, which did not materialize to their satisfaction. Patti omitted crucial information such as specific times, dates, locations, and other details from her book. Moreover, she did not mention that she was previously married to James F. DiPalma, a successful musician, nightclub performer, and radio entertainer before she married 19-year-old Jerry Lewis, a vaudeville novelty act. Interestingly, in her countless interviews dating back to her days as a singing star with the big bands, Patti never addressed the fact that she had been married to a show business entity before marrying Jerry. It is worth noting that when Jerry was six years old, James F. DiPalma, professionally known as Jimmy Palmer, was already an established entertainer.

Throughout her marriages to Jimmy Palmer and Jerry Lewis, the media never delved much into Patti's background, including her formal musical training. She played the piano, accordion, bass fiddle, slide trombone, drums, xylophone, and other band instruments. In addition, she became a radio personality, a recording artist, and a featured vocalist with some of the nation's top bands. The media never questioned the origin of the name Patti Palmer, which was directly linked to her first husband, entertainer Jimmy Palmer.

Born to Italian immigrants on November 20, 1921, Patti did not like her given name, Pasqualina, which in Italian means "Little Easter." Easter sounds like Esther in English, so Patti's strict Italian mother agreed to let her use the name Esther when Patti started school. However, Esther still preferred to be called Patti, a shortened version of Pasqualina. To reflect her Italian heritage, Patti spelled her name with an "i."

Growing up, Esther was dominated by her overbearing Catholic mother, Mary Rotellini Calonico. According to Patti's autobiography, Mary insisted that her daughter clean the house to her specifications, practice her music religiously, and avoid boys and sex. One night after Patti came home late from a club date, her mother beat her, accusing her of having sex. Exposure to her mother's abusive behavior made Patti more tolerant of the abuse she later faced from her husband, Jerry Lewis.

As a child, Patti was so instilled with fear of Jews that she would always run down the street when she passed the Jewish-owned grocery store. When Patti informed her mother she had married Jerry Lewis, who was Jewish, her mother was upset. To compound the situation, Patti was six months pregnant at the time of her marriage. To avoid social stigma and judgmental comments, Patti and Jerry told people they were married on October 3, 1944. In reality, they were married only once, in New York in April 1945, and their son was born in July three months later.

Patti was a highly talented student at Cass Technical High School in Detroit, which was a vocational school that focused on the performing arts. In 1939, she was awarded a scholarship to study music at the University of Florida, but her mother would not let her leave home. While studying at Cass, Patti was taught by Professor Clarence Byrne, whose son Bobby had previously been the bandleader for the school. Bobby Byrne went on to become a trombonist for Tommy and Jimmy Dorsey's big band when he was only 17 years old. Later, he formed his own successful orchestra and hired entertainer Jimmy "Palmer" DiPalma.

To help defray household expenses and to pay for her music lessons, Patti earned money after school playing the accordion at restaurants, small parties, picnics, weddings, and other local events. After graduating from

Dick Stabile & Gracie Barrie

high school, Patti began performing as an accordion soloist, trombonist, and vocalist with several bands in Detroit and became a member of an all-girl orchestra. Patti's music teacher, Professor Byrne, introduced her to his son, bandleader Bobby Byrne. Bobby subsequently introduced pretty, young Esther "Patti" Calonico to his new vocalist, Jimmy Palmer. Little did Bobby Byrne know he was introducing Patti to her first husband.

After Esther Calonico, age 20, married 28-year-old Jimmy Palmer, she began using the name Patti Palmer personally and professionally, even though her legal name continued to be DiPalma until her divorce. The name Patti Palmer was likely the only thing of value she took away from her short-lived marriage to Jimmy.

Born on October 31, 1913, in Canonsburg, Pennsylvania, James Frank DiPalma was nicknamed "Dancin' Shoes." Jimmy was a gifted bandleader, vocalist, musician, businessman, and multi-talented dancer. Winning a Paul Whiteman's Youth of America contest as a vocalist led to his own radio show on KDKA-Pittsburgh, the first licensed commercial radio station in the USA. Bandleader Dick Stabile heard Jimmy on the radio and hired him to sing with his band.

When the United States entered World War II, so many of Bobby Byrne's musicians were called to active duty that his orchestra disbanded. Bobby Byrne joined the Army as a pilot and bandleader. Jimmy, exempt from US military service due to a football injury, took a job with Gracie Barrie's band.

Gracie Barrie, who was an established singer and the wife of famed orchestra leader and saxophonist Dick Stabile, fronted her husband's band when he was called to serve a hitch in the military. On December 12, 1943, St. Louis' Tune Town advertised a dance with "Gracie Barrie and her famous all-male orchestra (formerly the Band of Dick Stabile), featuring Jimmy Palmer." While Dick Stabile was away on active duty, Gracie decided to part ways with her husband and the band to return to the New York stage where she was still a favorite. Before leaving, however, Gracie turned the baton and the spotlight over to Patti's husband, Jimmy Palmer, making him the interim conductor of the Dick Stabile Orchestra. Jimmy also worked as a vocalist with several other bands, including Blue Barron's and Les Brown's. Patti and Jimmy divorced in January 1944, and Jimmy started his own band in April of the same year.

When Dick Stabile's tour of duty ended, he resumed his position as bandleader, and Jimmy left the band, returning occasionally as a musician and vocalist. In 1946, when Dean Martin & Jerry Lewis began performing as a team, Dick Stabile and his orchestra became their exclusive band for nightclubs, radio, motion pictures, and television. Dick Stabile's byplay with Martin & Lewis made him like a third partner in their performances, a position he held for almost ten years. However, when Jerry Lewis became a solo act in 1956, Stabile was replaced by Lou Brown, who had previously served as the pianist for the orchestra. Because Jerry Lewis reneged on his promise to provide Dick Stabile with continued employment, Stabile sued Jerry for $40,000 and thus their relationship ended.

Patti Palmer, Jimmy Palmer, Dick Stabile, Joe Stabile, Ernie Glucksman, and Jerry Lewis form a chain as the lives of all these people, distant as they were from each other, found their way into *The REAL Jerry Lewis Story*.

The Divorce

Weeks after the marriage of Patti and Jimmy Palmer, he was on the road again, performing with bandleader Bobby Byrne and songstress Dorothy Claire. As a new bride left alone, Patti became disillusioned with her situation. Although Jimmy appeared with well-known orchestras and other female vocalists, there was no room for the pretty and multi-talented Patti Palmer, who had a beautiful voice and singing style. Home alone, Patti prepared her resumé and headshots for mailing, setting her sights on pursuing her career in show business with a dream of singing with the big bands. A year after she said, "I do," she said, "I don't." In January 1942, the Palmers separated, and the following year, Patti, a devout Catholic, filed for divorce. In her autobiography,

Patti wrote that for years, she refused to divorce Jerry because it was against her religion. What she forgot to mention is that 40 years earlier, she divorced her first husband, Jimmy Palmer.

Once on her own, Patti did what a performer should do to advance her career. She found opportunities to showcase her talents and notified agents of these appearances, sending out her professional photographs and resumés. Throughout the following months, Patti Palmer worked in a music store and performed at local venues until she landed a job as a staff singer on radio station WWJ, the NBC affiliate in Detroit, Michigan. She became a vocalist with the Sophisticats, WWJ's in-house singing group. Soon afterward, she was hired as the featured singer on the radio show *Two Pianos and Patty*; however, the station spelled her name with a "y." Her 15-minute daily program was elevated from the afternoon to a preferred evening time slot, airing from 7:30 to 7:45 p.m. on WWJ in Detroit and surrounding areas. It was heard and advertised in Windsor, Ontario, Canada. Patti gained international recognition, and her program was renamed *The Patti Palmer Show*. Broadcast opposite the popular comedy radio show *Easy Aces* on WJR and the hugely popular western adventure series *The Lone Ranger* on WXYZ, Patti's show had tough competition; however, WWJ believed the talented Miss Palmer would give the Lone Ranger and Tonto a run for their money.

According to Patti, during one of these broadcasts, Ted Fio Rito, the well-known musician, composer, and orchestra leader, heard her singing on the radio. He contacted the radio station, met with Patti, and offered her a contract to become his "girl singer." Known for giving Betty Hutton, June Haver, and Betty Grable their start in the entertainment industry, Patti was thrilled to have an opportunity to work with Ted Fio Rito and his A-class orchestra. Patti would have recording opportunities, gain national media coverage, and become more financially independent. It was her dream come true.

In November of 1943, Patti Palmer became a member of the Ted Fio Rito Orchestra and His Skylined Swing Band, which included other artists such as the Musical Pilots, Candy Candido, and Kay Swingle and Her Brothers. They performed at the State Theatre in Hartford, Connecticut. Patti, who felt accepted and respected in her chosen profession, occasionally sang with Kay Swingle and Her Brothers, forming a quartet called the Solidaires. Ted Fio Rito was instrumental in molding Patti Palmer into a star, as they often recorded in studios and made personal appearances at theaters. They also appeared on Coca-Cola's *Victory Parade of Spotlight Bands*, a daily radio broadcast with a live audience of hundreds of thousands of soldiers based in military installations. The show was heard across the country live and was available worldwide through recordings so that soldiers overseas could listen to it. Patti Palmer had hitched her wagon to a star, and now she was one of them. Patti was making quite a name for herself, a name that would be a topic of discussion in the media for the rest of her life and beyond.

On December 24, 1943, just a month after Patti Palmer officially became a big band singer, Jerry Lewis decided he wanted a big band singer for his bride. That

Christmas, Jerry was booked for a week-long engagement at the Central Theater in Passaic, New Jersey, where he performed his 12-minute record mime act before the band took the stage. When Jerry wasn't on stage, his mind was on the featured vocalist who sang with the band. As he watched each of her performances, he felt himself falling in love and wanted to marry her. The object of his affection was three years older than the 17-year-old comedian, but she did not consider him marriage material. Jerry had fallen in love with Louis Prima's female vocalist, Lily Ann Carol.

Lily Ann and her husband, Joe Barone, were a lively singing duo

Lily Ann Carol

reminiscent of Louis Prima and Keely Smith. Lily Ann Carol was Louis Prima's original girl singer from 1940 through 1946. Although the "deadpan" singing style is usually attributed to Keely Smith, it originally was Louis Prima's suggestion for Lily Ann and became a vehicle for his comedy. I knew all the players: Lily Ann, Louis Prima, Patti, and Jerry. The young Jerry Lewis seemed to like older women, and he was attracted to Lily Ann's looks, stage persona, and singing style, the same compelling traits that later drew him to Patti.

As far back as I can remember, any time an entertainer learned that I was connected with Jerry Lewis, inevitably, I was told some personal anecdote about him. While performing in the Catskills in the 1960s, I became friendly with Lily Ann Carol and Joe Barone. We spent a lot of time together, and she shared a particularly intriguing story with me. According to Lily Ann, she went out of town for an engagement. Jerry called her at her hotel and misinterpreted her amusement with him as a sign of her romantic interest in him. After his show, he took a bus to Philadelphia and knocked on her hotel room at 2 a.m. Concerned why he was there at this unusual hour, she invited him in to talk. However, when Jerry turned the conversation to romance, she asked Jerry to leave. Dejected, heartbroken, and horny, Jerry boarded the bus back to New York City.

On March 1, 1944, just 26 months after she took her first wedding vows, Patti was granted an unconditional divorce from Jimmy on the grounds of cruelty. As part of their divorce, the defendant, James F. DiPalma, was ordered to pay the plaintiff, Esther C. DiPalma, the sum of $215. It was a clean break. Although the court granted her request to resume her maiden name, she elected to be known as Patti Palmer. Patti was now free to look to the future as a single woman again.

The 20-year-old Lily Ann Carol had no romantic interest in the 18-year-old Jerry Lewis, and his attention soon turned to another band vocalist. Booked into the Downtown Theatre in Detroit on August 18, 1944, he again developed a crush on another girl singer. Just 17 days after her divorce from Jimmy Palmer was finalized, Cupid struck again, this time piercing the hearts of Jerry Lewis and the 23-year-old Patti Palmer.

The REAL Jerry Lewis Story

Patti & Jerry Lewis

How They Met

In 1944, Jerry Lewis was a record mime, and his manager and agent, Abner J. Greshler, was hard-pressed to find suitable work for his client, who did not want to speak on stage. Crafted as a novelty act, Jerry's 12-14 minute performance of mouthing and mugging to the songs of famous singers of the day fit perfectly into Greshler's corporate shows. As Jerry told me when I was on network TV with him in 1962, he used to do "strictly a dumb act." Jerry said, "I would just mime recordings of other artists. Years ago, they [record acts] were a dime a dozen." Jerry's pantomime performance, relying heavily on facial mugging, might not be appropriate for this entertainment palace, but Greshler, a creative showman and manager, "sold" Jerry to the Detroit Theater as an intermission act.

Built originally as vaudeville houses, movie palaces during the 1930s through the 1950s offered varied forms of entertainment. Many could seat thousands of people. Detroit's Downtown Theatre, with its opulent balcony, accommodated up to 3,000 patrons per show. Going to the movies during the Great Depression and beyond provided a form of escapism for hours. In addition to the films, there were live acts on stage, all at an affordable price with matinée discounts. People spent far more on food and candy concessions than on their admission tickets by design, and there was plenty of profit in popcorn.

© 2024 Rick Saphire

Patti Palmer

In this Detroit show, the opening performance was a live broadcast of a popular radio show, *Blind Date*. Next on the line-up was the Ted Fio Rito Orchestra. The stage crew needed about 10 minutes to set the stage for the musicians. When the main curtain closed, there was just enough room on the proscenium for Jerry Lewis to do his record act.

On this particular Friday, the broadcast of the road-company version of *Blind Date* was hosted by singer and actress Joy Hodges. Six local servicemen were selected from the audience to talk on the phone with three unseen ladies who picked the winners based on their conversations. The winning GI Joes got a chaperoned night out on the town with one of the ladies, plus $5 in spending money, which was a tidy sum in those days. In 1944, a full-course dinner cost about $1.45. The losers were also winners, as each got $15 in cash, tickets to a popular local theatre production, and a kiss from the hostess. Each lady was paid $50 for her appearance on the show, and the soldiers in the audience had a great time.

At the end of the broadcast, the curtains closed as the stagehands, musicians, announcers, and singers scrambled behind the scenes in preparation for the performance of Ted Fio Rito's orchestra. The intermission act was introduced to keep the audience entertained during this changeover. An offstage voice announced, "And now, Ladies and Gentlemen, please welcome, direct from New York City, Jerry Lewis and His Satirical Impersonations in Pantomimicry." In front of the curtain, alone on stage, Jerry Lewis appeared with his table of wigs, hats, and props, accompanied by the sounds of an offstage record player. Thousands of people watched him do what he loved most: make people laugh. All of the preparations for his act and all of his traveling boiled down to his 12-14 minute record act of fun and lunacy. His performance consisted of Jerry Lewis comedically exaggerating gestures to imitate famous opera stars and popular singers as he donned costumes and lip-synced to their songs in his uniquely outrageous way. As the curtain opened, signaling the end of his act, his impressive ovation died down. The audience's focus shifted to Ted Fio Rito and His Orchestra, featuring song stylist Patti Palmer.

For that short time on stage, Jerry Lewis forgot the pain of being a lonely, neglected child seeking approval from his parents. At that moment, the only approval that mattered to him was the audience's, which they gave through their laughter and applause. Being an intermission act was a lonely life for Jerry because once he was off the stage, he was alone again. This night, Jerry spied an empty seat in the audience and took it to watch the band.

Jerry's focus was drawn to the cute singer with the torchy voice. From Jerry's vantage point, Patti's dark brown hair was perfectly coiffed, her chiffon dress swayed with her every move, and the lights flattered her features. Looking and sounding like Lily Ann Carol, the songstress he had not yet released from his heart, Jerry once again felt himself falling in love.

Patti was a headliner, and Jerry was the intermission act, yet the difference in their show business status did not dissuade him from pursuing her. Patti was reluctant to enter into a relationship with this zany pantomimist, but Jerry's wit and persistence eventually won her affection. Even though Patti Palmer was nearly five years his senior, successful in her field, and earning a respectable income, those differences took a backseat to what they had in common. Each fulfilled the needs of the other. Jerry felt his home life lacked love; his parents shuttled him from relative to relative as they were on the road performing much of the time. Patti endured severe beatings and harsh scoldings from her mother as a child. After the birth of her half-sister, Anna May, Patti became the little girl's full-time nanny. When the child died from an illness, Patti suffered the loss and felt inexpressible guilt. Now newly divorced on the grounds of cruelty, Patti initially resisted Jerry's advances.

Patti and Jerry were well-matched because Patti needed someone to mother, and Jerry needed mothering. However, Patti's career had begun to skyrocket, and a romance with Jerry Lewis, or anyone else, could potentially interfere with her success.

The day after the first show, the newspapers described it as a hit. Ted Fio Rito, the Solidaires, and Patti Palmer received rave reviews. The most sparkling review of the

The night Patti and Jerry Met they both signed this page for an autograph collector at the Ted Fio Rito band concert

entire show went to an unknown, unadvertised novelty act. The *Detroit Free Press* wrote, "No ham in the entertainment sandwich is Jerry Lewis, who tears off terribly funny pantomime to recordings of operatic arias

Patti Palmer

and 'The Voice' [Frank Sinatra]." Although no one knows the outcome of the winners of *Blind Date*, we know the two "unofficial" grand prize winners that night were Jerry Lewis and Patti Palmer.

During the 6-day run of the show, Patti saw Jerry every day. She was charmed and flattered by his attention. The show closed in Detroit on Thursday, August 24, 1944. While Patti, Ted Fio Rito, and the band set off to spend the next week performing a series of one-nighters, Jerry returned to New York, where he performed his novelty act for Abby Greshler's private corporate shows. Their time apart from each other served to fuel their passion.

Unhappy about his star singer's involvement with a record mime, Fio Rito often chided Patti for dating Jerry, whom he referred to as "that Jew." Fio Rito blamed Patti's relationship with Jerry for infractions such as her lateness to rehearsal. Offended and disenchanted, Patti prepared to leave the Ted Fio Rito Orchestra. In November 1944, she accepted Jimmy Dorsey's offer to replace Anita Boyer as the lead singer of his big band.

On November 16, 1944, Patti Palmer debuted as the featured female vocalist for Jimmy Dorsey at the Capitol Theatre's 25th Anniversary Show with the world-famous Jimmy Dorsey and his Orchestra in New York City. Featured on the bill with Patti Palmer were vocalist Teddy Walters; America's most unusual dancer, Peg-Leg Bates; and Broadway's favorite comedian, Henny Youngman-in person! Kate Cameron of the *New York Daily News* wrote, "The Capitol Theatre selected a perfect picture for the gala premiere that set off its sixth War Loan Drive last night. Metro-Goldwyn-Mayer's production of *Thirty Seconds Over Tokyo* is one the most inspiring pictures of the war." As one of the live performers, Patti gave a pitch to collect money for the War Loan Drive, a campaign to encourage Americans to buy U.S. Treasury bonds to finance World War II. Patti Palmer was officially a singing star at the height of the Big Band Era with a step-up to the Jimmy Dorsey Orchestra and an extended engagement at the prestigious Capitol Theatre on Broadway.

During World War II, the big bands provided music for the younger generation, mainly servicemen and women on leave or preparing to embark. Bandleaders hired attractive female vocalists to appeal to men's fantasies. For the fairer sex, good-looking male vocalists crooned tunes. Although some reports claim Patti Palmer retired as a big band singer to raise a family, her fame was likely cut short when it became apparent that she was in a "family way."

Jerry and Patti were in love and expecting a baby; however, he knew his parents would not want him to marry a shiksa (a non-Jewish girl), and Patti's family did not want her to marry a Jew. Facing their respective parents was something neither wanted to do. Jerry's income was anemic, and his manager, Abby Greshler, encouraged him to expand his repertoire to include comedy and emceeing, but Jerry did not feel he was ready to speak in front of an audience. Many believe Jerry was paranoid about his past delinquent behaviors. It would be quite some time before he would reach his celebrity status, and the pressure was on him to be the family's breadwinner. Although Jerry could afford the bread, he could not afford the butter.

Journalists impacted show business careers in the 20th century, much like the 21st century Internet bloggers. Because of Patti's status in the entertainment field, gossip columnists frequently wrote about her, even if it wasn't true. On January 18, 1945, an article written by

Ann Robinson for the *Miami Daily News* read, "Patti Palmer, singer with the Jimmy Dorsey band at the Frolics Club, 'tis rumored, is making honeymoon plans with a bass player in the band…"

A month later, on February 19, 1945, one of the most respected nationally syndicated gossip columnists, Dorothy Kilgallen, reported, "Patti Palmer (Jimmy Dorsey's songbird) and Jerry Lewis the comic are Mr. and Mrs. after a quiet wedding…" It must have been a very quiet wedding because neither Jerry nor Patti attended it. Another case of misinformation.

The actual date of Jerry and Patti Lewis' marriage was purposely misreported. Twenty-three-year-old Esther "Patti Palmer" Calonico and 18-year-old Jerome "Jerry Lewis" Levitch were not married in October 1944 nor February 1945, as frequently reported. Credible columnists were purposely fed erroneous information about a marriage that had not yet occurred, although the honeymoon had. Attempts to mislead the public were done intentionally to protect the reputation of Patti, who was pregnant out of wedlock. Like so many things about Jerry Lewis' life, this, too, was clouded in contradictions and half-truths.

During the 1940s, Irving Kaye, a hotel bellhop and part-time comedian, was friends with Jerry's parents, Danny and Rae, who were not eager for their son to go into show business. Eventually, Jerry's parents relented to let their son go on the road, although in the resort town of Lakewood, "going on the road" meant traveling a few blocks. Lonnie Brown and her parents got Jerry Lewis his first paid bookings, even though Irving Kaye credited himself for "giving Jerry his start." Kaye became Jerry's unofficial road manager and traveling companion. Jerry was paid $3 for a midweek show and $5 for a weekend, which means Irving Kaye's average commission was $.40 per show. There was more money to be earned as a bellhop. Jerry let Irving Kaye bask in the glory that belonged to his close friend Lonnie Brown. Years later, Irving Kaye often misreported information for Jerry and bragged in several interviews that he did not have to worry about his future. As a teenager, Kaye claimed, Jerry Lewis promised to take care of him for life with a job and an annuity since he had given Jerry a break in show business by getting him some bookings. Irving Kaye, who knew more than he told, remained a lifelong member of Jerry Lewis' inner circle.

Inconsistencies, omissions, and misinformation have long clouded the facts about the date of Esther "Patti" Calonico's marriage to Jerome Levitch, that is, until now. In several 1960s interviews, Kaye claimed that on the evening of Monday, October 2, 1944, Jerry did not come back to the hotel room they shared. The next day, Jerry returned to the hotel, waving his hand in the air to show off his brand-new wedding band. Some versions of the "elopement" have Jerry waking Kaye to tell him the news, while others have Kaye meeting Jerry in front of the hotel. Decades later, Irving Kaye said Patti had sent Jerry money to buy train tickets to Connecticut, where they rendezvoused and got married. As his story continued, Kaye claimed Patti and Jerry then took a train to New Jersey and honeymooned at the Hotel Arthur in Lakewood, managed by Charles and Lillian Brown. Jerry and Patti selected an anniversary date to make it appear their son was conceived on their honeymoon, October 3, 1944, a date that will live in "infancy."

It is merely an urban legend that pantomimist Jerry Lewis and big band singer Patti Palmer took an overnight trip to Connecticut, where they tied the knot. In 1944, Connecticut law stipulated that a minor (under age 21) could not get married without written parental consent, and 19-year-old Jerome Levitch was underage and did not have his parents' consent.

Even under ideal conditions, getting a marriage application and applying for a marriage license took days, which meant they had to either remain in Connecticut or return once the paperwork was complete. Due to a major health crisis caused by the rise in venereal diseases in the 1930s, all states required couples to take a blood test, and it typically took three days to get the results. It wasn't until 2003 that Connecticut lifted the blood test requirement for a marriage license. In the 1940s, there was also a mandatory waiting period before a couple could get married.

To believe Patti and Jerry were married in Greenwich, Connecticut, on October 3, 1944, is to believe that 19-year-old Jerry did not need parental consent to get married, that no blood test was required, that there was no waiting period for a marriage license, and that Jerry Lewis held the deed to the Brooklyn Bridge. Once this yarn was spun, no one, before now, bothered to untangle it.

© 2024 Rick Saphire

Wedding Bells Again

In Patti's autobiography, she states that she did not think Jerry could have been anything but Italian. When she met Jerry Lewis, the 19-year-old looked like a character from a Damon Runyon novel with his slick, shiny black hair. Flinging around his ultra-high pompadour, his hair punctuated his comedy and became a prop in his record act.

Some resources claim Patti, who was Catholic, planned their Jewish wedding. Although it is common practice for the bride's family to handle the wedding arrangements, Patti's family was not even there. Both Patti and Jerry state in their respective books that Jerry's parents made them a traditional Jewish wedding, but the ceremony was not entirely traditional. According to Jewish law, two unrelated males must witness the betrothal. Officially married in a hotel room in Manhattan in New York, Esther Calonico and Jerome J. Levitch's marriage certificate was signed and witnessed by Rachel and Daniel Levitch, Jerry's parents, and that's not kosher.

Differing religious beliefs and practices often lead to prejudices and cultural misunderstandings. Patti, who claimed in her book that Jerry's grandfather was a rabbi, may have thought that because the elderly man went to the synagogue regularly and read the Talmud, or perhaps it was what she had been told. In the 1905 Census, Morris Lovitz's (aka Levitch) profession was recorded as a peddler. If Grandpa Morris was a rabbi, he likely would have officiated at his grandson's wedding, but he did not even attend it.

Accounts of Patti and Jerry's marriage are shrouded in subterfuge and ambiguities. Written after their divorce, Patti refers to Jerry in her autobiography as "Joseph" Levitch; however, on their sworn marriage application and official marriage certificate, his first name appears as Jerome, just as it appears on his birth certificate. On his marriage application and marriage license, Jerry identifies himself as Jerome "Joseph" Levitch, but the name on his birth certificate was simply Jerome Levitch.

On both her marriage application and her marriage license to Jerome Levitch, Patti swore on these government documents that she had not been married before, but her first husband, James F. DiPalma, might tell a different story. To willfully tell an untruth, especially after taking an oath, is to commit perjury, and excluding one or more facts to create a misconception is lying by omission.

The erroneous wedding dates and the stories accompanying them were originated and publicized to make it appear that Patti and Jerry's child had not been conceived out of wedlock. In this way, their baby would be spared any social stigma, and Patti's reputation would remain untainted. Jerry himself may or may not have invented the elopement fables, but he perpetuated them. Furthermore, when the newlyweds announced they were expecting a baby, their families could be spared social embarrassment if they supported the myth that the couple had previously eloped.

The REAL Jerry Lewis Story

[Image of marriage license document: NEW YORK STATE DEPARTMENT OF HEALTH, Division of Vital Statistics, MARRIAGE LICENSE No. 8860]

As Jerry Lewis became a known entity and gained popularity, keeping his image as an upstanding and devoted family man became more important to his handlers. Jerry reinforced and circulated the "elopement" tales to keep his reputation clean. For most of his life, their firstborn, Gary Lewis (born Cary), thought his parents' anniversary was October 3rd because Patti and Jerry went so far as to make the fantasy a reality by celebrating it at home on that date.

On April 16, 1945, Daniel and Rachel Levitch signed and submitted the Consent to Marry form permitting their underage son to get married. Before leaving the office on that day, Jerome Levitch and Esther Calonico filled out and submitted a sworn affidavit for their Application for a Marriage License in the state of New York.

Officiated by Cantor Rev. Hyman Lifshin, the wedding ceremony was witnessed by the groom's parents, Rachel and Daniel Levitch. Esther "Patti" Calonico and Jerome Levitch were officially married at 8 p.m. on April 30, 1945, at the Belmont Plaza Hotel, 49th Street and Lexington Avenue, Manhattan, New York, just three months before the birth of their son.

It is interesting to note that before Jerome Levitch, who was underage, could marry Esther Calonico, who was five months pregnant, he needed to obtain a Consent to Marry certificate. His parents signed the court's Certificate to Marry and marriage application in the New York County Clerk's Office on April 16, 1945, and submitted them on that day. However, the mandatory parental consent went missing for eight months. The papers were officially filed on December 20, 1945, when Jerry's baby was five months old. Equally notable is that my research unearthed an inaccuracy on the consent certificate where it listed Jerome Joseph Levitch's birth date as March 16, 1945. In reality, he was born on March 16, 1926. Could the error explain the delay in the filing of the document? Because parental consent was needed for the marriage to take place, was it marriage legal? If the date on the Consent to Marry Certificate was correct, Jerry would have married Patti when he was six weeks old, and Jerry would have been three months old when his son was born. Speaking of robbing the cradle.

The REAL Jerry Lewis Story

The Judy Scott Story

The Jerry Lewis Show, January 19, 1957
The Rick Saphire Collection

On January 13, 1957, I had the opportunity to attend Jerry Lewis' first TV appearance at the NBC Color Studio in Brooklyn, New York, after he parted ways with Dean Martin. During the show, I saw the fantastic performance of Judy Scott for the first time. More than a decade later, I worked as a comedy Master of Ceremonies at some of the top resort hotels on the East Coast and introduced Judy to appreciative audiences. My friendship with Judy gave me some interesting insights into her relationship with Jerry and Patti Lewis.

Jerry Lewis was renowned for being a career-maker, but he could also be a career-breaker. Jerry discovered Judy at the Copa Lounge in the Copacabana nightclub in Manhattan. He was originally there to hear a different singer but was so impressed with Judy's performance that he invited her to his table. Jerry then asked her to be his opening act in Las Vegas for his first engagement after splitting with Dean Martin. When Judy told Jerry she did not have a nightclub act, he scoffed, "Then get one." Once Jerry approved her song selections, he selected a new professional name for her, and Judy Gay became Judy Scott. Her last name was a tribute to his son, Scott Lewis. When Judy mentioned her nervousness about performing with an 18-piece orchestra behind her, Jerry joked, "Don't be nervous because the audience came to see me, not you." Judy felt that Jerry Lewis was her mentor. Jerry and his wife, Patti, were supportive of her, sending her flowers and gifts.

The critics praised Judy Scott, a young and talented vocalist, as Jerry Lewis's opening act at the Sands Hotel in Las Vegas and at the other venues on this tour. However, Jerry's dark side surfaced whenever he did not receive the rave reviews he expected. Before the tour ended, Jerry asked Judy to appear with him on his first solo TV special on NBC. Still needing a partner to bounce off of, comedian Jan Murray was hired to do the opening comedy sketch with Jerry. In contrast to Jerry's classic childish persona, Jan Murray, the popular host of the game shows *Dollar a Second* and *Treasure Hunt*, portrayed the host of a teenage rock 'n' roll dance party in the routine. Jan Murray's appearance enhanced the show, bringing Jerry Lewis the reviews he craved.

After these successful appearances, Judy was promised a featured spot on the bill with Jerry Lewis when he debuted at New York's renowned Palace Theater. Things were going well for the young songstress, but the 18-year-old was relentlessly teased by Jerry Lewis and his cast during the tour. This teasing was not because of something she did but because of something she refused to do. Judy had only one goal in mind and that was to always give an exemplary performance on stage. She was not interested in getting romantically or sexually involved with anyone on the tour, including the musicians, stage crew, other performers, or Jerry Lewis himself. Because Judy was a minor, her mother traveled with her. Despite this, some of the men teased Judy by calling her "Virgin," as if it was a bad thing, and ridiculed her prudish attitude. Jerry, in an effort to demean Judy, nicknamed her "Snot Nose."

Judy Scott was determined to put an end to the verbal abuse and outwit the men. To achieve this, she invited a few of her hometown girlfriends backstage to meet the troupe before their closing show in Vegas. She prearranged with her friends to casually mention to the others that Judy had been married, but the marriage had been annulled. She hoped this fabricated story of her "marriage" would put an end to the virgin jokes.

Jerry Lewis' reaction was unexpected. He got angry with Judy because he felt she deceived him into thinking she was a virgin. He then withdrew his offer to have her appear with him at the Palace. It is unclear whether the comedian was genuinely upset that his fantasy of being with a sexually inexperienced teenager was crushed or if he was using it as an excuse because the show's backers disagreed with his choice and decided to go with a female singer who had more marquee value. In any event, Judy's two-week run at New York's Palace Theater was canceled. Jerry pulled the rug from under her, breaking her heart but not her spirit. Oddly enough, Jerry invited Judy to be at the show on opening night, and she decided to attend.

Behind the scenes, there was drama. After Jerry reneged on his offer to have Judy Scott perform at the Palace, Teresa Brewer, a popular young singing star, was selected to replace her. However, Teresa wanted equal billing, and Jerry Lewis was not about to share the bill with her as he had done with Dean Martin for a decade. Eydie Gormé, chosen as the replacement for Teresa Brewer, had a strong fan base as a regular on *Tonight* starring Steve Allen. Her TV appearances also gave her a platform to promote the Palace show and potentially boost ticket sales. However, Eydie threatened to back out of the show because she insisted on singing her arrangement of "Rock-A-Bye Your Baby with a Dixie Melody," which was Jerry Lewis' only Top 10 hit recording, and he intended to sing it on the show. As a result of this conflict, Judy Scott was beginning to look good again.

Why did Jerry Lewis invite Judy Scott to the Palace opening night? Had Eydie Gormé gotten temperamental, Judy Scott could have taken the stage. Jerry's conductor, Lou Brown, and the musicians had previously played for Judy on their tour, so the show would have proceeded flawlessly. In the end, though, Eydie Gormé honored her contract and performed as planned.

SCOTT is Hot!
2 Great Sides by....
JUDY SCOTT
singing

On February 7, 1957, I was in the audience at Jerry's Broadway debut at the Palace Theater. This vaudeville-style show consisted of eight acts starring Jerry Lewis and featuring the multi-talented Wiere Brothers and songstress Eydie Gormé. What I remember most about Ms. Gormé's act that night, besides her extraordinary voice, was her dazzling costume. The reflection of the carbon arc spotlight bouncing off of the mini-mirrors adorning her dress sent blinding flashes of laser-like beams into my eyes. Jerry was charming and crazy, climbing up a long ladder to harass a lady in the box seats, but a subtle change in his style was very apparent to me. Without Dean at his side to react and ensure the laugh, Jerry began reacting to his own antics. Like a bad comic laughing at his own jokes, Jerry would punctuate each gag with an incongruous outburst of screaming and tongue-wagging. This change in performance style intensified over the years, becoming his "safety net" to cover up any lack of audience response.

Towards the end of the show, Judy, seated front row center, received a message saying, "Mr. Lewis would like to see you in his dressing room after the show." Thrilled and optimistic about meeting with Jerry again, she made her way backstage. However, what happened behind closed doors was completely unexpected. When she entered the dressing room, Jerry told everyone else to leave. Glaring at her, he proceeded to berate her, shouting at her, calling her a liar and a phony. For a split second, she thought he might be kidding. As his tirade ended, she was stunned that this superstar and one-time friend was so angry at her. This was a shining moment in Jerry's career as a solo performer. This was the Palace Theatre on Broadway. Why was he focused on her virginity? Judy left his dressing room confused, finding it hard to believe that Jerry Lewis, who once treated her like a daughter, could become so hostile and acrimonious.

Although the incident at the Palace happened a long time ago, Judy always wondered why Jerry's reaction to her was so extreme. Her thoughts have been haunted by Jerry Lewis shouting accusations at her on the night of his Broadway opening, a lingering and disturbing image that remained unanswered until now.

After the Palace, my family and I went to a local delicatessen, hoping that Jerry would join us, but he did not show up for our late dinner. He was too wound up and anxious about his pending show reviews, and his confrontation with Judy likely exhausted him emotionally. Jerry admitted to me that it was not unusual for him to explode in an angry rage if someone crossed him, but in Judy's case, it was a clear case of misplaced aggression.

During the 1940s, Jerry had a crush on two singers, Lily Ann Carol and Patti Palmer, and Judy Scott resembled both of them. The comment Judy Scott's friends made about her (fake) annulment made Jerry angry because he believed Judy had lied about her virginity. However, Judy Scott was not the real target of Jerry's aggression. Jerry was having a flashback. He had been deeply hurt and harbored animosity towards his own wife, Patti Palmer Lewis, who neglected to tell Jerry she was a divorcée. Although it is not clear when Patti disclosed to Jerry that she was previously married to Jimmy Palmer, it was certainly after they took their marriage vows. For whatever her reasons, Patti perjured herself on their marriage license by denying prior marriage and divorce. Jerry's vitriolic behavior towards teenage Judy Scott stemmed from his belief that she lied to him, just as Patti did.

Judy Scott had fooled Jerry Lewis, and she never worked for him again, yet she always felt fortunate to have been his protégé, if only for a little while. After all, Jerry arranged for her to appear at some prestigious venues, and those experiences started her on a lifelong career as a successful performer.

Judy Scott was not only a vibrant and talented young performer when Jerry Lewis considered her his protégé, but throughout the following decades, she made a name for herself around the country with her dynamic singing style. Judy told me about an interesting incident involving two comedians. One of the comedians was Phil Foster, known for his role as Papa Defazio on the television show Laverne and Shirley.

After appearing with Judy Scott at a New York club date, Phil Foster approached her and asked if he could recommend her for a popular television program called Arthur Godfrey's Talent Scouts. The program's premise was that entertainers, business people, or almost anybody in the mainstream could recommend a talented performer to appear on the show. Phil asked Judy if he could bring her on Talent Scouts as his protégé. Although she knew this would be an opportunity to get on network TV, she remembered that some years earlier, Jerry Lewis called himself her mentor, and she did not want to offend him. "I would love to do it," Judy told Phil, "but I need to run it by Jerry Lewis first because he always considered me his protégé."

Phil Foster understood, and Judy contacted Jerry Lewis, who surprised her, because he said, "Don't go on with Phil Foster. You are still my protégé, and I will bring you on the Talent Scouts program."

Judy was all set to sing once again on network TV under the auspices of Jerry Lewis. All seemed right with the world, except for one problem: Jerry Lewis never showed up.

The REAL Jerry Lewis Story

Taking the Pledge

SPECIAL GUEST ADMISSION admit bearer at any time to: RESERVED SECTION ORCHESTRA	JERRY LEWIS 1959 THANKSGIVING PARTY at THE ZIEGFELD THEATER — 54th Street & 6th Avenue for the benefit of the Institute for Muscle Disease
Continuous from 10:00 pm Saturday NOV. 21 Thru 5:00 pm Sunday 22	COMPLIMENTARY GUEST INVITATION	Continuous from 10:00 pm Saturday NOV. 21 Thru 5:00 pm Sunday 22

How It Came to Be

Since the early days of my relationship with Jerry Lewis, his fans and the media often asked me how and why he was so dedicated to the Muscular Dystrophy Association (MDAA/MDA). They asked me that question because Jerry never gave them a straight answer. Did he have a relative with that disease? Did someone close to him die from muscular dystrophy? Jerry's response was generally the same: "The important thing is that I do it, not the 'why.'" His response sidestepped the question. Like so many other things in Jerry's life, he loved creating an air of mystery. Jerry Lewis was a master at baiting the media. Yes, he was a master baiter.

The concise answer regarding Jerry Lewis' involvement with the MDA is: No, Jerry Lewis did not have a relative or friend who suffered from neuromuscular disease. Additionally, no one close to Jerry Lewis had died from muscular dystrophy. However, Dean Martin & Jerry Lewis had a stable of publicity agents, producers, and handlers who kept the comedy duo in the public consciousness. So, at least in the beginning, Jerry Lewis' commitment to muscular dystrophy was all about business.

To understand the underlying complexities of Jerry Lewis' association with the MDA, we need to sift through the details that unfolded in the early 1900s, beginning with a vaudeville and burlesque performer billed as comedian Ernie Gilbert. Ernie was my uncle. He eventually became Jerry Lewis' executive producer and personal manager after he found his true calling: writing, producing, and directing shows. When Ernie Gilbert stopped performing, he stopped using his stage name and started using his real last name, Glucksman. From the 1920s through the 1940s, he created countless high-end variety shows for major corporations and organizations each year, combining professional and amateur talents from New York and New Jersey. As an example of his prestigious work and reputation, just two years before he met the team of Martin & Lewis, Ernie and his first wife, Dorothy Sachs, were writing, choreographing, producing, and directing shows such as the 1948 variety show for New York's popular Abraham & Straus Department Store chain. One performance at Manhattan's Academy of Music boasted 20 scenes with a cast of 125 talented department store employees. He and Dorothy were responsible for the various comedy sketches and musical numbers, which received rave reviews. Employed by the country clubs, conventions, Yiddish theatres, and resort hotels in the Catskill and Adirondacks mountains in upstate New York, Uncle Ernie's impressive theatrical accomplishments grew.

The end of World War II heralded the beginning of the Golden Age of Television in the United States, which provided new opportunities for Ernie Glucksman's creative talents. To compete with the CBS hit variety show, *Toast of the Town* hosted by Ed Sullivan, NBC developed *The Colgate Comedy Hour*, starring a lineup of America's top entertainers who rotated each week. Live on television, celebrities included Eddie Cantor, Abbott & Costello, and Donald O'Connor, among others. Most significantly, the roster featured the sensational new musical comedy team of Martin & Lewis. Because of his vast experience producing top-flight variety shows, Uncle Ernie was hired by NBC to produce and direct Martin & Lewis' monthly appearances on this program. There were rumors that vaudeville had died, but it hadn't; it simply morphed into television. Unlike Ed Sullivan's show which presented a review of gifted singers, dancers, and novelty acts, *The Colgate Comedy Hour* resembled classic vaudeville and burlesque with its comedy sketches and musical routines. Under the guidance of Ernie D. Glucksman, America became enamored with Martin & Lewis' musical and comedy talents on *The Colgate Comedy Hour*. In 1955, as the audience's tastes in entertainment changed, it broadened its scope and became *The Colgate Variety Hour*.

Since the early 1930s, radio fundraisers have been part of the media landscape. Radio shows and their sponsors often relinquished commercial airtime to permit fundraiser programming. Telethons were an updated incarnation of this practice. Out of 150 million people in the US, only 6.5 percent of the population had television sets in those days. To stimulate television sales, TV stations needed to increase viewership as well as programming. After the playing of the National Anthem around midnight, TV stations went off the air, leaving viewers with white noise and a raster on the screen. Broadcasting resumed the next day. Having a 16-hour show that would run throughout the night was big news. At noon on April 9, 1949, comedian Milton Berle hosted an "entertainment marathon" to raise money for New York's Damon Runyon Memorial Cancer Fund. Milton Berle, also known as "Mr. Television," is credited with coining the term telethon. The term is a combination of "tele" from television and "thon" from marathon, which represents a long-lasting event. Pledges were made by phoning in donations, which made viewers feel they were part of the TV show. Associated Press columnist C. E. Butterfield reported, "The stunt Milton Berle is to pull on NBC television tomorrow is being called a 'telethon.'" Berle did not consider this new venture a mere "stunt." Convinced that this use of television would help humanity, Milton Berle promised to remain on the air until at least one million dollars in pledges were raised for the cancer fund. By the time the show ended at 4 a.m. on April 10, 1949, Berle, assisted by over 100 celebrities, had reached his goal. This first telethon served as the prototype for future televised fundraisers.

In 1950, my uncle Ernie was flown from New York to California and driven to the palatial offices of Music Corporation of America (MCA). This music and talent agency was one of the most prestigious and influential in the nation. There, Ernie was introduced to a group of people, all important in various capacities, who had assembled to meet with the zany comedy duo of Dean Martin & Jerry Lewis. Uncle Ernie encountered something he did not expect at this introductory meeting: a zany comedy duo. Martin and Lewis did not sit still, raucously making joke after joke and throwing punchline after punchline. When the meeting ended, my uncle questioned what he had gotten into. The next day, he had an appointment at Jerry Lewis' home, and Uncle Ernie once again encountered something he did not expect. Jerry was an entirely different person, a well-controlled, articulate individual. Considering his youth, he possessed much knowledge about the entertainment field. This marked the beginning of a close 14-year relationship between Ernest D. Glucksman and Jerry Lewis, which lasted until 1964.

Uncle Ernie developed many professional relationships throughout his career. Among his corporate associates and friends was a man named Paul Cohen. Paul Cohen, who suffered from a rare form of adult muscular dystrophy, was the president of a company that manufactured Tuck Tape, Scotch Tape's rival. In June 1950, Cohen and some other prominent businessmen founded the Muscular Dystrophy Association of America (MDAA). Their mission was to raise funds for research, provide support and resources for victims and their families, educate health professionals, and heighten public awareness to combat neuromuscular diseases. When Paul Cohen learned his friend, Ernie Glucksman, was in charge of NBCs bright new stars, Dean Martin & Jerry Lewis, he asked Ernie if they would be interested in accepting the honorary position as the national entertainment chairmen for his fledgling organization, and they accepted.

Meanwhile, as a result of a nationwide survey to determine the number of people with muscular dystrophy in the United States in October of that year, Paul Cohen set his sights on finding fundraisers for the MDAA. To aid his cause, my uncle went to NBC executives to arrange for Martin & Lewis to do a short "plug" for MDAA. During the broadcasts aired on their TV and radio programs, Martin and Lewis asked viewers and listeners to donate to this worthy charity. Similar to the pitches they had previously made for the March of Dimes and Easter Seals, Martin & Lewis made a plea for MDAA donations on *The Colgate Comedy Hour* on December 30, 1951, at the end of their program:

Jerry says, "We'd like to say that this is a very, very worthy cause and a very, very difficult illness. There's no cure, and there's no cause. They need money very, very badly within the next two months. If you could find it in your hearts to send just something to help children who may die any day."

Dean added, "There's supposed to be about, at least, 40 million people watching this show. Can you imagine if every person would send in just one penny? What would happen?"

Jerry interjected, "It'd be wonderful and help a lot of children. Do that for yourselves. Do that for us because we all love children, and we all have them."

Replicating Berle's successful recipe for a telethon, my uncle Ernie arranged for Dean Martin & Jerry Lewis to MC their first televised fundraiser. Seen only on New York's WNBT/Channel 4 on March 15, 1952, Dean and Jerry hosted a local 18-hour telethon, produced and directed by Ernest D. Glucksman, to benefit the proposed New York Cardiac Hospital. With 60 performers appearing on the show, they received over a million dollars in pledges. While many in the movie industry perceived television as a threat to their empires, Walt Disney and other insightful movie-makers saw this new medium as a vehicle to drive people to their theatrical releases. However, most in the film industry were not fans of this developing media. Nevertheless, television was the perfect vehicle to hold charitable benefits, raise money for worthy causes, and promote talent.

Hosted by Bing Crosby and Bob Hope, the goal of the next televised fundraiser of note was to fund that year's U.S. Olympic athletes bound for Helsinki, Finland. Held on June 21-22, 1952, at the El Capitan Theatre in Los Angeles, this 14½-hour marathon telecast, which marked Crosby's TV debut, was carried by both CBS and NBC. Hollywood responded with vast numbers of celebrities who volunteered their services and support. This was the first nationally broadcast telethon. Live on TV, luminaries accepted phone pledges, performed, and pitched for viewer donations. Crosby and Hope were contracted with Paramount Pictures, and so were Dean Martin and Jerry Lewis. Jerry Lewis was unleashed and uninhibited at this telethon, ad-libbing and creating pandemonium. He was so raucous that Bing Crosby left the stage, fearing Jerry would strip him of his toupée. Over a million dollars was pledged for the athletes to attend the Olympics. Although many phoned in bogus pledges, enough money was raised to send the team abroad.

Recognizing the promotional potential of the televised fundraisers, executives at Paramount Pictures suggested that Uncle Ernie find a national telethon for Dean and Jerry, as it would increase box-office sales for these stars. Given my uncle's relationship with Paul Cohen and the Muscular Dystrophy Association, the wheels were quickly put into motion for the first MDAA telethon hosted by Martin & Lewis.

The REAL Jerry Lewis Story

Star-studded telethons were gaining popularity as a means to raise money for charitable organizations; however, not everyone liked the idea of free entertainment for the good of the cause. Movie makers and theatre owners reportedly complained to the theatrical unions and guilds that their ticket sales dropped every time their stars appeared on a televised fundraiser. The implication was that telethons were taking away from their box office and popcorn revenue. The question was, "What did they expect the unions to do about the situation?"

Competition was nothing new to the entertainment industry. In the early 1800s, music boxes that could play various tunes in the home were introduced to America. Home entertainment advanced into the modern age with the invention of the player piano in 1901. Invented by Thomas Edison and manufactured by RCA Victor, talking machines, which included cylinder machines and phonographs, allowed people to hear artists such as Enrico Caruso, Sophie Tucker, Rudy Vallee, Paul Whiteman and His Orchestra, and other artists in the comfort of their homes. Since the advent of commercial radio in the 1920s, home entertainment has impacted ticket sales for movies, vaudeville, burlesque, symphony orchestras, and legitimate theatre.

Before the 1920s, movie palaces were not air-conditioned. The sweltering hot temperatures and summer humidity, combined with the audience's own body heat, created a sticky, uncomfortable environment for movie-goers, causing ticket sales and profits to slump in warm weather. After Willis Carrier installed the first air-conditioner in the luxurious Rivoli Theatre on Times Square in New York City in 1925, this new technology revolutionized the cinema as fans filled the movie theatres, sometimes just to cool off.

The movie industry employed many tactics to bring people back into their theatres. In the 1930s, the radio serial Amos 'n' Andy was so popular that movie houses turned off their projectors and turned on their sound system to broadcast the latest episode of that 15-minute program; otherwise, millions of people of all races and creeds across the country would have stayed home to listen to it on the radio. During that era, dialect humor was part of the American culture with radio programs like *The Goldbergs* (Jewish), *Life with Luigi* (Italian), *I Remember Mama* (Swedish), *Abie's Irish Rose* (Jewish/Irish), *Meet Me at Parky's* (Greek), *The Adventures of Charlie Chan* (Chinese), plus others. Many of the shows were multi-media in that a radio program became a television program, a Broadway show became a motion picture, and so on. Filmmakers and theatre owners were creative in reeling the public back to the cinemas. The Camden Drive-in, advertised as the first "automotive movie theatre" in the world, opened on June 6, 1933, in Pennsauken, New Jersey. For under $1, couples could enjoy talkies and do in their car what they could not do in the movie theatre balconies.

During the heydays of radio in the 1930s and 1940s, stars of the big screen might only appear in one or two films a year. To keep their names alive and their bank accounts solvent, they often performed on the radio as guest stars or in their own series. Frank Sinatra was a featured vocalist on the weekly radio show *Your Hit Parade*, and he also played the principal character in 25 episodes of a radio drama, *Rocky Fortune*. Mickey Rooney not only starred as Andy Hardy in that popular motion picture series but also portrayed the same character in the weekly radio adaptation of *The Hardy Family*. *The Six-Shooter* was a cowboy radio series starring Jimmy Stewart. Featured as a crime-fighting newspaper editor on the radio's weekly broadcast of *Big Town*, Edgar G. Robinson played the lead role. Humphrey Bogart and Lauren Bacall had a radio series called *Bold Venture*. Untold numbers of Hollywood celebrities appeared on the weekly anthology series *Lux Radio Theatre*. The 10 *Maisie* films, starring Ann Sothern, were so popular they were made into a spinoff of over 80 radio episodes called *The Adventures of Maisie*. Countless stars used radio appearances to promote their latest motion pictures. While the movie industry valued radio to draw people into the theatres, it feared television would drive them away.

As the public turned to television for entertainment and news in the 1950s, movie theatres devised ways to lure people away from their TV sets. Movie houses had "bank nights," where people put their names into a lottery to win prizes and giveaways of tableware like dishes and glasses for ticket stubs. Some movie theatre owners competed against television by providing live entertainment along with the cinema. In the early to mid-1960s, I was hired by local movie theatres to perform comedy and magic before the main feature as an incentive to draw youngsters away from Saturday morning TV shows. The first 500 youngsters to buy a ticket to the movies got a pencil box. It was commonplace for celebrities like Dorothy Lamour, the Three Stooges, or Jerry Lewis to make personal appearances in movie theatres to promote their latest films. Hollywood and movie moguls were very resourceful in securing viewership by showing double features, newsreels, and cartoons. Vista Vision, 3-D movies, CinemaScope, and Cinerama were all expensive gimmicks introduced to draw people to the silver screen. When TV sets became a fixture in nearly every household in the country, filmmakers, Broadway producers, and movie stars used telethons to generate interest in their talents to a vast audience. The performer's payment was in the form of publicity.

Representing unions and guilds of the theatrical community in the 1950s, Theatre Authority, Inc., acted as the clearing house for benefit performances. Not only did this non-profit organization scrutinize the legitimacy of charities, but it also established and oversaw regulations to protect performers and stage managers. Theatre Authority initially agreed to let members of these trade organizations make non-salaried benefit appearances. However, the motion picture studios, nightclub owners, and theatre companies supposedly badgered Theatre Authority to stop this practice because the public could see their stars for free. Theatre Authority claimed that the telethons kept people watching these lengthy variety shows at home. Before Martin & Lewis' 1956 telethon, the MDAA launched several televised fundraisers. From 1952-1953, these local fundraisers, hosted by celebrities like Dick Van Dyke, Robert Alda, and Virginia Graham were held across the country in Ohio, Georgia, Michigan, Wisconsin, and Washington, D.C.

In 1953, television was still in its infancy. The screen's small, black-and-white images were generally fuzzy and needed constant adjustments. If an airplane passed overhead in the middle of a double play in baseball, the picture would break up, and the viewer would miss the action. Despite television's technical limitations, Theatre Authority was seemingly wary of this new medium and took measures to stifle its development.

Theatre Authority dug in its heels to halt the 1953 Martin & Lewis MDAA telethon and refused to permit union and guild members to work without remuneration. To keep the telethon alive and to satisfy all parties, Paul Cohen offered to pay the talent, including Martin & Lewis. However, accepting money to host a benefit telethon for which they were fund-raising was morally contradictory. Most celebrities did not want to be paid for a benefit performance since they felt donating their time was contributing to the charity. Other artists had exclusive contracts that precluded them from working for pay elsewhere, but they could volunteer their time. Theatre Authority, nonetheless, stood their ground and put the kibosh on the telethon. When the MDAA informed Theatre Authority they had spent over $90,000 in promotional materials for this event, and the letter carriers had already agreed to deliver pledge envelopes and take donations on their own time, Theatre Authority organizers relented but imposed strict limitations: The planned 16-20 hour telethon was reduced to a 2-hour variety show with no opportunity for the viewers to phone in pledges. Simulcast on the ABC radio and TV networks, the program starred Martin & Lewis, Dick Stabile and His Orchestra, and far fewer celebrities than initially planned. The word "telethon" was intentionally omitted from the program's title, *Dean Martin & Jerry Lewis Present Their Radio and Television Party for Muscular Dystrophy Honoring the Letter Carriers of America for Their Volunteer March of Mercy*. Nevertheless, some media used the word "telethon" to refer to this program because it was a convenient and recognizable term. The program honored the letter carriers for aiding the collection of funds for MDAA.

Theatre Authority felt that a percentage of the money donated to the 1953 Muscular Dystrophy Association fundraiser should go to their professional charities. Without their cut, Theatre Authority would not permit the members of their theatrical communities to work for free. Reports in the early 1950s indicate an agreement was struck stating that 10 percent of the gross monies collected from the telethon would be paid to Theatre Authority to support their programs. While most donors thought all the talents who worked on the show did so gratis, that was not the case. Although many artists returned their earnings to the charity, some performers and their agents considered these appearances simply another engagement. The theatrical unions and guilds might have made good use of the monies they culled from the telethons; however, the benevolent listeners and viewers who sent in $1, $5, $50, or more were unaware that 10 percent of their donations was being diverted to the various actors' unions.

Complicating the situation, Martin & Lewis and their executive producer Ernie Glucksman were under exclusive contracts with NBC, and the proposed MDAA program was to be broadcast on ABC, a rival network. Uncle Ernie worked out an agreement with NBC granting them all permission to perform on ABC. Despite ongoing tension between Theatre Authority, the artists, the charitable organizations, and the film industry, numerous telethons were held throughout the country to support such causes as United Cerebral Palsy, Easter Seals, the American Heart Association, March of Dimes, and the Arthritis Foundation. In 1954, the following year, there was no Martin & Lewis telethon. However, Dean Martin & Jerry Lewis did appear in a series of filmed public service announcements thanking the firefighters and other public servants for collecting MDAA donations. As part of their thank-you, they made a plea for the public to continue to support this worthy cause. Broadcast in New York City on Channel 5 on September 10-11, 1955, the MDAA returned with a celebrity-packed 19-hour telethon that raised $225,000 hosted by none other than "The Toastmaster General of the United States," Georgie Jessel.

When Martin & Lewis assumed the honorary position as MDAA's national entertainment chairmen in 1951, which lasted until their first MDAA telethon in 1956, they had done one variety show, a few promotional spots, and some ads for the organization. Those first five years of planning were as rocky as the relationship between Martin and Lewis. Both on stage and off, they were barely speaking to each other. The first MDAA telethon I attended was at Carnegie Hall on June 29-30, 1956. This was also the first and only Martin & Lewis Telethon for MDAA. Televised on New York's WABD/Channel 5, the call letters stood for Allen B. DuMont, who established America's third television network. Channel 5 was the flagship station for the DuMont Network, consisting of several US stations. Only the local New York affiliate aired this telethon. I was there because Uncle Ernie was the program's executive producer. He knew how much I admired Martin & Lewis and arranged for me to work at the event. At nine years old, I had the job of "running" the pledge cards from the offstage telephone operators to my uncle. After I gave the cards to him, he sorted the pledges and handed them to Dean or Jerry, who would periodically mention the donors on the air. Running through the corridors of this theatre was fascinating because it had been temporarily converted into a television studio. There were hundreds of yards of cables, scores of hot video lights, boom microphones overhead, and large black-and-white WABD-TV cameras on dollies traversing the main stage, effectively blocking the audience's view. Video monitors were scattered everywhere. Surrounded by this jungle of electronics, it was hard for me to imagine that I was standing in the usually elegant and austere Carnegie Hall. As the first entry in *Rick Saphire's Book of World Records*, I am pleased to announce that Dean Martin holds the record for a famous singer to perform on the stage at Carnegie Hall for 21 straight hours.

On June 26, 1956, Martin & Lewis were on NBC's Today show, broadcast in part as a live remote from the 500 Club (formerly called the 500 Café) in Atlantic City. Their appearance was to celebrate their alleged 10th anniversary as a team, which allegedly began at the 500 Club, and to promote their upcoming MDAA telethon. Viewing the kinescope of this spot leaves no doubt that the relationship between Dean and Jerry was on "life support." When not needling or interrupting his partner, Jerry ignored Dean as he played to the glamorous actress and TV hostess Faye Emerson. Visibly aggravated, Dean Martin had little to say because he could not get a word in edgewise, and he walked off the set before the program ended. Part of the problem may have been that Martin & Lewis' appearance on the *Today Show* came at about 8:30 a.m., and most nightclub entertainers do not know there are two 8:30s in the same day. All joking aside, the real issue was that Jerry was essentially doing a single act and virtually ignoring his partner.

Ricky and Joanie Saphire at the 1957 MDAA Telethon

On With the Show...

The artists on this program appear with the cooperation and permission of Theatre Authority, whose member unions are:

ACTORS' EQUITY ASSOCIATION
AMERICAN FEDERATION OF TELEVISION AND RADIO ARTISTS
AMERICAN GUILD OF MUSICAL ARTISTS
AMERICAN GUILD OF VARIETY ARTISTS
SCREEN ACTORS GUILD

Rebroadcast or reuse of artists' performances is prohibited without the express written consent of Theatre Authority and the Muscular Dystrophy Association of America.

So began the 1956 MDAA telethon with Martin & Lewis. Tension between Dean and Jerry was palpable from the start. I was backstage as ominous rumors circulated that this could be Dean's last television appearance with Jerry. Halfway through the program, my uncle told me this was, in fact, the truth. This was to be Dean and Jerry's TV swan song. As the news spread among the staff, I saw shock and sadness on their faces. Even though the duo had been feuding for years and were no longer socializing with each other, their break-up was still hard to believe. I loved the team of Martin & Lewis, and they always seemed to love each other. In my mind, Dean symbolized the patient father, who was always amused by the shenanigans of Jerry, the kid every kid wanted to be.

Following the 1956 telethon, Martin & Lewis had only one more live performance together at the Copacabana Night Club in Manhattan on July 24, 1956. While singer Dean Martin prepared to re-establish himself as a solo performer, Jerry, who began his career as a record mime act, had to re-invent himself without a partner or an off-stage phonograph. Jerry Lewis went on to host the 1957 MDAA Telethon, while Dean Martin hosted a similar 19-hour televised fundraiser on May 25-26, 1957, sponsored by the Dean Martin Blood Disease Center at the City of Hope to combat childhood leukemia. Dean Martin's telethon was to benefit a single hospital in California, yet, strangely enough, nobody outside of the New York metropolitan area could view this program.

Performers can be altruistic and give of themselves without expecting anything in return. On October 8, 1957, a month before that year's MDAA telethon, Jerry Lewis' team arranged to have several celebrities join Jerry at an NBC television studio to greet and entertain a young victim of muscular dystrophy, celebrating his 9th, and possibly his last, birthday. This lonely boy, nicknamed Francis X to protect his identity, was in the hospital, gravely ill, and felt no one cared about him. His father was in prison for killing his mother. Having heard about the child's situation, within 27 hours, Jerry spearheaded the production of an instant show featuring Jimmy Dodd along with Walt Disney's Mouseketeers, Darlene Gillespie, Bobby Burgess, and Doreen Tracey; singers Mary Costa, Dinah Shore, and Eddie Fisher; actor Hugh O'Brien, star of TV's *Wyatt Earp*; comedians George Gobel, Pinky Lee, and Eddie Cantor. The celebrities quickly rehearsed for this private show that was beamed directly to a television set in Francis' hospital room via closed-circuit TV in Hollywood. NBC, the MDAA, and Jerry contributed to the cost of the show. When asked why he did it, Jerry said, "I just thought it would be a nice gift." Although making a sick child happy is often ample payment for an artist, it also makes for good press.

The 1957 Jerry Lewis Thanksgiving Party for Muscular Dystrophy Telethon was held on November 30-December 1 at the Hotel Roosevelt Ballroom in Manhattan, where Guy Lombardo and his band played every New Year's Eve for over 40 years. At this telethon, I spent most of my time bringing pledge cards from the off-stage phone banks to the stage area for Jerry to read on the air and doing magic tricks backstage for the MDAA's poster child, who was in a wheelchair. My sister Joanie went on camera with Jerry Lewis to donate the $209.00 she had collected designing, producing, and selling MDAA badges. My mom worked the telephones taking pledges, and my dad managed pledge cards. He was on camera updating the tote board numbers, which were manually operated in those days. The famed "tote board" was not an exacting science. The audience was often reminded that the money tallied during the show only reflected donations from viewers during the telethon. Usually, cash collected by organizations like the firefighters was added to the tote board, but what was not reflected here were the millions of dollars paid to the MDAA by corporations. Businesses paid large sums to be classified as corporate sponsors, which entitled them to be mentioned on the air. For the privilege of presenting the check to Jerry Lewis live on camera, the corporation had to pay the MDAA an additional sum.

Because my sister was going to present her donation to Jerry on the air, my cousin, watching the show on TV at home, made an audiotape of telethon segments using my Webcor tape recorder. Listening to the audiotape vividly brings back those memories. Jerry Lewis was known to have a sharp tongue and a temper to match. He usually vented his anger just out of the earshot of people in the studio, but the star lashed out directly at his audience that night. My sister Joanie had just presented Jerry with a donation check. During my break, I sat in the hotel ballroom, which had been converted into a TV studio for this event. Jerry introduced Milton Berle to a room full of adoring fans. As the orchestra played Milton's theme song, "Near You," the people around me were on their feet. The cheers and whistles were deafening. Seeing Milton Berle in person was a surprise to many in attendance, who were buzzing with excitement. When the first sound emerged from Berle's mouth, Jerry Lewis upstaged him with a loud, long, "Shush." as he instructed the people in the audience to be courteous. When Milton Berle opened his mouth to speak again, Jerry Lewis interrupted his guest by saying, "Wait." With no respect for Berle's ability to control an audience, Jerry Lewis drew all of the attention onto himself as he walked to the proscenium to admonish those sitting around me. His tone was vitriolic as he declared that Milton Berle earns more money than the telethon, and Berle was here as a favor. This did not sit well with the people who just wanted to see "Uncle Miltie," but it effectively kept all of the attention on Jerry. The audience grew louder, showing their displeasure with Lewis' interruptions and reprimands.

At this point, a well-meaning, uniformed serviceman turned to the people around him, close to where I was sitting, and motioned them to be quiet. Jerry Lewis saw this and went ballistic. The enlisted man's involvement infuriated Jerry. His face became red, and he exploded. "Soldier, right here. Soldier, don't help." Lewis screamed at the top of his lungs, "Sit down, and let's have quiet." The soldier sat down, but the rumblings of displeasure continued. The ugly and unprofessional scene was being played out to millions of New York viewers. As Jerry stepped in front of Milton Berle, "Mr. Television" was left alone and looking helpless at center stage. Jerry Lewis was precisely where he wanted to be, in the center of a self-imposed controversy. Jerry's yelling became even more intense as he lectured the crowd about Berle's emergence from a sickbed to appear on the telethon.

The older and more experienced star finally elected to shut down Lewis. Milton Berle did not want to solicit his fans' affection by complaining about his hardships, so he ended the whole episode by interrupting Jerry Lewis, saying, "All right, all right, Jerry." Finally, having the spotlight to himself, Berle did what he had come there to do: appeal for the needed donations. As a 10 year old, it was hard to understand how Jerry Lewis could be so charming when the cameras were on him and then abruptly shift into a screaming tyrant when they were off. In this case, witnessing his tirade on stage was even more shocking.

Although Jerry Lewis did not host any MDAA televised fundraisers in 1958, he returned for *The 1959*

Thanksgiving Party Telethon at the Ziegfeld Theatre in New York City to benefit the Institute of Muscle Disease, an affiliate of the MDAA. This telethon was again a family affair, with all of us volunteering to do our parts. On a personal note, at 12 years old, I could hardly imagine the next Jerry Lewis telethon I would attend would be in 2005 as Jerry Lewis' theatrical representative.

Many of the early MDAA fundraisers kicked off their campaigns around Thanksgiving. In 1960, the famous New York rock 'n' roll DJ Bruce Morrow, known to his fans and the music industry as Cousin Brucie, hosted a televised fundraiser advertised as a 2-hour MDAA "telethon." The show was on WATV/Channel 13, an independent Newark, New Jersey, station. In 1961, a three-hour MDAA fundraiser titled *The Jerry Lewis Thanks-for-Giving Party* featured dozens of show business celebrities who appeared to make a pitch for contributions. This spectacular was broadcast to the New York tri-state area on WNEW-TV Channel 5 and produced by Ernest D. Glucksman. Mr. Landau of Beacon Wax arranged for his company to help defray production costs of the program, and Paul Cohen, whose Technical Tape Corporation had manufactured "Martin & Lewis" Tuck Tape in the 1950s, arranged for print advertisements promoting this event. Reminiscent of their two-hour 1953 "telethon," people could not phone in donations. Instead, they were asked to mail in contributions or donate when an official volunteer knocked on their door.

In 1962, Jerry Lewis hosted a special one-hour variety show, *From This Moment On*, sponsored by MDAA and produced by my uncle, Ernest D. Glucksman. Jerry's wife Patti was seen sitting in the balcony with the MDA poster child, Lola Lucus. Jerry asked the wheelchair-bound little girl if he could kiss her on the cheek, remarking, "All I have is boys."

Jerry Lewis agreed to host the 1966 telethon for the newly reorganized Muscular Dystrophy Association (MDA) to be aired Labor Day weekend. Seen only on New York's Channel 5, this program was so successful that it became the vanguard for more than 40 years of annual telethons as the fundraiser appeared on the ever-growing network of stations across the United States, Canada, and eventually worldwide on the Internet. The MDA assembled a network of local stations nationwide, identified as the Love Network, making the Jerry Lewis' Labor Day Muscular Dystrophy telethons an annual national event that lasted until 2010.

For many years, the MDA telethons were broadcast from New York City with a signal that covered the New York metropolitan area, the most densely populated region in the country. Aside from its vast viewership, it provided access to abundant talent from nightclubs, Broadway, and television. Once the MDA established its own TV network across the country, it didn't matter where the show originated. After becoming recognized as the Entertainment Capital of the World, the MDA telethon moved to Las Vegas in 1973 for its talents, glitz, and ever-growing popularity. Not surprisingly, after Louis Prima finished his last show, he could take a short taxi ride to be on national TV with Jerry Lewis. Stars like Frank Sinatra, Steve Lawrence and Eydie Gormé, Don

Rickles, Charlie Callas, and Rip Taylor frequently "dropped in" on Jerry between or after their shows. Ed McMahon heightened the excitement in the telethon promos as he announced, "Stay up and watch the stars come out on the Jerry Lewis Labor Day telethon." The 1970s was the most exciting and glamorous era for these televised fundraisers. Jerry was still young and energetic, and the celebrities who appeared appealed to a cross-section of generations.

One night during the summer of 1976, I received a call from Uncle Ernie with a cryptic message. "Ricky," he said, "make sure you watch the telethon when Frank Sinatra comes on around 3 a.m. your time. I can't tell you why, but make sure you're watching." Although he and Jerry had parted ways 12 years earlier, my uncle was still very active and well-connected in the entertainment business. The fact that he would not divulge any information convinced me that he must have gotten exciting news from an insider. Something was about to happen, and I was intrigued. My uncle didn't say the words, but my first thought was, "It has something to do with Dean." Setting up my Panasonic reel-to-reel videotape machine, I hit the record button as soon as "Old Blue Eyes" appeared on the telethon. Accompanied by saxophonist Sam Butera, Sinatra finished singing and called Jerry to join him center stage. Frank Sinatra read off the names of some donors. Then, he casually remarked, "Jerry, I've got a friend who likes your work." Speaking to no one in particular, Sinatra said, "Could someone send out my friend?"

Frank Sinatra then supposedly surprised Jerry by bringing out Dean Martin. Supposedly, Martin and Lewis had not been in each other's company for 20 years. Uncle Ernie knew weeks before the 1976 Jerry Lewis MDA telethon that Frank Sinatra would be introducing Dean Martin on the program. Quite a few people were involved in planning this "surprise" for Jerry, and I am sure Jerry knew about it. After all, I knew about it. Insiders knew the best way to get thrown under the bus by the "King of Comedy" was to surprise him. Jerry hated surprises and would not tolerate them. At that moment, show business history was made, or at least, that's how it appeared.

Let's Go to the Tote Board

Herb Saphire at the tote board during the 1957 Jerry Lewis MDAA Telethon

After Jerry Lewis' effectiveness as a comedian peaked, the MDA kept his star shining, and Jerry Lewis kept those televised fundraisers growing. With over 200 local stations carrying the live feed, the Love Network was one of the largest independent television networks. The telethon feed from Las Vegas ran for 45 minutes per hour, providing 15 minutes per hour for the network affiliates to run their own local MDA fundraisers. For the stations that could not afford a live 15-minute production per hour, MDA provided them with a 15-minute fill, primarily made up of clips from past telethons.

In the 1980s and 1990s, telethons flourished amid pockets of protests, lawsuits, controversies, and criticisms. Underlying tensions in the 2000s mounted during Jerry Lewis' last decade of association with the MDA, and the popularity of the telethons waned. I witnessed conflicts firsthand that exacerbated the already emotionally charged situation, which led to Jerry Lewis' termination as the host of the MDA fundraisers and stripping him of his title of MDA National Chairman.

In those early days of the telethons, Jerry Lewis would be on camera round the clock. As he got older and faced health issues, he would open the show for the first few hours, introduce his fill-in host, and return for the final several hours before singing "You'll Never Walk Alone." By the 2000s, the A-list of stars had dwindled, and Jerry had no reason to stay up through the off-peak hours. Although Frank Sinatra, Wayne Newton, Milton Berle, Sammy Davis, Jr., Totie Fields, Liberace, and other legendary performers were no longer finishing up their shows in Las Vegas with just enough time to "drop in" and join Jerry on camera, they sometimes appeared on the telethons via cut-aways and remotes. During the final years, local acts, dancing schools, and the Muppets carried on throughout the night as Jerry recharged his batteries.

When Jerry approached me to represent him in the early 2000s, I felt comfortable and well-equipped to accept his offer. I understood Jerry Lewis' erratic temperament and realized his earning potential, so I took him on as a client for two reasons: bread and butter. Actually, there was a third reason; he was still my hero. Jerry was looking for someone who could understand him, represent him, and find work for him. He also sought me out because he felt nostalgic about carrying on our "lineage." After all, my uncle, Ernest D. Glucksman, helped craft the TV careers of Martin & Lewis and Jerry's as a solo performer throughout the 1950s and 1960s.

For almost a decade, I brought celebrities I represented to DragonCon, a popular convention in Atlanta, Georgia, that draws thousands of fans of the film, gaming, art, comic, and television industries. Held over the long Labor Day weekend, this multi-genre event provides a venue where current and nostalgic icons sell their autographs, and convention vendors sell their treasured memorabilia. During one of my visits, I was approached by the head of DragonCon and asked if I could arrange to have their event mentioned on Atlanta's local cut-away of the national "Jerry Lewis Telethon." I recommended having a celebrity memorabilia auction and donating the proceeds to the MDA. The idea quickly became a reality with the assistance of one of my clients, Cathy Garver, best known for her portrayal of Cissy on the sitcom *Family Affair*. Collectibles were donated by the attending stars and sold, amounting to over $7,000, and DragonCon's management added to the funds, rounding the sum up to an even $10,000. With this sizable donation in hand, I contacted the Atlanta Broadcast Center. Grateful for the funds, they agreed to put me on the air on behalf of DragonCon. Arriving at Channel 69, Cathy and I presented the corporate check to the TV host on the air. Invited to join Jerry Lewis in California for the remainder of the telethon, I flew out to the home base for the national 2005 broadcast. Jerry was not in a good mood.

Against his better judgment, the show had been moved to the Beverly Hills Hotel, a smaller venue that lacked the show business excitement Jerry Lewis was used to.

When the 2006 Jerry Lewis MDA telethon returned to Las Vegas, I returned to Atlanta for DragonCon. Appearing in the Atlanta cutaway of the telethon were the TV sitcom *Happy Days* stars Erin Moran, Don Most, and Anson Williams, as well as my good friend and client, the wild and unpredictable comedian Rip Taylor. To the delight and benefit of the Atlanta Muscular Dystrophy Association, I was accompanied by one of the most iconic movie stars and entertainers of all time, Mickey Rooney, escorted by his talented wife, Jan. At the request

Rick Saphire's friends and clients in Atlanta, Rip Taylor and movie icon Mickey Rooney

of the Atlanta producers, I arranged to have Mickey make an on-camera plea for donations.

Mickey Rooney's appearance at the telethon was not without some challenges. It seemed that Mickey suffered from a type of mild dementia. While rehearsing his speech, he often became overly emotional and said things that honestly made little or no sense. When I suggested revising some of what he was planning to say, Mickey became upset, loud, and argumentative. Finally, Jan and her son Chris Aber, Mickey's stepson, came to my rescue, and we calmed him down together.

While this scene unfolded in the lobby, a member of the telethon production crew was unobtrusively looking on. As a result, Mickey's spot on the show was cut from 5 minutes to 90 seconds. They probably would have canceled his spot if they hadn't already announced that Mickey Rooney would be on the bill. As Mickey Rooney's representative, I had to break the news to him. After I told him he would only have 90 seconds on the air, Mickey was angry and in tears and wanted to leave the building. Just then, Mickey noticed uniformed members of the Atlanta Fire Department, who were there to deliver collected donations. Mickey wanted to meet the firefighters. Knowing they were ready to go on the air, Jan and Chris lovingly restrained Mickey. I approached the firefighters and asked if they could spare a moment before they went on camera to meet Mickey Rooney. Surprised and thrilled, we brought Mickey over to meet them. Mickey's "man-child" came to the surface, and it was a wonderful sight to behold. There were smiles all around. But now we had to face Mickey's appearance on the live broadcast, aware that whatever happened would be seen by millions of local TV viewers and the press. Mickey sat in a chair provided by the stage crew, and then he insisted another chair be set next to him for his wife Jan, since he wanted her by his side.

The countdown coming out of the commercial dwindled to only a few seconds; there was terror in the hearts of everyone in the studio. The red light on top of the TV camera lit up, indicating Mickey and Jan were live on TV. That's when a miracle happened. This small, hard-to-control, unpredictable, agitated elderly man became "Mickey Rooney." In stunned disbelief, we heard a most eloquent, soft-spoken, well-rehearsed, compelling, sympathetic, and passionate man give the most heartfelt plea for the needed donations. Mickey's allotted 90 seconds became several minutes of heartfelt drama, bringing tears to the eyes. If I were an atheist, I would now believe in God because God surely had His hand on Mickey Rooney's shoulder.

The Mickey Rooney MDA saga did not end there. On the heels of his sensational appearance on the telethon in Atlanta, Mickey and his wife Jan asked if I could arrange to have him appear on the national broadcast with Jerry Lewis in 2007. I was ready to pitch the idea to Jerry. The telethon would have two of Hollywood's greatest stars, Mickey Rooney, whose body of work dated back to the silent era, and Jerry Lewis, who gained international popularity in the late 1940s with *My Friend Irma.* In 2007, both of these superstars would be live on the same stage. They could do a song and dance routine together. It would be a historical event.

I called Jerry and told him about Mickey's appearance in Atlanta. Before I could ask him, Jerry asked me, "Would Mickey be interested in coming on with me next year?" Of course, I told Jerry that his idea was great, assuring him Mickey would love to do it. Jerry told me he would make a few calls and let me know for sure. When Jerry called me back, he was sullen. Someone in Atlanta had spoken to someone at the MDA about Mickey's "uncontrollable" behavior before he went on the air. "Jerry," I said, "I was with Mickey every minute in Atlanta, and his behavior was a bit erratic. Mickey was excited and worked up, but as soon as the cameras went on, he was nothing less than perfection." Jerry countered that the telethon entertainment booker was unwilling to take a chance because Mickey had been so hard to control.

My reply to Jerry was somewhat sarcastic: "Jerry, you don't manage a charm school, either." I reminded him that it does not matter what happens in the Green Room and off camera. I reminded him that we were all professionals who could handle entertainers' temperaments. Although Jerry agreed with what I said, adding that he loved Mickey and the whole idea, he could not fight the system. The idea was shelved forever.

The accounting I just detailed was my first indication of the depth of the breakdown in Jerry Lewis' position within the MDA. Behind the scenes, there was infighting on several fronts as the players vied for power. Shortly after my conversation with Jerry, I encountered Eddie Foy III, the MDA entertainment booker who nixed Mickey Rooney's appearance with Jerry. Apparently, Foy hated

Jerry Lewis and would have done whatever he could to come between Jerry and the MDA.

There were many other Foy vs. Lewis incidents. I had been friends with Rip Taylor for over 40 years, and he called to tell me he had been replaced on the MDA telethon. His spot had been given to another prop comedian. When I spoke to Jerry, he verified what Rip had told me, explaining that the MDA was looking for younger talent to appeal to younger viewers. Jerry sounded unhappy about this decision because he liked Rip.

Mallory Lewis, the daughter of the famous ventriloquist Shari Lewis, was a client of mine. My connection to Mallory went beyond representing her. In the 1950s, when I was a boy who wanted to become an entertainer, I was introduced to Dr. Abraham Hurwitz, who was a professor at New York's Yeshiva University for 47 years and was well-known as Peter Pan, the Magic Man. Doc Hurwitz was my magic teacher, Shari Lewis' father, and Mallory's grandfather. Mallory was a highly qualified entertainer. Upon her mother's death, she gave life to the beloved sock puppet, Lamb Chop, created by her mother.

Even the most discerning fan of Lamb Chop would be hard-pressed to hear a difference between Lamb Chop's voice from the days of Shari Lewis to those of Mallory. As Mallory Lewis' representative in the mid-2000s, I recommended her for a spot on the 2007 MDA Telethon. After Jerry saw Mallory's promotional video, he was sold and wanted both the ventriloquist and her famous alter-ego, Lamb Chop, to appear with him in primetime during the opening hours of the telethon. Jerry then instructed me to sell the idea to Eddie Foy III, the MDA's talent coordinator, since he and Foy did not see eye-to-eye on many issues.

I found myself in the middle of their power play as the referee. Eddie Foy III, who had come from a renowned show business family of actors, had made a name for himself as a casting director with an extensive and impressive list of credits. In my first conversation with Foy, I was taken aback when this man bluntly stated, "The fuckin' old man [referring to Jerry] has no taste in talent." He continued, "How can he [Jerry Lewis] ask me to put on a pretty little bitch with a sock on her hand?" His characterizations, replete with expletives, continued for 10 minutes. I assured him I knew Mallory and that she was very talented, adding that most adult telethon viewers grew up watching her mother on TV. He responded, "Now, her mother is a different story. I knew Shari Lewis and would have loved to fuck her." This was my last conversation with Eddie Foy III, as I had no desire to talk with him again. He had been the telethon entertainment coordinator for many years and made no secret of his disdain for Jerry Lewis. I found him to be far less professional than the people he disparaged. What I

Mallory Lewis and Lamb Chop

found amusing was the idea that Eddie Foy III would have wanted to go to bed with Shari Lewis even though she also had a sock puppet on her hand.

In a way, Jerry Lewis won the battle. Grudgingly, Eddie Foy III agreed to have Mallory Lewis appear on the telethon, but he scheduled her appearance as far away from primetime as possible. Mallory Lewis and Lamb Chop appeared on the show in the wee small hours of the morning while the telethon's star was fast asleep. I was not in attendance at the 2007 MDA telethon; however, I stayed up all night to catch my client on the show right after the cloggers. A few days after Mallory's outstanding performance, Jerry called to thank me for suggesting her for the show and to apologize for her unsatisfactory treatment. Sometime later, I learned just how unsatisfactory Mallory's treatment was. The fight between Jerry Lewis and Eddie Foy III got down and dirty. Mallory Lewis, along with her traveling companion, actress Jane Damian, were transported from the Las Vegas airport to the hotel/studio, not in a limo but in the back of a large, empty cargo van, where they had to sit on the floor with no seatbelts or windows. This contemptible act of retribution against Jerry Lewis was the brainchild of Eddie Foy III. Mallory Lewis remained the consummate professional through it all, performed her spot on the show with humor and class, and Lamb Chop followed suit.

In 2007, I was representing both Jerry Lewis and Gary Lewis, who was Jerry's eldest son and the popular lead singer of Gary Lewis & the Playboys. I arranged for Gary Lewis to cohost a few hours of the Atlanta local cutaway of the MDA telethon, and he was looking forward to doing it. When I told Jerry about the idea he said that it was genius and offered to contact the MDA home office to have them put out a press release. A few weeks later, out of the blue, Gary called to say his spot in Atlanta was cut. He did not know why his appearance was canceled and was unhappy about it. Faulting his father, this put Jerry and Gary's shaky relationship on even shakier grounds.

On July 31, 2007, I was on Jerry's boat and asked him why Gary's Atlanta appearance was canceled. Jerry sidestepped the question by asking me a question. "What do I think would be better for Gary's career? For him to be with me on the national feed of the telethon with 50 million people watching [Jerry might have been confusing his viewership with the Super Bowl] or the local Atlanta cutaway with a few million people tuned in?"

As Gary's manager, the decision was elementary, and I replied, "There is no contest. Appearing for three to four hours on Atlanta TV as a genial host and fundraiser in his own right would undoubtedly be better for Gary's career than appearing on the national MDA broadcast doing two songs and having nothing to say." Gary Lewis & the Playboys had appeared many times on his father's telethons, and Gary was ready for a change.

In the end, Gary performed on the nationally broadcast telethon in Las Vegas and did his two songs. However, the band was not given rehearsal time or a sound check, and during their appearance, only one of the microphones worked. This was not a great showcase for Gary and the band. In all candor, I do not know who was behind the cancellation of Atlanta. If it was the entertainment director's decision, that meant Jerry was no longer in charge.

In 2008, I booked Gary and the band for a two-week concert tour in the Philippines. We were scheduled to leave the day after Jerry's 2008 telethon, which would have enabled Gary to make an appearance. However, Gary asked if I could arrange for us to leave for Manila a day earlier than initially planned so he would be unavailable for Jerry's telethon. After the 2007 telethon fiasco, Gary Lewis had no desire to speak to his father again.

On the day of the telethon, Gary and I were sitting at a café in LAX, where a big-screen TV was broadcasting Jerry's annual event. When our waiter came over to our table, he looked up and said, "Hey, that's the show Jerry Lewis does every year. Have you guys ever watched it?"

And Gary responded, "Oh, yeah. I've seen it before."

The waiter then went about his business, and a few hours later we were on our way to the Philippines. To this day, the waiter probably has no idea he was speaking to the first-born son of the guy he was watching on television, unless, of course, he is reading this book.

Jerry Lewis' telethons advanced many an entertainer's career, but not always. Back in 1966, while I was working as an entertainer on the social staff at the Catskills' Concord Hotel, a bellhop told me that Philly Greenwald, the entertainment buyer at the Concord, wanted to talk to me. I was taken by surprise because, up to that point, Greenwald had never spoken two words to me. Calling him on the house phone, he began, "Rick, you know Jerry Lewis, right?" I immediately thought he wanted to book Jerry into the hotel, and I assured him I knew Jerry. Then, Philly asked, "Rick, can you come to the nightclub show with me tonight?"

I jokingly said to Philly, "This is very sudden, isn't it?"

He laughed and answered, "No. Are you familiar with a comic named Charlie Callas? Jerry Lewis is using him in a movie." I admitted I did not know Charlie and asked him what was happening. Philly replied, "The Charles Rapp Agency wants me to sign Callas to a multi-show contract for the summer."

In those years, the *Guinness Book of World Records* listed the Concord Hotel's Imperial Room as the world's largest nightclub, with a seating capacity of over 2,500. It was a very important booking for any entertainer. Philly Greenwald continued, "The Rapp office says he's a fabulous comedian and is just like Jerry Lewis. Rick," he confessed, "I hate Jerry Lewis, and I have Charlie opening tonight. I'd like you to come with me and give me your opinion."

Charlie Callas was no newcomer to show business. After serving in World War II, he returned home and found work as a drummer with the big bands but was now diving head-first into comedy. A multi-show deal at the Concord would mean Charlie would have many shows in various hotels in the East Coast's resort circuit through

Charlie Callas with author Rick Saphire

the prestigious Rapp Agency. A good contract like that would not only be lucrative for the summer but could be a springboard for advancing his career. That evening, Philly and I sat off to the side at a small table in the Imperial Room, watching as Charlie Callas was introduced.

When the band played his walk-on music, Charlie entered from stage left. The audience immediately began laughing hysterically during his long walk to center stage. There was no doubt that they were looking at a comedian. Charlie, who had long dark hair in keeping with the times, wore a black suit that seemed two sizes too large. He was so skinny that I wanted to throw him a sandwich. His comedic facial expressions and gestures would have scared the life out of any blind date. After staring at the audience for 20 seconds, waiting for the laughter to subside, Charlie's opening line was, "Well, did you ever see a fat greyhound?" Within 30 seconds of his introduction, the audience had made up their minds about him. He was funny, different, and likable.

Fifteen minutes into Charlie's performance, Philly Greenwald took his face out of his hands and asked me what I thought of the act. It was quite evident that Mr. Greenwald did not enjoy the comedy of the comedian whose mannerisms resembled Jerry Lewis. I told Philly it didn't matter what I thought of Charlie. "Look at the audience," I said. "They haven't stopped laughing."

Philly told me he couldn't take anymore. As he got up from his seat to leave the theater, he sighed, "Okay, Rick, I'll sign him." Philly left me in the theater to enjoy the rest of Charlie's act.

There was a lot of Jerry Lewis in Charlie Callas' performance, but Charlie was not a Jerry Lewis clone. Jerry could be imitated but never duplicated. The 1966 Charlie Callas was funnier than the 1966 Jerry Lewis. That summer, Charlie and I frequently crossed paths. We became friends and shared something in common, Jerry Lewis.

By 1967, Charlie had seemingly outgrown club dating in the Catskills and "went Hollywood," becoming friends with the Rat Pack and influential West Coast TV and film producers. By the time I reunited with Charlie, Hollywood was in his blood. He acted more sophisticated. On stage, he now wore beautifully tailored suits and was well-groomed. He insisted on framing his comedy routines with stories about how his friends Frank, Dean, and others enjoyed his bits. As with Jerry Lewis, Charlie

Callas was often funnier than his material. However, Charlie Callas lacked Jerry Lewis' long history as a beloved talent. Charlie's swift metamorphosis from the zany comedian into a sophisticated, seasoned legend came too soon, and he had lost some of his "funny."

Charlie Callas, a popular and charming comedian, managed to get booked as a regular guest on many network TV shows. In 1984, when Jerry Lewis was offered a syndicated talk show for Metromedia, he asked Charlie to be his announcer and sidekick. I was surprised Jerry had taken such a liking to Charlie because typically, Jerry did not like "Jerry Lewis act-alikes." Martin & Lewis' performances worked well because there was a contrast between the two men. Callas and Lewis were too much the same. After the week-long audition, plans for this program were canceled.

Over the years, I remained friends with Charlie Callas and eventually represented him. When I asked Charlie if he would appear at a celebrity autograph show, he did not understand how he would fit into a sci-fi and animation collectors' convention. I reminded him that he appeared in Disney's live and animated film, *Pete's Dragon,* starring Mickey Rooney, who was live on screen. In the movie, Charlie provides the voice for Elliott the Dragon, who makes nonsensical and unintelligible sounds. Charlie was surprised and happy that his fans recognized him at the convention and lined up to meet him and purchase his autographed photos.

I had Charlie scheduled to go to the DragonCon convention in Atlanta, Georgia, on Labor Day weekend.

When Jerry called to ask me if Charlie was available for the telethon, I told him about Charlie's upcoming appearance, adding, "If you need him for the telethon, I will release him." Then, Jerry asked me if Charlie stood to lose much money by giving up the convention. The answer should have been an unequivocal "Yes," but I told Jerry I would discuss it with Charlie and get back to him. I already knew what the answer would be. Charlie, who had been on the telethon many times before, was ecstatic when he heard Jerry's request, but as a friend, he told me that if I needed him at DragonCon, he would not let me down. I knew what had to be done.

While in my hotel room in Atlanta, I watched Charlie's appearance on the telethon. Damned, if he didn't go Hollywood! Jerry waited for Charlie to get funny, but it was slow in coming. Eventually, Charlie stepped out of his staid persona and did a pantomime to a recording of "Yes, I Remember It Well," playing both the parts of Maurice Chevalier and Hermione Gingold, which he had done in prior telethons. Jerry was livid because Charlie did not come on as the fun-loving, silly comedian he and the audience expected.

Jerry Lewis had pushed hard against the rising oppositional forces at the MDA to get Charlie Callas back on the show, and Charlie disappointed and embarrassed him. Later, Charlie called me, "Rick, have you been in touch with Jerry?" I told him I always talked to Jerry and asked why he wanted to know. "I've been phoning Jerry, and he doesn't return my calls," he said.

When I relayed my conversation with Charlie to Jerry, all Jerry said was, "Thanks." I knew Jerry was pissed and why. Jerry Lewis always fought hard to keep the old-timers on the show, and this was not the Charlie Callas he had booked for the telethon. Where was "the funny"? Jerry couldn't forgive his friend for wanting to appear more sophisticated than his comedic character. Ironically, Jerry had often been accused of the same thing, even by me. Jerry never spoke to Charlie after that appearance, and Charlie Callas, who had been on the MDA telethon countless times, never appeared on it again.

The telethon returned to Las Vegas in 2006. However, the studio audience attendance had decreased, so the organization hired professional actors as extras to pose as audience members. Two of them were my clients, who were hired through a Las Vegas casting company. Actress Beverly Washburn, a former child star, appeared in over 500 TV shows, radio programs, and films, including Cecil B. DeMille's Academy Award-winning movie *The Greatest Show on Earth*. She was also featured in Walt Disney's film *Old Yeller*, the cult classic *Spider Baby* with Lon Chaney, Jr., and, among others. My other client, Cynthia Pepper, starred in her own ABC-TV sitcom *Margie*, had a regular role on TV's *My Three Sons*, and shared a love scene with Elvis Presley in *Kissin' Cousins*. Filling the 2006 MDA telethon as studio audience members at Las Vegas' South Point Hotel was not a typical booking for either of them.

Cynthia had heard Jerry Lewis was hard to get along with, so the negative comments people made about him were no surprise to her. She found it endearing that he spoke lovingly about his adopted daughter. "If he adored that little girl that much," Cynthia commented, "he couldn't be all that bad."

Although Beverly had never met Jerry Lewis, she had been a fan of his since she saw his films as a child and was looking forward to seeing the telethon and Jerry Lewis in person. She was disappointed when she heard the crew and audience members disparaging him. "What an atypical booking. We were considered extras," Beverly said, "and when we left the show, we were given our pay and a boxed lunch."

Beginning in the 1950s, the Muscular Dystrophy Association arranged for Jerry Lewis' face to become the symbol of their organization. Throughout the years, Jerry's image appeared on posters, ads, and collection canisters in stores nationwide. When Labor Day came along, it was hard to cross the street without seeing Jerry Lewis' picture promoting the MDA telethon on the side of a passing bus. Between 1970 and 1980, Jerry Lewis did not make any movies. His appearances in nightclubs and on television were few and far between. While Dean Martin carved out a successful career in television, recordings, films, and personal appearances, the MDA was Jerry Lewis' mainstay and his claim to fame. During the telethon airing, business executives handed Jerry Lewis donation checks adding up to millions of dollars with grateful comments like, "We love you, Jerry." It is inarguable that Jerry Lewis gave life to the MDA, and the MDA gave life to Jerry Lewis.

© 2024 Rick Saphire

In the latter years of his association with the telethon, Jerry Lewis' dependence on the MDA seemed far greater than the MDA's dependence on him. By the 1970s, Jerry Lewis' box office draw was over, and his theatrical appearances were minimal except for the highly-rated MDA telethons. Early on, Jerry started calling the victims of neuromuscular disease "my kids," and the media began referring to these children as "Jerry's kids." Over the years, the MDA developed into a massive corporate structure, and Jerry Lewis gave it the much-needed personal touch and heart. When Jerry's tenure with the MDA ended in 2010, it was apparent that "Jerry's kids" had become simply a catchphrase.

As a fundraising host and iconic figurehead of a charitable organization devoted to curing muscular dystrophy and related childhood diseases, Jerry Lewis had a degree of impunity. Throughout the decades, the MDA tolerated Jerry Lewis' issues as long as his work benefitted the organization and its cause. Jerry jeopardized his career with comments he made on the syndicated program *That Show with Joan Rivers*, which aired on September 17, 1968. The show's theme on this day was children in show business. Jerry Lewis was questioned about growing up in a show business family and asked how he felt about his son Gary following in his footsteps. Claiming he would support whatever career choice his eldest son made, Jerry manipulated the conversation so that he could brag about his strict parenting skills, justifying this ongoing practice of corporal punishment and bragging about how he secretly turned on a listening device to hear his child's cries. Was the MDA unaware of what their national chairman said on a nationally televised program, or did they ignore it? At this point, the organization may still have been afraid to lose Jerry Lewis, but the tides turned.

As Jerry Lewis' influence within the organization decreased, his fear of losing his franchise increased. Over the years, tensions mounted as times changed, and Jerry's fear of anything and anyone interfering with his position with the MDA compounded his paranoia. When I began representing Jerry Lewis, he stipulated he wanted to be paid for print and media interviews regarding his life and career. There was one caveat: Any interview regarding the MDA must be approved and scheduled by the organization. Vetting these offers, however, was sometimes a challenge. I was once contacted by a freelance writer who was supposedly doing an interview with Jerry Lewis for *Newsweek Magazine*. I knew this guy was a phony because *Newsweek*'s journalists would contact the MDA or Jerry Lewis directly. As per Jerry's instructions, I told him Jerry's fee for an interview and advised him that a story on the MDA would have to go through them. My suggestion evidently ruffled his feathers because the man called the offices of the MDA, misrepresenting himself as a writer for *Newsweek* assigned to do a story about Jerry Lewis and the telethon. He complained that I told him there would be a fee for an MDA interview. According to my attorney, who contacted Newsweek, the freelancer did not work for them, and their publication had no plans to do a story about Jerry's life, the MDA, or the telethon. The freelancer created a very uncomfortable situation between Jerry Lewis and the MDA by conniving to get a free interview for his blog and website. Once the dust settled and the truth surfaced, our attorneys worked things out, and I continued representing Jerry. However, I did not appreciate being drawn into the ever-widening rift between Jerry Lewis and the MDA. It is undeniable that Jerry Lewis and the Muscular Dystrophy Association both benefitted from his effective fundraising, which spanned seven decades. Sadly, Jerry's quest for personal publicity often alienated him from the MDA.

Jerry could be kind and generous, yet there was always the underlying tendency for him to be an unreasonable, spiteful brat. Just as he could not explain his comedic talents, he could not explain his compulsion to be mean-spirited. His undeniable talent as a comedian often outweighed his negative traits. As he aged, however, he became more cantankerous, pompous, intolerant, and less funny, and he knew it. In a series of speaking engagements over the final years of his life, he showed a lack of patience with his adoring audience, often making them uncomfortable with his offensive comments.

According to Joan Rivers, a feud between them erupted in the 1960s. She was at an MDA telethon and was appalled when Jerry used a sick child as a prop to solicit donations, subsequently describing him as an "unfunny, lucky, stupid asshole."

Jerry "took umbrage" at her description of him and the implications of the situation. "Joan attacked me in the press, and all she said was, 'Jerry Lewis has to be thankful that he has the telethon because it helps his career.'" According to Jerry, that night he wrote her a letter, saying, "We never met, and I'm looking forward to keeping it that way. If you find it necessary to discuss me or my kids ever again, I promise you I will get someone from Chicago to beat your goddamn head off." Jerry further threatened that even if he was imprisoned, her life would still be in danger due to his connections. He affirmed, "It wasn't a joke. She said that what I do helps my career. In other words, if I didn't have the crippled children, I'd be out of the business, and that's pretty strong."

During a July 1, 2014, interview on *Unmasked* with Ron Bennington, Joan Rivers confirmed Jerry's allegations, admitting she took his threat seriously. "He meant it. My husband had to get security guards…This was a threat." She commented, "I couldn't believe anyone would be stupid enough to voluntarily admit to sending a genuine death threat." Interestingly, the threatening note never surfaced.

Jerry's reaction to Joan Rivers' statement garnered him some brief media publicity, but the punishment did not suit the crime, if there was one. Jerry Lewis must have forgotten he'd been on *That Show with Joan Rivers* in 1968, and she had been on his MDA telethon. He conveniently forgot that on April 21, 1974, he hosted *The Tonight Show* with Joan Rivers. He also forgot that on January 5, 1978, he and Rivers appeared at *The 3rd Annual People's Command Performance* hosted by Alan King. They often appeared together, but Jerry exercised selective forgetfulness and frequently rewrote history to suit his needs.

My last attempt to secure a substantial appearance for Jerry came in 2015, just two years before his death when promoters from Canada wanted to book him for a multimedia speaking engagement for a fundraiser. I had negotiated a substantial six-digit payday for Jerry, and he willingly signed the contract. Although the promoters also signed it, they still needed to send me their deposit. When the deadline passed, I reminded them that they were in default of the agreement. They explained that they were blindsided by several scathing reviews about Jerry Lewis' recent similar engagements, and the Canadian promoters decided they could not risk a fundraising disaster. I could not argue with them because they were right, and I released them from the contract. Although I continued to represent Jerry Lewis on paper, our professional relationship could no longer exist without the mutual trust we shared for over 60 years. It was easy to understand why the MDA lost faith in their one-time guiding light.

The 2000s saw a decline in the earning power of televised marathons. Younger people were no longer interested in this type of programming and turned to other channels or the Internet for entertainment. Interested viewers who did not wish to stay up all night to watch the telethon could record the show and watch it at their convenience. Since the telethon was not on the air, they were unable to make an impromptu pledge. Based on the needs of the MDA and its local network affiliates, the MDA scaled back the Jerry Lewis telethons to 6 hours. This decision was rightly made to save the telethon; however, it angered Jerry. The bad blood that had been brewing between Jerry and the organization boiled over and resulted in the demise of Jerry Lewis' MDA telethons. An insider told me that at a pivotal meeting with an MDA decision-maker, Jerry exploded, yelling at the executive, "You, and not the kids, belong in a fuckin' wheelchair."

Diehard fans may choose to believe that Jerry Lewis' departure from the MDA telethon was responsible for its ultimate demise. However, telethons had been on a downward spiral, and Jerry Lewis' continued appearances on this annual program would have had little to no positive impact. To answer the original question regarding how and why Jerry Lewis got involved with the MDA; it was a good business deal for the team of Martin & Lewis. For decades after Martin & Lewis broke up, Jerry's star continued to shine brightly in the entertainment world, as his superstar status was sustained through the MDA and its telethons. It was also true that Jerry's involvement with the MDA and its annual telethons was a great asset to the Association. When Jerry's health declined, and his judgment began to fail, the MDA telethons kept his star shining.

Jerry Lewis told me, "The donations generated under my watch amounted to over two billion dollars." Throughout the years, Jerry's dedication to improving the quality of life for the victims of neuromuscular diseases while searching for a cure grew stronger and deeper. What began as a smart business move for Jerry Lewis ended when it was no longer a smart business move for the Muscular Dystrophy Association.

Jerry Lewis' MDA telethons came to an end for many reasons. Most importantly, times were changing. Jerry Lewis no longer had a younger fan base and was unwilling and unable to change with the times. When the MDA telethon had to be cut down to six hours, it was done so without consulting Jerry, triggering massive feuding. The fights between this legendary superstar and the organization's corporate powers escalated to an untenable level. When the irresistible force met with the immovable object, the immovable object was removed. In 2010, the MDA did not allow Jerry Lewis to say "Goodbye" to his followers. My sources disclosed that the organization did not trust him on live TV because Jerry had a record of saying inappropriate things. A vicious diatribe could have done irreparable damage to the image of the MDA. It is possible the organization was also concerned that if Jerry made a pre-recorded "goodbye," it would tear at the viewers' heartstrings, causing a negative backlash by garnering sympathy for the host and disapproval for the MDA. However, I believe Jerry would have called on his lifelong experience as a professional, and his farewell speech would have been as memorable as Mickey Rooney's plea for donations. With God's hand on Jerry's shoulder, he would have "walked through the storm with his head up high." But, Jerry Lewis did not have an opportunity to say "Goodbye."

The REAL Jerry Lewis Story

Dean Martin & Jerry Lewis

A Myth is as Good as a Mile

Jerry Lewis deserves all of the accolades he received throughout his career with Dean Martin and beyond for being a comedy force whose effect still reverberates worldwide. However, Jerry was never satisfied with his fame and spent a lifetime embellishing his biography with incredible stories. Although he earned his place in show business history, that never fully satisfied him. From the time the team of Martin & Lewis began their legendary climb to fame, Jerry was driven to reinvent the history of how it all began.

Jerry Lewis told and retold his tale about how he masterminded the comedy duo of Martin & Lewis in the early days before they had teams of writers like Ed Simmons, Neil Simon, and Norman Lear and producers and directors like my uncle, Ernest D. Glucksman. Looking back to the start of Martin & Lewis, Jerry Lewis liked to say he befriended a singer named Dean Martin and got him work.

For 60 years, Jerry told a tall tale about how he and Dean became Martin & Lewis. According to Jerry Lewis' fable, alleged racketeer Paul "Skinny" D'Amato, who ran the 500 Café in Atlantic City, asked the 20-year-old record mime if he could recommend a replacement act for vocalist Jack Randall, who, depending on when Jerry told the story, either suffered from a strep throat or just left. In response, Jerry told Skinny about his friend who was currently out of work but was a terrific singer. When D'Amato replied that he was not looking for a singer, Jerry pitched the act. "He's more than a singer. We do funny bits together." How remarkable that on the say-so of this 20-year-old neophyte, crooner Dean Martin was hired as the featured act at the height of the season and first performed with Jerry Lewis on July 25, 1946, even though D'Amato did not want a singer.

Like many show biz anecdotes, which should be taken with a grain of salt, this one should be taken with the entire salt shaker. Jerry Lewis often added details to his story, saying that on opening night, Dean Martin did three songs, and then Jerry did his mime act to three records, and that was it. Jerry neglected to mention that Jayne Manners was the star of the revue and its closing act. Although Skinny was a young man at the time, Jerry characterized him in his storytelling like Marlon Brando's character in *The Godfather*. According to Jerry, he was approached by Skinny who asked, "Where's the funny stuff you do with him?" Jerry explained that they just had to warm up, and Skinny added, "Warm up? If on the next show, which is in an hour, you don't get it together, you'll both have cement shoes," implying they would be murdered mafia-style.

As his tale unfolds, Jerry claimed he was sitting in the dressing room recalling all the comedy routines he professed to have learned by watching his dad perform years earlier. Desperate for paper, Jerry said he wrote all those jokes on a stained pastrami sandwich wrapper from his lunch bag. Luckily, Jerry had the foresight to know he and Dean would be so successful that he not only saved that grubby paper bag but put the tattered paper in his bank safe. Jerry then shared these bits with Dean. Due to Dean's natural ability to catch on quickly, Jerry was able to teach him a few routines in the dressing room. And, just like that, Jerry created the greatest comedy team in history.

Oops, the lie detector just went off. The story you have just read is Jerry's fable. Only the facts have been changed to protect the truth.

The REAL Jerry Lewis Story

Jerry's myth of how he and Dean Martin became a top-flight act in the entertainment field lacks several essential facts. Although Jerry Lewis often took the credit, Dean Martin, an accomplished entertainer, was well-known and well-liked in show business years before he met Jerry Lewis. While Jerry always insisted he taught Dean a plethora of "double routines" he learned by watching his dad, who did a single, it was actually Dean Martin who had the experience performing on stage with a host of well-established comedians. A decade before he began performing with Jerry, Dean did routines on stage with comedian Buddy Lester and comedian-actor Zero Mostel. Being part of a comedy team was nothing new to Dean Martin, who, from the start, was the team's pace-setter as he held the zany Jerry Lewis at bay.

Although often called the 500 Club, the nightclub in Atlantic City, where Martin & Lewis allegedly got their start, was initially named the 500 Café. Paul "Skinny" D'Amato did not produce the shows nor did he book the talent. That job belonged to Skinny's partner, Irvin Wolf. Additionally, Jerry Lewis and Dean Martin both had personal managers who also acted as their theatrical agents. To perform at an established venue like the 500

© 2024 Rick Saphire

Café, an act would have to come through an agent, and only a respected agent could supply talent to this prominent nightclub during the height of their summer season. This was Jerry's first appearance at this nightclub, and he had only been there for two weeks when he said he convinced "Skinny" to hire Dean Martin as a featured act. Jerry overlooked the fact that the star of the show was actually the lovely and unpredictable Jayne Manners, a singer and sexy comedienne. Anyone believing that Jerry Lewis was solely responsible for Dean Martin's appearance at the 500 Café in 1946 would have a naïve understanding of the workings of the entertainment industry. There is no truth to the story that a singer got sick, and either "Skinny" D'Amato or Irvin Wolf approached Jerry Lewis for a recommendation and, on his say-so, hired Dean Martin.

The show's format was usually a balance of music, comedy, and a novelty act, and a singer leaving the revue would generally be replaced by another singer. Display advertising requires lead time to keep it up-to-date. A prestigious nightclub would not hire an untested unknown as a featured act. Dean Martin's appearance at the 500 Café had been negotiated well before he stepped onto the stage on Thursday, July 25, 1946. Although Jerry claimed that during the weeks they were at the 500 Café together when they teamed up and created pandemonium, there are no newspaper reviews to support his contention. The *Press of Atlantic City* reviewed the opening and reported, "Dean Martin is the newest Broadway song sensation." The article continues, "The M.C. is none other than that zany New York comedy star Jerry Lewis, who offers satirical impressions in pantomimicry."

The earliest indication of Dean Martin teaming up with Jerry Lewis was in September 1946 at New York's Havana-Madrid.

Martin & Lewis' REAL Beginning

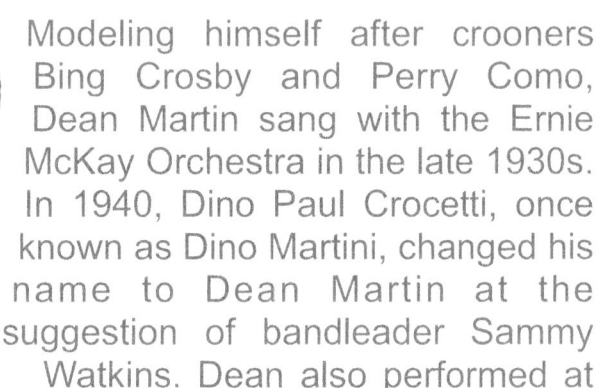

Dino

Modeling himself after crooners Bing Crosby and Perry Como, Dean Martin sang with the Ernie McKay Orchestra in the late 1930s. In 1940, Dino Paul Crocetti, once known as Dino Martini, changed his name to Dean Martin at the suggestion of bandleader Sammy Watkins. Dean also performed at private engagements for notable companies such as Curtiss-Wright, sponsor of the 1942 war fundraiser at the Buffalo Memorial Auditorium, where admission was one pack of cigarettes per person. As a popular vocalist, Dean Martin was heard nightly on WMCA, a New York radio station. One of Dean Martin's regular bookings in the early days was at the Riobamba, a famous New York night spot. In October of 1943, Dean Martin appeared there as a solo performer. In November 1943, the club featured songstress Frances Faye, comedy star Gene Baylos, and Dean Martin. As a side note, some of the

The REAL Jerry Lewis Story

comedians who partnered with Dean in his pre-Jerry Lewis days were invited to reprise their comedy bits with him on TV's *Dean Martin Variety Show* during the 1960s and 1970s. Although Jerry Lewis credited himself with teaching Dean Martin comedy routines and timing for their act, Dean had a wealth of experience performing with top-notch comedians even before Jerry entered the business.

Singers and comedians were often paired in nightclubs, and Dean Martin worked with many of them. In an interview, comedian Alan King remarked that before Dean Martin met Jerry Lewis, Dean enjoyed performing with comedians on the bill with him. Given equal billing, Dean Martin and comedian Sonny Mars were first teamed together at the Tic Toc Club in Montreal, Canada on March 8, 1944. Dean Martin's manager and agent, Lou Perry, booked him for a return engagement to El Morocco in Canada with Sonny Mars on May 30, 1945. "Both performed admirably, but the points at which their acts merged were described as the brightest spot in the show." Montreal's *Gazette* continued, "Martin sang in a manner that had the ladies swooning, and Mars sat [in the audience] demonstrating how the men felt about it. Mars dressed as a baby and asked the questions while Martin crooned 'Sonny Boy.' In other ways, these two combined their talents to make a team, which kept audiences howling."

Nine years older than Jerry, Dean had experience working outside show business as a welterweight boxer billed as "Kid Crocetti," a croupier at an illegal gambling house, and a steel mill worker. From band singer to featured singer, Dean Martin was a headliner in New York City supper clubs and high-profile nightspots in 1945.

On August 9, 1945, a year before his performance at the 500 Café, "romantic singing star" Dean Martin appeared with comedy talent Jackie Green, billed as the master of satire, at the Chanticleer, a well-known nightspot in Baltimore, Maryland. On September 1, 1945, Dean was on the *Tuneful Trolley* radio show featuring Zero Mostel to promote their joint appearance at the Chanticleer. Mostel, a brash, unpredictable comedian whose presence filled the stage, later became known for his 1965 Tony Award-winning portrayal of Tevye in *Fiddler on the Roof* on Broadway. Dean excelled when teamed with entertainers who contrasted with his smooth, calm style as he came off as the grown-up in the room. In reality, it was Dean Martin who came to the 500 Café armed with a well-stocked arsenal of comedy bits culled from his years of experience billed together with talented comedians.

Nevertheless, there was magic in the chemistry between Dean & Jerry.

In May 1946, Dean Martin, advertised as one of the best-liked singers, appeared at the Chanticleer with Buddy Lester, advertised as one of the greatest comedians. In May 1946, billed as the "Bright Boy from Broadway," Jerry Lewis was doing his record act and acting as Master of Ceremonies at the Gayety, a striptease joint, in Montreal, Canada. The *Baltimore Sun* wrote on June 11, 1946, "Buddy Lester and Dean Martin are breaking records at the Chanticleer, headlining one of the greatest floor shows of the year." The following day, an article from the *Baltimore Sun* read, "Don't miss Buddy Lester's entertaining comedy and Dean Martin's really wonderful singing at the beautiful Chanticleer." No one reviewed Jerry's mime act. This was one month before Jerry Lewis allegedly got Dean Martin his "big break" at the 500 Café in Atlantic City.

While Dean Martin was receiving accolades, Jerry Lewis was still receiving second, third, and fourth billing. Under contract with Diamond Records, Dean Martin recorded "Which Way Did My Heart Go?" on July 1, 1946, just days before he appeared at the 500 Café where pantomimist Jerry Lewis was on the program but not always advertised on the bill. Once Martin & Lewis gained fame, Jerry found ways to take credit for Dean's success. Dean was publicly tolerant of his partner and never contradicted or corrected Jerry's fictional stories despite history to the contrary. This accounting of true facts is not intended to undermine Jerry Lewis' talents but to finally give Dean Martin the credit he deserves.

While Dean Martin was co-starring regularly with some of the country's top comedians, Jerry Lewis was "working" together with superstars Enrico Caruso, Betty Hutton, and Carmen Miranda, all of whom were on 78 RPM records. In 1941, Jerry Lewis began his show business career doing a "dumb act," which meant the performer was silent. As an off-stage phonograph played tunes, Jerry mouthed the words to these songs. Imagine a zany Jerry Lewis lip-syncing to "Indian Love Call," playing the roles of both Nelson Eddie and Jeanette MacDonald. Jerry was comfortable with this because he was uncomfortable speaking to large groups of people in his own voice as this hid his identity. When Jerry Lewis' father realized his son was pretty funny and had his mind set on a career in show business, Danny Lewis introduced his son to an agent from New York City, Abner J. Greshler.

Abby Greshler's forte was producing corporate variety spectaculars, which were unadvertised entertainment revues for private companies. Reputed to be an innovative agent, Greshler sometimes used deceptive and unethical means, at least in Jerry's case, to bolster his successes. One of Abby Greshler's mainstay acts for his corporate shows was the Wesson Brothers. When Greshler found out that Dick and Gene Wesson, who sang and did impressions, planned to leave his talent agency and head for Hollywood, Greshler hatched a plan of his own. Like the Fagan character in Charles Dickens' *Oliver Twist*, Greshler instructed young Jerry to steal Dick Wesson's characters covertly. In a conversation with Dick's daughter, Eileen Wesson confirmed that her father was naïve about Jerry and Abby. In later years, when he realized what they had done, he felt betrayed, and that led to his nervous breakdown. Dick was the skilled "idea man" who had an innate ability to create materials and develop a character in a story for the Wesson Brothers' team. My friend, comedian Bobby Ramsen, witnessed Jerry Lewis going to the theatre, nightclubs, and conventions with a pad and pencil in hand to take notes on Gene and Dick's act.

As Jerry's confidence grew, Abby Greshler saw qualities in young Jerry Lewis' stage persona similar to the successful comedian Richard "Dick" Lewis Wesson. Regulars on the *Chesterfield Supper Club* radio show with Perry Como, Dick and Gene Wesson were famous personalities and recording artists for National Records and under contract to Greshler as nightclub and stage performers.

Impressed with Jerry's talent, Greshler took a keen interest in the boy and swiftly signed him to a management contract. Initially, the agent was interested in Jerry's pantomime act as an add-on to his vaudeville-style convention shows. Because the real story of how Jerry Lewis got his start was not compelling, Greshler began engineering a tale of Jerry's entrance into show business. Investigation, though, suggests that Jerry had his own personal reason for embracing fiction over fact. Over time, a history evolved, and everyone went along with it. For this reason, the facts in *The REAL Jerry Lewis Story* may differ from the more commonplace folklore, media, and print versions of Jerry Lewis' showbiz beginnings.

When Gresher told Jerry that he would like him to serve as an emcee for his variety shows and club dates, in addition to his record act, Jerry felt the first pangs of stage fright. Until now, Jerry Lewis was not a comedian; he was a mime and had virtually no professional experience speaking to an audience. The threat of unemployment was an incentive for Jerry to find his voice, which, to his surprise, came naturally.

Comedian Bobby Ramsen knew Dean Martin and Jerry Lewis before they formed the team of Martin & Lewis. Bobby told me that Jerry was under contract with Abby Greshler and how he transitioned from a "dumb act" to one of the noisiest acts in show business. Greshler felt Jerry Lewis had potential and invested time and money in developing his show business talents.

While Jerry Lewis took notes and perfected his imitation of Dick Wesson's squeaky voice, stage persona, and his characters, Greshler searched for the other half of this future musical-comedy team. A Broadway, radio, and Jewish theater veteran, Marty

Dick Wesson, the original Jerry Lewis

Drake became Jerry Lewis' first theatrical partner. Billed as Marty Drake and Jerry Lewis, they were the headliners at the Chanticleer. As part of their routine, Marty Drake, the straight man, sang the popular song "Sonny Boy" while comedian Jerry Lewis sat on Drake's knee, mugging like a child while smoking a cigar. This act was similar to one performed by Dick and Gene Wesson and the routine done by Dean Martin and Sonny Mars. Although the team of Drake and Lewis was well-received, they went their separate ways after this engagement, leaving Greshler in search of someone to fill the bill as the other half of the team.

> **A Bright New Day . . . Bright New Fun**
> **At the Air-Conditioned Chanticleer**
> **Starring Marty Drake and Jerry Lewis**
> **Two Bands—Continuous Dancing**
> **Charles at Eager**

Abby Greshler's wife had seen Dean Martin perform at the Havana-Madrid in New York City and thought this smooth, sophisticated singer would be an ideal replacement for Gene Wesson. Her husband contacted the nightclub's owner, Angel Lopez, and arranged for Jerry Lewis to perform his 12-14 minute comedy act there in January 1946, marking the beginnings of Martin & Lewis as a duo.

For the first quarter of 1946, Dean Martin, represented by theatrical agent Lou Perry, and Jerry Lewis, represented by theatrical agent Abner J. Greshler, appeared nightly at the Havana-Madrid; however, they were not advertised as a team. Angel Lopez, owner of the club, should be credited with creating the team of Martin & Lewis since it was there that Dean Martin and Jerry Lewis were first advertised on the same bill together. Over those three months, Martin and Lewis performed over 150 shows together. Culling from his experiences performing with other comedy talents like Gene Baylos, Sonny Mars, Buddy Lester, and Zero Mostel, Dean Martin shared his knowledge with the fledgling comedic pantomimist Jerry Lewis, who learned quickly. Jerry Lewis also shared with Dean the information he had acquired while taking notes on the Wesson Brothers under the direction of Abby Greshler. At the end of their respective performances, Dean and Jerry returned to the stage for what appeared to be an impromptu after-show performance. They developed and refined their material from January to June to make it look unrehearsed. Undoubtedly, many of their ad-libs were from what Dean had done with well-known comedians. Dean and Jerry honed other bits, many of which were lifted from the Wesson Brothers' acts. Much of their clowning occurred at the end of the late show since there were no time constraints.

Although most accounts of Martin & Lewis' start foster the legend that Dean and Jerry began working as a team at Atlantic City's 500 Café in July 1946, Martin and Lewis first performed together on the same bill at Angel Lopez's Havana-Madrid in New York City in January 1946. While they were on the same bill, Angel Lopez encouraged the two to perform as a team during the after-shows, which were impromptu performances after the last show.

Multiple forces interacted to create the perfect storm. Angel Lopez, Lou Perry, Abby Greshler, and others had the foresight to see the potential of Martin and Lewis. Dean Martin had experience working with top-notch comedians, and Jerry Lewis had an innate sense of comedy and timing. All the elements combined to form the Martin & Lewis musical-comedy team. When this joint booking at the Havana-Madrid ended, Dean Martin returned to the Chanticleer teaming up with Buddy Lester, and Jerry Lewis resumed his record act as a single. However, after performing as a team for three shows nightly plus an after-show, seven days a week for three months for Angel Lopez, their act was set for their appearance at the 500 Café in Atlantic City where they did the same "spontaneous" after-show act they had developed during the time spent at the Havana-Madrid.

In the years before Dean Martin and Jerry Lewis appeared at the Havana-Madrid together, Dick and Gene Wesson were regulars on the NBC radio's *Chesterfield Supper Club* and clients of Abby Greshler. Up to this point, Martin & Lewis was a local act that was gaining popularity; however, their exposure was limited. In order to develop a fan base, Martin & Lewis, who were largely unknown to the general public, needed national exposure, which came in the form of radio. Martin & Lewis' talent agent, Abner J. Greshler, arranged for the duo to be guests on several radio shows, including *Sealtest Variety Theatre* hosted by Dorothy Lamour and The Bob Hope Show. Hope supported Martin & Lewis and appeared on their first audition radio broadcast. Originally called *The Martin & Lewis Show*, it was soon renamed *The Dean Martin & Jerry Lewis Show*. Initially, the show was sustaining (funded by the station); however, several sponsors picked it up when the program's popularity increased. From 1949 to 1953, the show's main sponsor was Chesterfield Cigarettes, the same company that sponsored the Wesson Brothers' appearances on the *Chesterfield Supper Club*. Copying Dick Wesson's baby voice, Jerry excelled as the puerile dunce, and Dean distinguished himself as the sauve, tolerant straight man.

Behind the scenes, Greshler saw Dean Martin and Jerry Lewis as a profit-making team and a replacement for the Wesson Brothers in his corporate show lineup. From vocal intonations to facial expressions, Jerry followed in Dick Wesson's footsteps, tailoring the bits to his style. Once Greshler bought out Dean Martin's contract from Lou Perry in 1946, his plans for Martin & Lewis were underway. Although Martin & Lewis were billed as a team, Dean Martin and Jerry Lewis did not become legal partners until 1950, after they left Greshler.

Martin & Lewis: For the Record

Martin & Lewis became a musical-comedy team whose performance depended on live music and byplay with the band, which was an integral part of their act. In 1951, the duo's popularity grew as Martin & Lewis regularly appeared on NBC TV's *The Colgate Comedy Hour*, topping the ratings of *The Ed Sullivan Show*. Dean & Jerry's national NBC radio show gained popularity, and they were making two films a year released by Paramount Pictures.

The REAL Jerry Lewis Story

In the early 1950s, *Life Magazine* reported that Dean Martin and Jerry Lewis were among the world's most successful and highest-paid performers. At the height of their partnership in 1951, the comedy duo signed a contract for a return engagement to appear at New York's prestigious Copacabana nightclub the following year (1952) for a whopping $24,000, quite an impressive amount in those days. However, the details of their contract with the Copa paint a different picture stating that the team of Martin & Lewis would perform for four consecutive weeks, seven days a week, three shows nightly, with their last performance each night ending after 3 a.m. During their 60-90 minute performances, Dean and Jerry would sing, dance, clown, take pratfalls, and give it their all. That grueling commitment was for an exhausting 84 shows without a day off, for which they were each paid the shockingly small sum of $142.86 per show.

Although the Copacabana had its own highly regarded orchestra, Martin & Lewis always augmented the musicians and paid out-of-pocket for their conductor Dick Stabile, pianist Lou Brown, and drummer Ray Toland. Deducting 20 percent for union fees, taxes, housing, transportation, and other expenses, Dean Martin and Jerry Lewis each likely netted about $114 a show. Even in 1952, that salary was comparable to a magic act or a local stand-up comic.

Within the industry, it was general knowledge that the team of Martin & Lewis left Abby Greshler and was being represented by the Music Corporation of America (MCA), the country's premier theatrical agency. Yet, Dean Martin and Jerry Lewis signed this particular Copacabana contract without the advantage of an agent. In all likelihood, MCA would not have condoned such a demanding schedule for so little money for this popular act, reputed to be the top moneymaker in the entertainment field. The usual practice would have been for MCA to negotiate Martin & Lewis' contract with the Copa. However, both Dean and Jerry acted as free agents because they needed the money, and MCA would not have agreed to this deal. When the Copa presented the duo with a standard AGVA contract, they signed it.

In addition to their live performances, Martin & Lewis' fan base expanded its appeal to include children with the introduction of *The Adventures of Dean Martin & Jerry Lewis* comic books. Published by DC Comics, these were published from 1952 through 1957. The year after the team split, the comic book was renamed *The Adventures of Jerry Lewis*, running from 1957 through 1971. Many children did not realize the characters in the comics were based on real people.

While Dean Martin, under the Capitol Records label, performed songs that appealed to adults, Capitol Records also put out a series of children's records starring Jerry Lewis with various songs and storylines designed to appeal to the kiddies. The National Mask & Puppet Corporation manufactured the Martin & Lewis Puppet Show, which included one Dean Martin and one Jerry Lewis hand puppet, a curtain imprinted with pictures of Martin & Lewis that served as a puppet stage, and a two-sided 7-inch vinyl record with selected audio clips from their radio show, providing Dean and Jerry's actual voices. Another hand puppet that gained mild popularity was two-faced because it had the face of Jerry Lewis on one side of the head and the face of Dean Martin on the other. Adult merchandising by the Tuck Tape Company included Dean Martin & Jerry Lewis cellophane tape and other products bearing their likenesses. Martin & Lewis were highly marketable, even marketing themselves with giveaway souvenirs such as Zippo lighters, Cross pens, and other advertising specialties, which became highly collectible.

Jerry Lewis fabricated stories about how he and Dean Martin came to be because he was driven to tell stories that made him sound like the driving force behind the team. He wanted to prove to the public that he was smart. Plus, he was still living in fear of his past catching up to him. Instead of enjoying the fruits of his labor, Jerry's ego drove him to prove to his fans that he was not only the brains behind his success but also the brains behind his partner. Dean never contradicted him because, for Dean, Jerry represented a payday.

The public likes to think of celebrities as well-to-do, and Dean Martin and Jerry Lewis gave that impression of having wealth. Wearing designer clothes, living in expensive homes, socializing with the social elite, buying costly jewelry, joining posh country clubs, and taking exotic vacations contributed to the impression that they were high-class and important. When I was in Germany with Jerry Lewis, he spent $5,000 on a piece of Louis Vuitton luggage he already had at home. To the world, Martin & Lewis were well-to-do, but in reality, they were "well-to-don't." To paraphrase Will Rogers, celebrities often spend money they haven't yet earned to buy things they don't need to impress people they'll likely never meet.

Martin & Lewis: Un-vestigation

On the Air

Professional entertainers should follow this Golden Rule: "If there is a microphone in the room, NEVER say anything you would not want others to hear." Another bit of advice is: "If there is a camera in the room, keep your clothes on." There is no argument that Martin & Lewis had unrivaled talent and timing, and there is also no argument that both Dean Martin and Jerry Lewis often suffered from a lack of sound judgment.

Back in the 1950s, family members often visited our suburban New Jersey home from their city apartment in the Bronx, New York. Occasionally, after a cook-out on the patio, we kids would be banished from the living room while our parents listened to adult party records. As the grownups sat on the couch near the phonograph, I could hear the music coming from the record player and everyone laughing.

Before the advent of home video and audiocassettes, party records were all the rage. In many cases, stores openly sold bawdy recordings by Belle Barth, Redd Foxx, Pearl Williams, and Woody Woodbury. On the black market, 78 RPM recordings contained obscene material featuring men and women acting out sexually explicit vignettes. Commercial record labels did not produce these black-market pornographic recordings. In most cases, they were individually cut as 78 RPM transcriptions. Generally, a person had to know somebody who knew somebody to acquire one of these records.

One day, when I was home alone, I made a beeline for my father's "secret" record cabinet to find out what was so funny. In all candor, at seven years old, listening to a lady named Ruth Wallis singing about a man who had "the cutest little dinghy in the Navy" or some guy nibbling on her cupcakes meant absolutely nothing. Why the grownups found this record, among others, so hilarious and kept us from them was beyond me. As I sifted through my dad's collection of 78s, I found one that intrigued me because it was unlabeled. Placing the needle on the 78 RPM transcription, I heard what sounded like a commercial for Martin & Lewis' movie *The Caddy*. As the recording played, I was shocked and confused to hear my heroes, Dean and Jerry, exchanging insults and spewing forth vulgarities like "shit," "cocksucker," and "fuck." To this point, my perception of these two entertainers, in my innocent mind, was that my idols were above reproach. I knew that type of language was inappropriate, and to my young ears, it sounded as if they were angry with each other, and I didn't see any humor in it.

In 1953, Martin and Lewis made an audio-only recording to promote their upcoming motion picture release of *The Caddy*. However, the obscenities on this record were outtakes, which should have been remanded to the cutting room floor and destroyed. In those days, the studio recording processes employed one of three methods:

1. Magnetic recording on thin wire in low-fidelity was still available but outmoded and could not easily be edited.
2. Electrical transcriptions (ETs) were recorded onto a disk in real-time and could be played back on a turntable but could not easily be edited.
3. Reel-to-reel magnetic audiotape was the technology of choice since it recorded in high-quality sound and could easily be edited.

In the early 1950s, most audiotape was made of magnetic metal particles affixed to a paper backing. Editing was done with a razor blade and cellophane tape. The simplest and most time-efficient recording process was to record continuously, without stopping and re-starting. The benefit of magnetic audiotape was that the editing process could easily correct imperfections occurring during recording. When the tapings were complete, the next step was entrusted to the audio technicians, who finished their work by editing out flaws and destroying the outtakes. After editing, the final tape recording was transferred to 78 RPM or 33⅓ RPM discs for distribution to broadcast stations. The 1953 promo heard by the general public for *The Caddy* was flawless.

Throughout the years that followed, this illicit recording session made its way around the world. It was first available on records, then audiocassettes, next digital MP3s, and ultimately the Internet, where millions could hear the "naughty" promo outtakes. Because of its low sound quality, casual listeners might assume only Martin and Lewis were on the recording. In reality, there were others in the room interacting with Dean and Jerry:

Take One

MARTIN - Hi, everybody! This Dean Martin

LEWIS - …and Jerry Lewis.

MARTIN - We'd like to tell you all about our latest and funniest picture for Paramount.

LEWIS - Of course, you mean *The Caddy*.

MARTIN - Of course. Jerry, I don't remember the last time I had so much fun making a picture.

LEWIS - Boy, I'll say. How about the scene when I wreck the department store that I'm working in?

MARTIN - What about the time when I come home and find a strange, and I do mean strange, man in my bed, and it turns out to be you?

LEWIS - Tell them about a terrific game of golf I play. Go on, tell them, tell them.

MARTIN - Terrific? I never saw golf played that way before. Crazy man, crazy!

LEWIS - I hate to brag, folks, but I think *The Caddy* is the funniest picture we made. No kidding, it's got 90 riotous minutes of howls, gags, fun, and more heartwarming entertainment than you and the family ever saw.

MARTIN - You'll love Jerry and me in *The Caddy*.

LEWIS - Take my word for it. *The Caddy* is the most hilarious picture we have ever made. Come on and join the fun. See Paramount's *The Caddy*.

MARTIN - Yeah, The Caddy.

MARTIN (to audio technician) - Is that all right, you cocksucker?

LEWIS (to audio technician) - How was that, you shitheel?

MARTIN - Without reading it?

AUDIO TECHNICIAN - I'm with you.

LEWIS (to audio technician) - Okay! Next. You still rolling?
MARTIN (to audio technician) - Still rolling?
LEWIS (to audio technician)- All right. All right. Start.
AUDIO TECHNICIAN - Okay, I will.
MARTIN (to audio technician) - You can cut that bit out.

Take Two
MARTIN - Now, this is Dean Martin
LEWIS - ...and Jerry Lewis asking you to see our newest and funniest picture to date.
MARTIN - Of course, you mean The Caddy.
LEWIS - You bet I do. *The Caddy* is filled with 90 hilarious minutes of howls, gags, fun and heartwarming entertainment that the entire family will enjoy.
MARTIN - Crazy man, crazy.
LEWIS - No doubt about it, Dean, this is the funniest picture we have ever made. No kidding, folks, we're sensational. Take my word for it. Come on and join the fun. See Paramount's *The Caddy*.
MARTIN - Yeah.
LEWIS - It will make you shit. [Laughter in the background]
MARTIN - Cut out "make." [Laughter increases.]
MARTIN (to audio technician) - You ready? He ain't doing a fuckin' thing. He's just standing there.

Take Three
MARTIN - Now, this is Dean Martin
LEWIS - ...and Jerry Lewis (tongue-tied noises), you cocksucker. [Laughter]
MARTIN (to no one in particular) - Wait till this guy with TB [twisted balls] gets through here.

Take Four
MARTIN - Ready? Now, this is Dean Martin
LEWIS - ...and Jerry Lewis with a reminder to see our newest and funniest motion picture ever, *The Caddy*.
MARTIN - He's right, folks. Come on and join the fun in the most "right-you-us" 90 minutes of howls.
LEWIS (interrupting Dean) - "Right-you-us"? Where the fuck do you see "right-you-us"? [Laughter in the background]
LEWIS (to Dean) - That's riotous, you greaseball. [Laughter increases]
MARTIN - (to Jerry) Righteous! What is this, a religious picture?
MARTIN - (to no one in particular) This is religious Martin and Jerry Lewis. We've got five fucking lines, and we can't get through with it.

Take Five
MARTIN - This is Dean Martin
LEWIS - ...and Jerry Lewis with a reminder to see our newest and funniest motion picture ever,".
MARTIN - He's right, folks. Come on and join the fun and the most wonderful 90 minutes of howls and gags you ever saw.
LEWIS - We'll be seeing you in Paramount's *The Caddy*.
MARTIN - Yep, *The Caddy*.
LEWIS - With a big cock on it. [Voices and laughter]
UNKNOWN VOICE #1 - All right, let's go.
UNKNOWN VOICE #2 - All right, let's go to lunch.

When the promo for *The Caddy* was made, Dean Martin and Jerry Lewis were in a professional recording studio with other adults, and they started clowning around. My father gained possession of this record through an insider in the mid-1950s. Careful listening to this recording makes it apparent that Dean and Jerry requested and expected their playful exchange to be cut and destroyed. They didn't know they would be double-crossed by one or more studio technicians who saved the outtakes and produced a separate master tape that included the offensive language. What resulted from the distribution of the recording was much more serious than a blemish on Dean's or Jerry's reputation. In the 20th century, transporting and selling such obscene material across state lines was a felony. Little did anyone know that a copy of this illicit recording would find its way to the desk of FBI Director J. Edgar Hoover, who opened an intense FBI investigation on Interstate Transportation of Obscene Matter.

When Martin & Lewis broke the Golden Rule, it turned around and bit Jerry in the end. Four years after the promo was made, Martin & Lewis' indiscretion in the recording studio resurfaced, effectively ending Jerry's plans for his future.

In 1956, Dean Martin and Jerry Lewis publicly announced the dissolution of their partnership, and fans began wondering, "Why did Martin & Lewis break up?" People asked me that question when I was nine, and I had no answer, except that I saw them at the MDAA Telethon and observed how they deliberately avoided each other when they were not on camera. Years later, when I learned the complicated truth about their split, I sidestepped the question by responding, "The real question should be, 'How did they manage to stay together for ten years?'" I gave that glib response because the real reason for the breakup was highly complex and filled with unexpected entanglements.

It was widely known that Dean Martin and Jerry Lewis were often at odds with each other during the last few years of their partnership. For extended periods, they did not perform together outside of their motion pictures, and there were times on the studio set when they did not talk to one another. A case in point: They appeared together on NBC's *Today* program in June 1956 to promote their upcoming MDAA telethon and celebrate their tenth anniversary as a comedy team. This live broadcast occurred at Atlantic City's 500 Club, where Jerry claimed Martin & Lewis got their start. Within moments of the broadcast, it became apparent Jerry was in his "take-over" mode, and Dean wished he was somewhere else. Before the program ended, Dean walked off the stage, and Jerry finished the show without his partner. Not long afterward, they did their first and last MDAA telethon, which was also their last scheduled TV appearance together.

Jerry Lewis was adept at writing and rewriting history. He often touted how he and Dean broke up "10 years to the day" that they had gotten together at the 500 Club in July 1946. Those in the know, know that was far from the truth, but it made for good press.

The 10-year partnership of Martin & Lewis was becoming old hat. The original magic of their unpredictability was becoming very predictable. They were both too old for their "ad-lib" zaniness to be believable, and laughs were harder to come by. Having reached a point where nothing they did on stage was unique, it was time to either radically change their style of comedy or move on. Although Paramount director Hal Wallis believed they could transition to a new era of film comedy, Dean was no longer interested in being Jerry's straight man. While Dean was tired of being the heavy in the movie plots, Jerry wanted more songs and more involvement with the production of their films. With Frank Sinatra's moral support and the confidence that he could always fall back on his singing career, Dean was ready to try his hand at dramatic acting.

After Dean Martin passed away in 1995, Jerry Lewis began discussing their partnership. In the days following their break-up, I remember someone asking Jerry if he ever talked to Dean Martin, and his response was, "Oh, you mean the Italian kid who used to work for me?" Of course, Jerry meant to be funny and got a laugh, sidestepping the question. On the other hand, Dean Martin never had any problem talking about Jerry Lewis in a complimentary manner. Although Jerry never mentioned Dean in his solo performances, Dean often mentioned Jerry's name in his. Dean had a staple joke on stage with Frank Sinatra, Sammy Davis, Jr., Joey Bishop, and Peter Lawford, collectively known as the Rat Pack. Picking up the microphone stand and moving it off to the side, he'd say, "Now, you stand over here, Jerry."

After he and Jerry split up, Dean Martin was featured on Edward R. Murrow's *Person-to-Person* TV show on

February 7, 1958. Murrow asked, "Dean, what do you regard as the biggest break of your life?"

Aware that Martin & Lewis fans were upset that the team went their separate ways, Dean remained a diplomat and replied, "The biggest and most wonderful break in my life was meeting Jerry Lewis. We had 10 wonderful great years, and I enjoyed every minute of it. And I think that was a real lucky, lucky break for me."

Once Dean and Jerry went their separate ways, Dean's name was not mentioned in the Lewis household until Jerry succeeded as a single in his movies. While Jerry no longer kept pictures or memorabilia pertaining to Dean Martin displayed in his house, Dean had a portrait of Martin & Lewis hanging on his wall.

Die-hard Martin & Lewis fans were collectively surprised and saddened by the news of the unofficial dissolution of their partnership in July of 1956. Many refused to believe the duo would not be performing together anymore. Even Hal Wallis, who directed all of their Paramount productions, expected both of them to return to the set to film the next Martin & Lewis movie, *Sad Sack*. However, Dean never looked back. Instead, he looked forward to his acting career. While Jerry's future as a single act was uncertain, he did have a secret dream.

Reveling in the media attention the breakup generated for him, Jerry was poised to set the show business world ablaze by reinventing himself as a serious television producer. While the entertainment industry and Jerry's fans were wondering if he would be a success without his partner reacting to his well-rehearsed comic idiocy, Jerry Lewis was planning a radical departure from what he knew best: making people laugh.

Jerry Lewis had also been eager to end his theatrical relationship with Dean Martin and to have Dean step down from his position as an executive within their company, York Productions. On January 1, 1957, their contractual ties were resolved, making the break-up of Martin & Lewis official, and Jerry Lewis now had the freedom to implement the vision he had been secretly developing during the months before the final Martin & Lewis appearance at the Copacabana on July 25, 1956. It is unclear if Dean Martin knew about Jerry's radical new ambitions, but it was clear that Dean was out.

Jerry Lewis planned to produce a series of TV docudramas based on actual cases from the Department of Justice (DOJ) and the Federal Bureau of Investigation (FBI) files. Under the banner of his company, York Productions, Jerry could model his series after programs such as *Dragnet* and *The FBI in Peace and War*, which were popular during the era of dramatic radio and the early days of television.

At the end of World War II, America needed to laugh and enjoy some light-hearted entertainment. After years of uncertainties, losses, and fears brought on by the Depression and war, the musical comedy team of Martin & Lewis provided a welcome escape. Much of Dean & Jerry's initial success was timing. The country needed to laugh at something completely inane, and Jerry was there to serve. In the late 1940s, radio's National

Broadcasting Company (NBC) was in search of new comedy talents to fill the voids created by the Columbia Broadcasting System's (CBS) "talent raid." With so many of their comedy programs lost to CBS, NBC needed comedic replacements to fill the gaps. Abby Greshler, who was managing the musical-comedy team of Martin & Lewis, arranged for them to do a spot on October 26, 1948, on NBC radio's *The New Swan Show* starring Bob Hope with Doris Day, Irene Ryan, and Les Brown and His Orchestra. Their theatrical personas and their voices were distinctively unique from each other, making them a perfect duo for radio. Looking to the future, NBC executives believed their music, comedy style, and physical stage presence would fit the new medium, television.

A decade after World War II, Jerry once again relied on timing. No, he was not attempting to alleviate the nation's hardships with music and laughter, which had propelled Martin & Lewis' popularity starting in 1946. Jerry's new dream was to rouse the country's emotions by recalling some of the darkest days of the Holocaust and the war-ending A-Bomb attack on Japan. Unlike Jerry's ill-conceived, ill-fated Nazi-style World War II motion picture of the early 1970s, *The Day the Clown Cried,* this new "reality" series was Jerry's secret. Jerry Lewis and his production staff worked behind the scenes to gain the cooperation of the Justice Department and FBI Director J. Edgar Hoover. Jerry was confident the first episode in his new series would generate overwhelming publicity, and all the pieces seemed to be falling into place.

The REAL Jerry Lewis Story

Jerry Lewis was determined to prove to the world that he was much more intelligent than the silly, bumbling character his fans adored. The risks for Jerry were great. If his debut episode met with audience approval, his dream of establishing himself as a highly-regarded documentary producer would be realized; however, Jerry Lewis was playing with fire. If he misjudged the public's appetite for this type of docudrama, it would be a career-ending disaster for the comedian. Jerry should have taken Papa Geppetto's fatherly advice to his little creation, Pinocchio. "Schmuck, stay wood."

As of January 1, 1957, Dean Martin was officially out of York Productions and out of Jerry's way. Stepping out of his area of expertise, the comedian wasted no time getting involved in negotiations with the DOJ for York Productions to produce his new reality-based documentaries, and the department approved the series in concept. Things looked promising. The next step was to gain approval from the director of the FBI, J. Edgar Hoover. As early as 1950, the FBI had been scrutinizing the activities of Dean Martin and Jerry Lewis, interviewing people and alleging Jerry Lewis had been involved with some nefarious activities with Dean Martin and on his own. Hoover was familiar with Lewis' files, including that obscene promo for *The Caddy*. A government memorandum in 1961 confirmed, "In August 1957, the Department of Justice signed a contract with York Pictures Corporation to produce a series of films on the Department. Jerry Lewis, the comedian, handled the arrangements for York. Lewis was president of York Pictures Corporation in 1957. York Productions was found to be a front organization for Jerry Lewis, handling only his television, movie, and personal appearances. It was not a production company, and the productions were actually made through Paramount Pictures. Dean Martin and Jerry Lewis initially established the corporation. After Paramount Pictures took over the controlling interest, Lewis was no longer president."

FBI Director J. Edgar Hoover's disdain for Jerry Lewis and his general mistrust of the comedy star's judgment was no secret within the FBI and DOJ. Although Jerry Lewis initially received approval for his project in concept from the DOJ, when the information reached the desk of Hoover, the series was rejected. Jerry's attempts to further ingratiate himself with these agencies were unsuccessful. On January 28, 1958, J. Edgar Hoover sent a letter expressing his bitter disapproval of the entire project to the Attorney General of the United States and other members of the Department of Justice. Hoover wrote: "This afternoon, while in conference with the Attorney General, I talked with him about my concern over the contemplated TV program being developed by the York Pictures Corporation headed by Jerry Lewis. I stated that, excluding the unsavory background and reputation of Lewis, I was particularly concerned about the fact that I understood that their first TV production was to be on the Rosenberg case, and I thought that this was most undesirable and dangerous." Hoover continued, "I also pointed out that many aspects of the Rosenberg case are still current, in that David Greenglass and Harry Gold, who were convicted along with the Rosenbergs, are in the penitentiary, and their cases will shortly be considered for parole, and that Morton Sobell, another one convicted in that case, was now in Alcatraz and the communists planned to start a worldwide campaign for their release within the next few weeks. I stated that for a picture to be portrayed dealing with this case and sponsored by the Attorney General would inevitably result in repercussions." J. Edgar Hoover added, "I also stated there was danger in that suits would be brought by relatives of the Rosenbergs and other defendants who might tend to embarrass the Department." At the end of this particular letter, Director Hoover made it quite clear that "the Attorney General did not desire to have the Rosenberg case portrayed on TV by the York Pictures Corporation at this time or at any time in the near future." Signed, John Edgar Hoover, Director

J. Edgar Hoover deemed all agreements with Jerry Lewis null and void. Jerry Lewis, America's zany TV and movie funnyman, wanted his premiere episode to be an intense docudrama detailing the divisive and controversial 1951 "Trial of the Century." Convicted of espionage, the Jewish husband and wife "spy team," Julius and Ethel Rosenberg, were executed by electrocution in 1953 at Sing Sing Prison. An important factor in Hoover's decision to thwart Lewis' new venture came uncomfortably close to impacting current events. In the days of dramatic radio and the early days of television, programs like *Dragnet* and *This Is Your FBI* were quite popular and produced in cooperation with the Los Angeles Police Department and the FBI. Following in the footsteps of former comedian turned producer and dramatic star of *Dragnet*, Jack Webb, Jerry Lewis was taking a giant leap from comedy to tragedy.

Debates over the 1951 trial and the swift 1953 execution of the Rosenbergs have transcended time. Their execution left their two children, Michael and Robert, orphaned. In preparation for this book, I was in contact with the Rosenberg's younger son, Robert (nee Rosenberg) Meeropol, who believes that Soviet secret documents, which the US now has, indicate his father, Julius, was ignorant of the atomic bomb project, and his mother, Ethel, did not spy in the 1940s. According to Robert, his father was a military-industrial spy, not an atomic spy, and his mother was not a spy at all. In the aftermath of World War II, Americans in the 1940s and 1950s considered Soviet espionage and Communism as significant threats. As of 2023, efforts to posthumously reverse Ethel Rosenberg's conviction have failed, and the debate continues.

Despite Jerry Lewis' continued efforts to ingratiate himself with the Departments, it was a fait accompli. In June 1961, an FBI official sent a memo: "The arrangements which the Department made with Jerry Lewis the comedian were not discussed with us beforehand, and when we brought to the Department's attention information available to us concerning Jerry Lewis' background and moral character, they were successful in having the program plans canceled." In his letter to the Attorney General, the Director stated, "I would be unwilling to have the Bureau associated in any way with an individual such as Mr. Lewis." After Hoover's directive, the only thing for certain was that Jerry was out.

The Bare Facts

I first met comedian Bobby Ramsen in 1963 when I was an emcee in the Catskill Mountains, and we remained close friends until his passing in 2017. Beginning in the 1940s, Bobby began acting in many dramatic radio shows and soap operas broadcast on network radio emanating from New York City. In the late 1940s, he became a busy New York comedian, working in nightclubs with his well-organized comedy material. Twenty years my senior, he shared countless show business stories with me, and we had many laughs together. Well-read and knowledgeable about show business, I considered Bobby an entertainment authority and show biz historian.

The REAL Jerry Lewis Story

Bobby Ramsen shared a startling story with me about Dean and Jerry. The incident took place at a Hollywood-style party, where the men were attired in their finest tuxedos with shiny patent leather shoes, and the ladies wore designer gowns replete with Tiffany's inventory. Suddenly, without warning, Dean Martin and Jerry Lewis burst into the room completely nude. As Dean held onto Jerry's "manhood," he pulled him through the party like a dog on a short leash. All of the attendees, who were quite hip, broke into uncontrollable laughter as Martin and Lewis circled around the room. With Dean still holding the lead, the naked pair walked towards the door and left the party. It was a hysterical story, but I didn't believe it. It sounded more like folklore than fact.

In 2022, nude pictures of Dean Martin with Jerry Lewis surfaced online for sale from a private estate. Some of the photos showed the duo clowning together in a stall shower and steam room. In other photos, their private parts were kept private. These were posed pictures showing Dean Martin and Jerry Lewis sitting with Howard Ross, a Jerry Lewis insider, smiling into the camera, as Dean's bodyguard sat on the steam room bench. Shot with high-quality photographic equipment, these nudes were probably taken in 1952 or 1953 because Jerry still had a mole on his chin. The clear, sharp pictures were being sold on the Internet as part of the estate of Frank Branda, one of Jerry's longtime friends, or so it seemed. Dean was fully exposed in one photo, whereas Jerry Lewis had his hand covering his pee-shooter. In another shot, while Dean was again fully exposed, Jerry kept his back toward the camera, his backside in full view. In that photo, the shower was running while Dean scrubbed

Jerry's back with a shower brush. After seeing these photographs, I immediately changed my opinion about Bobby Ramsen's story of Dean Martin leading Jerry Lewis around by the "nose" at the party.

During the height of their careers in the early 1950s, Dean Martin & Jerry Lewis frequently pushed the boundaries with their nightclub act and on their live TV appearances, often leaving their sponsors biting their nails down to the knuckles. There was a time when nothing Martin & Lewis did surprised me, although they came close to breaking the rules. They knew their limits and remained consummate professionals. Had those photographs been leaked to the public, it could have been devastating to the reputations and careers of Martin & Lewis. Their employers could have overlooked the indiscretions in *The Caddy* promo because the technician was responsible for the production and distribution of the obscene record. In that situation, Martin and Lewis were only guilty of ignoring the entertainers' Golden Rule: "If there is a microphone in the room, NEVER say anything you would not want others to hear."

During the time when Martin & Lewis' nude photos were taken, the moral standards of the industry were quite strict, and such photos could have severely impacted their TV, radio, recording, and film contracts. Many radio, film, print, and television contracts included a moral stating, "The contract can be terminated if the person does or says anything that could harm the employer's business. Engaging in misconduct that disregards public conventions and morals or doing anything to degrade himself in society is a violation of the morals clause and may annul the contract and hold the person accountable for investment losses."

Martin & Lewis' reckless behavior might easily have ended their deal with D.C. Comic Books, caused the cancellation of their personal appearances, and thwarted their fundraising efforts. This was a time in our history when such behavior was not tolerated. Notoriety of this caliber would have offended their adoring fans, destroying their reputations and careers. The billions of dollars raised on behalf of the Muscular Dystrophy Association over the decades through the efforts of Jerry Lewis would have been sacrificed. Considering that those revealing photographs were not exposed to the salivating media, some entities may have profited by keeping the nude photos of Martin & Lewis under wraps.

Back then, if a celebrity was photographed without his knowledge, he could only be accused of forgetting to draw the window shade. However, in the case of the Martin & Lewis nudes, it was apparent that the photographs were taken intentionally. The images were professionally lit and meticulously posed. It is difficult to comprehend what motivated Dean Martin and Jerry Lewis to agree to the photo shoot.

Did Jerry Lewis live his life in fear of being "exposed"? Had the nude pictures of Martin and Lewis ever been made public during their careers, it would have been a disastrous case of double exposure.

Jerry and Me on Network TV

Photographed off of a studio monitor. Rick Saphire on The Tonight Show with guest host Jerry Lewis. Broadcast on NBC, July 6, 1962

Jerry Lewis had an absolute rule: No surprises. However, life doesn't always follow our rules, and sometimes the unexpected is positive and sometimes negative. One of the most bizarre events involving Jerry Lewis and me occurred during the early summer of 1962. Interestingly, I only fully understood the true story of what had occurred a decade after it happened.

On Monday morning, June 25, 1962, my mother and I boarded the bus from Livingston, New Jersey, to Manhattan, where I was to spend one week with my uncle, Ernie Glucksman. During that week, I also spent

The REAL Jerry Lewis Story

time with Jerry Lewis, his wife Patti, and Jerry's entourage. Among the group staying in New York with Jerry was a young writer named Peter Bogdanovich. Peter, hired to write a major story for *Esquire Magazine*, followed Jerry around, day and night, for two weeks. Jerry Lewis was in New York because he was sitting in as guest host of NBC's *Tonight* show during the interim period between Jack Parr's exit and Johnny Carson's debut, which would happen on October 1.

On the first night, we all went by limousine to the NBC Studios at 30 Rockefeller Plaza. *The Tonight Show* was recorded on videotape during the early evening hours for broadcast beginning at 11:15 p.m. Eastern time. During the late 1950s into the early 1960s, *The Tonight Show* was broadcast from 11:15 p.m. to 1:00 a.m.; however, the first 15 minutes were only seen in the New York metropolitan area. Starting at 11:30 p.m. local time, the show aired in various time zones across the country. After the program's taping, we all returned to our 4th-floor hotel suites, where there was tremendous activity. Our room was next to Jerry's. Whereas Uncle Ernie and I had a two-bedroom suite, Jerry's suite must have had at least four bedrooms, a sitting room, and an office area. Having been in Jerry's company in the past, I was used to the fact that there was always activity surrounding him, which included plenty of media and production staff, depending on what he was doing at the time.

On Tuesday afternoon, June 26, Uncle Ernie, Jerry, and the entourage left the hotel for an activity I could not attend. I was 15 years old, and Uncle Ernie felt I would either be bored or unwelcome at a high-powered business meeting. I stayed behind while Uncle Ernie, who was Jerry Lewis' personal manager, and the rest of the crew left the hotel. Jerry's wife, Patti, was dressed beautifully for a luncheon she was attending. I was content to stay by myself in the hotel room because Uncle Ernie's business phone book was on his desk. Before leaving, he deputized me to answer the phone in our suite, take messages, and jot them down on the notepad next to his coveted telephone book. Well, I could not help but open his phone book, and the first name I saw was Milton Berle, with Uncle Miltie's home address and telephone number. In flipping through the book, I found the names, addresses, and phone numbers of almost every important entertainer in the business. I loved show business, and sifting through the pages of that coveted book just made me feel a little bit closer to all the people I admired.

That afternoon, there was a knock on the door. Uncle Ernie had advised me not to let anyone in the room but did not tell me to refrain from answering the door. Cautiously, I opened the door a crack, and there, standing outside the room, were two men and a woman. Looking absolutely shocked and somewhat confused when I appeared in the doorway, the woman asked, "Are you Jerry Lewis' son?"

"No. Can I help you?" I answered.

The woman started to talk, but before she could say an intelligible sentence, one of the men gently pushed her aside and asked, "Is this Jerry Lewis' suite?"

Naïvely, I told him it was next door, and they were expected back in a little while. When I asked if they wanted me to write down their names and phone numbers, one of the men answered, "No, that's all right." Without another word, they turned and walked away as I shut the door.

Jerry and Patti returned from their separate activities, and we got ready to go to NBC for the taping of Tuesday night's broadcast. At the show that evening, I was seated in the audience with my mother, father, and sister, who had come in from New Jersey to watch it live with me. After the taping, my family went home, and I returned to the Essex House with Jerry's entourage.

Shortly after we arrived back at the hotel, we heard a commotion coming from Jerry's suite and noticed a sudden flurry of activity. Uncle Ernie dashed down the hall while I stayed behind. Whatever was happening grew louder by the minute. Peeking out the door, I saw several uniformed police officers and several men in business suits. Concerned that something might have happened to Jerry or Patti, I walked into the hall to get a closer look. Peering into the open door of Jerry's suite, I saw Jerry and Patti sitting together on the couch, surrounded by police, reporters, and photographers. They looked grim. It appeared as though Patti had been crying. When Uncle Ernie saw me standing there, he left Jerry's suite and immediately escorted me back into our room. He told me I would have to stay in the room because while we were all at Studio 6B at NBC, Jerry's suite was broken into, and some things were stolen, which was why all the police and detectives were there.

Without giving it much thought, I remarked to Uncle Ernie, "I wonder if it was those people?"

Uncle Ernie reacted, "What people?" That's when I told him about the three strangers who had knocked on our door earlier in the day. I had not mentioned anything to him about those visitors before because I didn't think much about it since they left no message and just walked off. Uncle Ernie looked concerned and closed the door to our suite, then walked me into the bedroom. He asked me what the people looked like and what they wanted. I explained how they seemed surprised to see me when I opened the door and asked if I was Jerry's son and if this was his suite. He then asked me to describe their appearance and the lady's hair color, etc. At that point, I admitted to him that I was not a very good witness because I was colorblind, which had created problems for me in school.

Uncle Ernie was very kind to me, and he told me not to tell anybody about the incident with the three people in the afternoon. I thought I might be helpful, so I asked him why he didn't want me to mention them. He implored me, "Ricky, please, don't say anything. If anybody asks you any questions about this, tell them to talk to me." Uncle Ernie hugged me, thanked me for telling him what I knew, and returned to Patti and Jerry's room.

On Wednesday morning, June 27, 1962, we all went shopping. Actually, Jerry went shopping, and we all walked with him from the hotel to Tiffany's, where Trump Tower was erected in 1979. Jerry always needed a crowd of insiders around him. Once at the jewelry store, Jerry bought himself a watch, possibly to replace the stolen one, and then we all walked back to the hotel. After lunch, Uncle Ernie had to go out for a short time. He told me to stay in the room and reminded me not to let in any strangers. He didn't have to tell me that. I was 15 years old and knew how it felt to be scared.

Left alone in the suite, I was somewhat uncomfortable, but five minutes after my uncle went out, there was a knock on the door. I opened it slightly and was taken aback to see Jerry Lewis standing there. I let him in, and he greeted me cheerfully saying, "Hi, Ricky!" I returned his greeting. Considering the robbery had been the night before, Jerry seemed in good spirits and did not let it knock him off his stride.

As I was closing the door, I heard familiar footsteps. It was a click, click, click sound. A voice from the hallway called, "Don't forget Mother." Yes, it was my mother.

Jerry, who was standing next to me, squealed, "Rosie. Hello, Rosie." Putting his hands on her shoulders, he kissed my mother on the cheek and guided her into my suite. For an instant, I wondered why Jerry was so familiar with my mother. He called her by her nickname, Rosie, and kissed her. She never mentioned that she knew Jerry Lewis, but he obviously knew her pretty well. Under the circumstances, I was not about to question her. Within seconds, I was sitting in the hotel room with my mother and one of the most famous people in the world.

I was surprised to see my mother there that afternoon. It was quite coincidental that the three of us were present together, especially considering Jerry's hectic schedule. Jerry wanted me to show him a few magic tricks (I always traveled prepared), and then he asked to speak with my mother privately for a few minutes. I went into the bathroom and washed my hands...several times...until I was summoned back into the sitting room. Then, Jerry asked me if I would like to perform as his guest on *The Tonight Show*. I was stunned. When I looked at my mother, she gave me a smile of approval, and I gave Jerry a big YES and a handshake. Jerry explained he would have to use his best judgment regarding the date and timing of my appearance, adding that he might not be able to get me onto the show. Nevertheless, my one-week stay in New York with my uncle and Jerry was extended for another week.

I had some theatrical training and experience. Since the early 1950s, I had been developing my talents as a singer, tap dancer, and comedy magician. When I was in my early teens, my credits included performances at the Mosque Theater in Newark, New Jersey; the Flagship Theatre Restaurant in Union, New Jersey; and many private and community functions. Jerry and I discussed my upcoming appearance on *The Tonight Show* several times. Whenever I said something funny, Jerry quipped, "Remember that for the show." He never instructed me what to say but rather encouraged me to ad-lib. I was so excited that I could not think about what I was going to say on the air. Instead, I decided to focus on my magic tricks.

On Thursday afternoon, June 28, 1962, as Patti and I were leaving her suite to go to lunch together, the phone rang. Patti asked me to answer it, and I did. The person on the other end said, "Hi. This is Gary. Could I speak with my mother, please?" Although it was a short conversation, it was significant because I had just spoken to my future friend and client who, two years later, would become the rock 'n' roll star, Gary Lewis.

After briefly speaking to her son Gary, Patti and I left. This was one of several lunch dates I had with Jerry's wife during those two weeks. Patti was pretty and charming, and when she talked to me she made me feel far more important than I was. While we were dining at the Stage Delicatessen, a woman recognized her and approached our table. After exchanging pleasantries, the woman asked if I was Patti's son. Patti politely replied, "No, this is Ricky Saphire, and he's the nephew of Ernie Glucksman." Her friend knew exactly who Uncle Ernie was, and then Patti added, "Ricky is a friend of Jerry's and a terrific magician."

In the evening, after we returned from NBC, Uncle Ernie informed me that he had to leave for a few hours, but someone would be staying with me. Just before he left, Billy Richmond, who had been Jerry's drummer, showed up to keep me company. Billy, who had an uncanny resemblance to movie comedian Stan Laurel, eventually became one of Jerry's leading comedy writers, appearing on screen with him several times. That night, while keeping me company, I entertained Billy with a few card tricks, and we chatted.

Enter Peter Bogdanovich. It was like a tag team. Peter came in, and Billy went out. Peter sat quietly in the suite, reading and working on his article, so there wasn't much conversation. Years later, after Peter Bogdanovich became an award-winning film writer, director/producer, actor, and historian, I jokingly bragged to my friends that he had also once been my babysitter. He stayed for about an hour.

Enter the stranger. As Peter was leaving the hotel suite, a serious-looking man wearing a tie and jacket arrived. He exchanged a few words with Peter before greeting me, and we engaged in small talk. I felt uncomfortable because I didn't know this stranger and felt like I had to entertain him. A few hours later, Uncle Ernie returned to the suite and the stranger left. It wasn't until years later that I discovered his identity.

That first week in New York was filled with nonstop excitement and surprises. After the show on Friday, June 29, 1962, I went home with my family to the quiet confines of Livingston, New Jersey. On Saturday morning, I told the entire story to my dog Rocky, who listened patiently, licked my face, and went outside to pee.

Rick Saphire on TV with Chuck McCann on July 2, 1962

Throughout the remainder of the weekend, I rehearsed my magic, rested, and relived that fantastic week over and over in my mind. However, my thoughts were interrupted by a phone call from Uncle Ernie, who asked if I knew the local New York TV personality, Chuck McCann. "Yes," I said, "I watch him every day." Chuck hosted a children's program that featured the films of Laurel and Hardy, puppets, and numerous commercials. In preparation for my appearance on *The Tonight Show*, Uncle Ernie and Jerry Lewis arranged for me to be on Chuck's program. After Uncle Ernie asked me if I would like to appear on the show, I got approval from my mother, and we set the date. Knowing that I would be on at least one TV broadcast over the next few days, I updated Rocky. I could hardly sleep that night, as I was eagerly looking forward to the upcoming week, where I might also appear on *The Tonight Show* with my hero, Jerry Lewis, and I might have another luncheon date with my latest crush, Patti Lewis.

On July 2, 1962, my mother came to New York where I was scheduled to appear on *Laurel and Hardy and Chuck* in the afternoon. We first went to the Essex House Hotel and then took a cab to WPIX, a TV station in New York. Chuck, who was much taller than he appeared on TV, made me feel at ease despite my nervousness and excitement. I was stunned that the studio was so small. At the beginning of the program, Chuck and I did an impression of Stan Laurel and Oliver Hardy. Next, he interviewed me, and then I performed a few magic tricks with him live on the air. As we were coming down the escalator just moments after the show, I asked Chuck if there was a newsstand nearby. When he asked me why I wanted one, I told him I wanted a copy of *Variety* to read my review. He laughed, and from that day on, Chuck and I were lifelong friends.

During my second week in New York City, my days were busy and fun-filled as I hopscotched around the town with my uncle, Jerry, Patti, and the entourage. Each evening, I looked forward to returning to NBC. My mother had cautioned my father about bragging to his friends that I would be on TV with Jerry Lewis since it was not definite. However, as the days passed, my father got angrier and angrier with Jerry for not putting me on the show. He felt Jerry kept me dangling. Despite the uncertainty, I was thrilled to be a part of the action and around big-time showbiz. Like a racehorse at the starting gate, I was champing at the bit every night.

Jerry expected to introduce me sometime during the second week but couldn't say precisely when. I was dressed and ready in the Green Room every night because I had no idea if I would be on or not. Each time Jerry began an introduction, I thought, "This is it." Throughout the week, backstage at the studio, Jerry looked right through me, not giving me a smile or a word. Even my uncle, who was the associate producer of *The Tonight Show* for those two weeks, admitted that he was uncertain about Jerry's intentions. In all probability, Jerry was unsure of the timing because he was searching for a sponsor for my 10-minute spot. However, once Paul Cohen, owner and president of the Tuck Tape Corporation, agreed to buy advertising, my appearance was set. It's worth noting that Paul Cohen was not only the founder but also the president of the Muscular Dystrophy Association.

The REAL Jerry Lewis Story

One evening before *The Tonight Show*'s taping, I stood in the hallway between Studio 6A and 6B. Initially used for radio programs, Studio 6B had a rich history because that's also where *The Howdy Doody Show*, Milton Berle's *Texaco Star Theatre*, and *The Tonight Show* were often broadcast. I was very familiar with the smaller studio, 6A, across the hall, where I was occasionally permitted to sit in on the live broadcast of the *Huntley-Brinkley Report*. My reverie was interrupted when I saw Jerry Lewis in the hallway, holding a cigarette in his mouth. Like flashes of lightning, a half dozen lighters flickered in his face, making a flame so bright that it looked like his head was on fire. This was not spontaneous combustion; it was Jerry's entourage. Each member was vying for the honor of lighting his cigarette.

On Friday, Jerry Lewis gave me a "deadpan" wink. Perry Cross, *The Tonight Show*'s producer, put his hands on my face to wish me luck, and Uncle Ernie smiled and patted me on the back. This was it.

On Friday, July 6, 1962, I debuted on national television. I was already a veteran, having appeared on one local New York TV program, but this was the Big Time… network TV.

Jerry was very considerate toward me. His introduction was so impressive that, for a moment, I was not sure it was for me. I was his only guest on the panel, and my first impression when I sat in the chair next to that famous desk was that the studio lights were very hot. The scene was surrealistic. There I was, sitting in a chair,

The REAL Jerry Lewis Story

surrounded by blinding lights, cameras, and men in suits, all plugged into headphones. Three cameras circled about the stage, and the boom microphone above my head was wiggling around to catch my words. Thankfully, I had had the experience of being on television before, or I might have fainted. Though the audience was invisible, hidden in a black hole behind the lights and cameras, I could see Skitch Henderson fronting the NBC Orchestra with Doc Severinsen, lead trumpet, on my left. Turning a bit more, I was face-to-face with Jerry Lewis in his formal attire, interviewing me. We ad-libbed as he asked me about my desire to be in show business. I then noticed my face on the TV monitors as the camera came in for a close-up, and I thought, "Wow! Right now, I'm the only person in the entire country being seen on the NBC Network." I was only 15 years old and living my dream.

After an amusing interview, Jerry asked me to do a magic trick. The handkerchief I was trying to make vanish kept clinging to my sweaty hands. Magicians are uniquely prepared if something does not go right, so I looked at Jerry Lewis and said, "I just washed my hands, and I can't do a thing with them." I was astonished at the reaction I got. The crowd laughed and applauded, Jerry smiled broadly, band leader Skitch Henderson chuckled, and most importantly, the NBC orchestra gave me my first official rim shot, and then the magic trick worked.

During my performance, Jerry commented that I reminded him of a young Jerry Lewis, although Jerry noted he had begun performing as a "dumb act" (record mime), and I was a magician. At that point, I was officially the youngest comic to have appeared on *The Tonight*

Show. Backstage, I was greeted by my parents, comedian Henry Gibson, who had also been on the show, and, of course, the man from AFTRA (American Federation of Television and Radio Artists). With pen and application in hand, he arranged for me to receive the standard $320.00 less tax that every guest of the show was paid.

While I was waiting in the wings to appear with Jerry Lewis on TV, I felt fortunate and couldn't help but wonder, "Why me?" Each night of the two weeks Jerry Lewis hosted *The Tonight Show*, the ratings climbed higher and higher. When I appeared with him on the final Friday, it was reported that there were over 36 million viewers, the biggest audience in *The Tonight Show* history to that date. That record was only broken in 1969 when Tiny Tim and Miss Vicki got married on the show. Why did Jerry Lewis take such a big gamble on a 15-year-old boy with limited TV experience and have him sitting on the panel with him one-on-one?

The REAL Jerry Lewis Story

Did Jerry Lewis have me on the program because my uncle was his manager and the show's associate producer for those two weeks? Absolutely not. My uncle would never have used his relationship with Jerry to impose on him like that. Could it have been because Jerry thought I was "The World's Greatest Magician," as was printed on my letterhead? Of course not. That was a blatant publicity scheme. Could I have secretly been related to Jerry? Since my early childhood, rumors have circulated among some family members and senior members of the show business community that I was related to Jerry Lewis; however, the matter remains unresolved.

During the summer of 1973, I visited Aunt Judy and Uncle Ernie in Beverly Hills, California. It had been 11 years since my two-week stay in New York with Jerry. Although Uncle Ernie had long since parted ways with Jerry, he was still very involved in TV and theatrical productions. Catching up on news, we reminisced about *The Tonight Show* events. When I asked my uncle what happened to Jerry's belongings after the robbery in 1962, I found out that Jerry had made a public plea on national television. He requested the thieves to keep everything they had taken except for a particular ring that Patti had given him, which held great sentimental value. Uncle Ernie told me that years after the robbery, Jerry's limousine was parked outside a TV studio in Los Angeles with the back passenger window open. Upon his return to the car, he was surprised to find the treasured ring sitting on the backseat with no explanation.

© 2024 Rick Saphire

I then asked Uncle Ernie about the stranger who stayed with me in the hotel suite in 1962. To my surprise, Uncle Ernie revealed he had shared my concerns about the suspicious suspects with the police. Apparently, I was considered a potential witness, and my safety could have been at risk. Uncle Ernie left me with the three men as he was part of the police's plan to set up a money drop in exchange for the stolen goods. My uncle acted as the decoy while the police and federal agents surrounded the designated area. The thieves did not show up. In hindsight, I am glad I was kept in the dark. Ernie Glucksman, Jerry Lewis, Patti Lewis, Billy Richmond, and Peter Bogdanovich were aware of the identity of the third man. Even after a decade, I still found my uncle's explanation unsettling. Billy and Peter were requested to stay with me until the third man arrived. Uncle Ernie informed me that the stranger who sat in the suite with me that night was an undercover FBI agent stationed in our hotel room for my protection.

My uncle told me Jerry Lewis invited me to appear on the program with him because he wanted to present himself as a caring and empathetic interviewer who could match up to Jack Paar, a sensitive humorist and former TV show host. Jerry was advised to target a younger audience as he was being considered for a high-paying contract to host a late-night talk show on CBS or ABC. Jerry believed I was talented but lacked the ego and glossy polish of professional child actors. He thought I would be a good fit. My presence on the show was supposed to showcase Jerry's sensitive side, and it worked like a charm. The audience and the networks saw a facet of Jerry Lewis' character that was unexpected and compelling, and he elevated himself to a top TV personality with all the elements working in his favor during those two weeks. As a result, he was offered lucrative deals.

On September 21, 1963, ABC-TV premiered *Jerry Lewis Live!* This was the first of a 40-show contract that paid Jerry Lewis over $40 million to host a two-hour live interview and variety show every Saturday night with an almost unlimited budget for talent. Uncle Ernie was brought in as its executive producer, Perry Cross left *The Tonight Show* to become the program's producer, and Dick Cavett was hired as a writer. Complying with Jerry's demands, a control panel was built into his desk, allowing him to override the director's shots. Besides rehearsing a few songs, Jerry refused to discuss what he would do on the show, which was of enormous concern. Things fell apart so rapidly on opening night that the show was canceled after the first live broadcast.

Whatever Jerry thought would work didn't. Since most TV shows of that era had equipment that blocked part of the audience's view, Jerry ordered a large TV projection screen, which was supposed to let the people on the balcony see the action. However, the big screen went out, and then the sound system failed. Jerry had immersed himself in the technical aspects of the program, confident that he would rise to the occasion when on the air. Neglecting the theatrical concerns, much to the frustration of others, Jerry Lewis created an artistic disaster. His ego had gotten the better of him, resulting in a fiasco. The wrap-up party after the show resembled a wake.

Jerry Lewis Live! was dead, and *The Hollywood Palace* was born. This highly successful midseason replacement ran every Saturday night on ABC for six years.

Did my appearance on *The Tonight Show* with Jerry Lewis help my career? Absolutely. Did my appearance on *The Tonight Show* help Jerry Lewis' career? Absolutely. Do I believe that, in some roundabout way, I had something to do with the birth of *The Hollywood Palace*? Absolutely not… but it's fun to think about.

The Catskills: My Alma-Matzoh

Even before I was born, my roots were intertwined with show business and the Catskill Mountains. The Catskill Mountains is an area in upstate New York that once boasted having hundreds of large and small resort hotels and bungalow colonies. Jewish families owned and operated most of these establishments, giving their guests the finest food and entertainment. Passed down from one generation to the next, these incomparable summer retreats thrived from the turn of the 20th century till their decline in the 1960s.

In the early 1900s, Eastern European Jews immigrated to the foothills of the Catskill Mountains as farmers. As these Yiddish-speaking entrepreneurs attracted more and more city-dwellers seeking fresh air and good food, they expanded their farms and built rooming houses. Charging guests for an overnight stay supplemented their incomes. Reinvesting the profits, these room rentals burgeoned into the larger, popular summer vacation spots. With many upscale hotels and beach areas in the United States "restricted," which meant "no Jews allowed," the Catskills became a Mecca for opulent and not-so-opulent Jews. Hotel advertisements promoted access to trains, bus lines, and convenient free parking. A single room with a shared bath on the floor cost $5 per person in 1920. Deluxe accommodations for a single room with a bath, running water, and an electric light cost $7 a day, which included three meals a day replete with a menu of farm-fresh produce, daily activities, and the use of the facility, plus nightly entertainment.

In the 1920s, after World War I, my father's family purchased a small Catskill hotel called the Grandview House. Dad's parents had ten children who all helped run the place together. The whole family kept this popular 40-room "mansion" alive with a warm spirit of family living in this country haven miles away from the steamy East Coast cities.

The Saphire family Catskill hotel

The 1929 stock market crash heralded the start of the Great Depression. The decade-long "crash" affected everyone to some degree, but people have an indomitable spirit and found ways to have fun and enjoy life. Money was tight, times were in flux, and jobs were scarce, but people saved pennies to fund a getaway. For most, a vacation to the Catskill Mountains was an affordable form of escapism.

In 1935, Mom's sister Selma, known professionally as Judy Allen, and her first husband, Buddy Allen, auditioned as a dance team for Ernest D. Glucksman, the entertainment director at the Flagler Hotel in the Catskills. The duties of the director of entertainment ranged from hiring all of the athletic staff to producing theatrical extravaganzas for the hotel guests' enjoyment. When

The REAL Jerry Lewis Story

Judy and Buddy Allen, who often worked in the Mountains, were not entertaining in the United States, they performed for European audiences. Through a series of bizarre events, Aunt Judy and Uncle Buddy performed for Benito Mussolini, founder and leader of the Italian Fascist Party, fighting on Germany's side during World War II in 1940. My aunt and uncle were then summoned to entertain the Chancellor of Germany and head of the Nazi Party, Adolf Hitler. Before doing so, they were required to sign a document swearing their veins contained no Jewish blood. Considering that they wanted to keep the blood they had, they found it wise to flee Europe immediately.

By the time I was born in 1947, the Grandview House was only a memory, but my family's ties to the Catskills continued. Mom, Dad, my aunts, my uncles, and their families rented a cottage at some quaint bungalow colony every summer. I sang and danced in the casino, a large multi-purpose hall with a stage, at the Pine Knoll Bungalow Colony in Monticello. I loved to entertain, and the guests were always a receptive audience. For each performance, I received crisp, new dollar bills from friends and family staying there. It was not a bad way for a five-year-old kid to make a living.

Produced and directed by the hotel's social director, the social staff performed original skits and sketches to amuse the guests. As time went on, hotels began to enhance their in-house entertainment by recruiting professional performers from established New York City talent agencies, giving rise to the "Catskill Entertainment Circuit."

Borscht, a favorite soup served at the hotels, was initially brought to this country by Ashkenazi and Slavic Jews. The term circuit referred to the countless theatres that circulated contracted performers to locations across the United States. In the heydays of vaudeville, fortunate entertainers got a contract with one of the reigning booking agencies: the Keith Circuit, the Albee Circuit, or the Orpheum Circuit. The "borscht circuit" was an unofficial term used to describe a region in the Mountains where a small group of performers entertained a specific ethnic group. The area was sometimes referred to as the "borscht belt," a term that mimicked colloquial names of other American regions like the Bible Belt in the South or the Rust Belt in Pennsylvania and Ohio.

I do not know of any hotel that ever advertised being located in the scenic "Borsch Belt." When a newspaper review referred to a performer as a "Borscht Belt" comedian, it implied that the entertainer was only suitable for a Jewish audience, and the terms "borscht circuit" and "borscht belt" were ethnic slurs. I have known hundreds of entertainers in my lifetime and represented scores of them. A Las Vegas emcee might introduce comedian Shecky Greene by saying, "Let's welcome our comedy star direct from a successful two-week engagement at the Copacabana in Manhattan," but no one would ever say, "Let's welcome our comedy star direct from a successful one-nighter at Rabinowitz's Bungalow Colony in the 'Borscht Belt.'" An entertainer who put "Borscht Belt" on his resumé would get a ticket back to the "Borscht Belt."

Jerry Lewis said, "The Catskills gave comedians a place to fail," but he was wrong. By and large, Catskill vacationers were sophisticated and worldly. They had seen it all. New performers could not understand the ambivalent reactions they received from the people seated in the first few rows, who were the season guests and occupied the same spot for two months. To be successful on stage, a performer had to be talented, fresh, clever, and, above all, respectful to the audience. If the act was using material gleaned from another Catskill artist, the audience would sense it and could "eat you up alive." Performers needed to be genuine, prepared, and seasoned. Catskill audiences were branded as tough, but I disagree. They were receptive, albeit highly discerning.

Many acts received a modest remuneration per show. However, New York talent agencies like Charles Rapp and Jack Segal would book an act as a double or a triple; that is, the act would be scheduled for multiple appearances at different hotels on a single night, making the 100-mile drive from Manhattan profitable for the performer. In that way, the artists earned a good living, and the hotels could afford to offer their guests a variety of quality shows. As the years passed and business became more profitable and competitive, the establishments began booking big names. Although the hotels in Lakewood were a significant distance from the Catskill venues, they were still considered part of the "borscht circuit" because they used the same booking agents.

Offering their guests a tranquil retreat from hot city life with its fresh mountain air, eclectic activities, friendly staff, and good food, the Catskills provided top-notch entertainment, including big-name talents such as comedian Jan Murray, female celebrity impersonator Lynne Carter, comedienne Totie Fields, Vegas lounge favorite The Trenires, comedian Red Buttons, comedian Nipsey Russell, musical comedian Mr. Kerri April, singer Eddie Fisher, and impersonator Marilyn Michaels.

Social staff members could hone their comedic skills in the Catskill hotels. Entertainment was not confined to the nightclub or theatre. Anytime a group of people were seen sitting quietly in the lobby or at the pool, an instant comedy routine could break out. There were always pockets of guests staying there, ready to be entertained. This was an opportunity for aspiring comedians like myself to gain confidence and try out material. Hotel owners encouraged this as it was part of the Catskill experience. Whether conducting a Bingo game, performing a magic routine, or managing a guest-staff talent show, my role was to engage the guests, make them laugh, and ensure they had fun. Here is where a comedian could try out material…not in the big room.

Because the majority of the audience in the Catskills spoke only Yiddish in the early days, the comedians had to be skilled in delivering their jokes in Yiddish with a hint of English. The Jewish clientele enjoyed the Catskills not only for the fresh air and kosher food but they also shared a culture which the entertainers understood. Over time, people assimilated. When performers told their jokes in Yiddish, there would be laughter and mumbling in the audience as people who spoke Yiddish explained the joke to those who did not. By the 1950s, entertainers told their punchlines in a combination of Yiddish and English. By the mid-1960s, if the comedians told their jokes in Yiddish, they did not work. Originally, "borscht belt" meant "We speak your language." Nowadays, the term means "Jewish."

In order for Catskill hotels to compete with other resort areas, such as the Poconos and Atlantic City, they needed to attract regional and national conventions. Although most Catskill hotels maintained a kosher menu and observed Jewish holidays, promoting themselves as Jewish resorts severely limited their business. Ironically, when Italian singer Enzo Stuarti incorporated many Jewish tunes into his repertoire in 1964 to please the guests at Brown's Hotel, the audience was disappointed because they wanted to hear him sing in Italian.

In 1963, less than a year after I was on *The Tonight Show*, Uncle Ernie called with another proposal. Jerry had spoken to Charles and Lillian, the owners of Brown's Hotel, and they were interested in having me work at their famous Catskill resort for two weeks. Uncle Ernie had spoken to my parents to get their approval. The arrangements were in place, pending my consent. Was I interested in a job at Brown's? I sure was. This turned out to be a major step forward in my entertainment career.

My family took the two-hour ride from Livingston, New Jersey, to drop me off at Brown's in the Catskill Mountains in upstate New York. We passed countless signs along the highway that showed a picture of Jerry Lewis with a slogan that read "Brown's Hotel, My Favorite Resort." These iconic signs were a win-win deal for Jerry

Lewis and Brown's Hotel. The Browns benefited from the use of Jerry Lewis' name, and Jerry benefited from the Browns' advertising Jerry Lewis. One of the funniest things I remember Jerry saying was, "Brown's is my favorite resort. I know that because I read it on a sign."

My first day working at Brown's was memorable. As my family and I pulled into the parking lot at this lavish resort, I could hear the echoes of a strong man's voice giving commands: "Left-right-right, companyyyy halt." Where was I going to work? It sounded like an army base. Approaching the hotel, I could see a large group of women and men marching in place, fronted by a short, muscular man wearing shorts and a baseball cap biting a long cigar. The hotel's activities director, Sam Tolkoff, coached the daily calisthenics class.

As we approached the front desk, the Brown's Hotel lobby was bustling with activity. While waiting to check in, a man strolling through the lobby approached my father. Acting like he had known my dad for years, they shook hands, and the man asked, "How are you today?"

Puzzled, my dad said, "I think you have the wrong person. I don't think I know you."

The elegantly dressed man smiled back at my father and said, "Oh, I know everybody here. Everyone here is my guest. I'm Charlie Brown." That said it all. The personal touch came from the top down and contributed to the hotel's success.

The REAL Jerry Lewis Story

Mr. Tolkoff (nobody called him Sam) was to be my immediate supervisor, although he wasn't pleased about it at the time. Mr. T, which is what you got to call him after he got to know you better, was a highly regarded physical education instructor for the New York City school system and worked at Brown's during his summer vacation. His staff was comprised of boys from his school whom he brought to the Catskills to live and work during the summer. Some kids came from difficult home lives, had committed crimes, and were on the brink of disaster. Sam Tolkoff would rule them with an iron hand, shaping them quickly into respectful men. Maybe that was why his students affectionately called this Jewish man the "Priest in Sneakers." Before the end of a 12-week summer season, most of Mr. Tolkoff's staff could perform just about every job in the hotel, including running contests, teaching shuffleboard, guarding the pool, working in the coffee shop, running the hotel switchboard, and filling in behind the front desk. Everyone multi-tasked and became a trusted and valued part of the hotel.

On the other hand, I was a "Jerry Lewis contract." I was there to perform my magic act for the teenage guests a few times a week and to socialize with them in the dining room. Mr. Tolkoff and his staff truly resented this unable-to-be-fired, 16-year-old, 117-pound, less-than-athletic string bean. However, I quickly learned about the resort hotel business and did almost every job there. Within the first few weeks, I had fallen head over heels in love with every phase of the resort hotel business and with a 14-year-old guest from Philadelphia named Sheila, who would become important to my future. My two weeks on the staff at Brown's were extended through the remainder of the summer season.

Entertainment was not confined to the nightclub or theatre. There was always an opportunity for aspiring comedians like myself to gain confidence and try out material. For example, Ike Reeves, whose parents ran the snack bar at the Pine's Hotel in the Catskills, worked with me at Brown's in the summer of 1964. Ike was a personable young man, a singer, a musician, a fledgling comedian, and an excellent impressionist. His "stage" was the massive hotel lobbies replete with plush carpeting and cozy lounge chairs with matching sofas, or the austere convention meeting rooms or one of the pool areas. Whenever more than three people congregated, they risked becoming an audience. Hotel owners encouraged this as it was part of the Catskill experience. While running the B-I-N-G-O games, which were called B-R-O-W-N, so winners yelled out "Brown," Ike added some impressions, a song or two on the accordion, and some well-received humor. On sunny days, Ike provided musical entertainment poolside by singing and playing the piano or accordion. He also accompanied me for our pool closing jingle, which we wrote together. Sixty years later, Ike, who cut his teeth in the Catskills, continues entertaining audiences.

After running an afternoon guest-staff talent show in the Jerry Lewis Theater Club, I might be found putting the lounge pads away at the outdoor pool or cleaning the scum gutters with a scrub brush after the guests had left the area. Even on my nights off, I was at the hotel running the show's spotlight or setting up chairs for an evening activity. There was no room for egos in the hotel business in those days. We all worked together because we loved our jobs, respected our employers, and knew everyone had to pitch in and keep the hotel running smoothly.

Everywhere guests turned at Brown's, there were signs of Jerry Lewis. His likeness was emblazoned on ashtrays, napkins, menus, activity schedules, shot glasses, t-shirts, and sweatshirts. One season, there was even a Jerry Lewis lookalike on the entertainment staff. Martin Abrahams, a personable teenager whose face and body bore an uncanny resemblance to the young Jerry Lewis of the 40s and 50s, reminded me of Jerry as depicted in the Jerry Lewis comic books. Marty Abrahams' uncle, Mack Gray, was a popular Hollywood entity, having once been a personal manager and confidant to screen actor George Raft. In the 1950s, Mack became Dean Martin's fill-in double and bodyguard. As a favor to Mack, Dean, who had taken a liking to Mack's nephew, arranged for Marty to work at Brown's during the summer of 1964. Lillian Brown, who loved Jerry, loved the idea of having this young clone at the hotel. I worked with Marty that season, and he became a favorite among the guests. As an adult, Martin Abrahams, whose son is actor Jon Avery, became an actor and a highly sought-after futuristic pop artist.

If some people considered the hotel owners "The Royals" because they were the kings and queens of their own private domains, I would call Charlie Brown a benevolent dictator. He was, in fact, the owner of the hotel, and he called the shots. But his concern was always for the hotel and its guests. One day when Mr. Brown was doing his daily tour of the outdoor pool area, he mentioned that there were some cigarette butts in the crack of one of the steps and asked me to get a broom and pan to clean them up. I was very willing to accommodate him, but I wasn't doing a very good job sweeping the cigarette butts into the pan. Mr. Brown took the broom and pan to show me how to hold the broom sideways so it could sweep the butts out of the crevice of the pavement and into the dustpan. As he plunked it into the container, he looked up and realized he was standing in front of 700 guests at the outdoor pool. A little bit embarrassed, he quickly handed the dustpan and the broom back to me, and we both laughed about it. This type of staff treatment was typical of the owners, their families, and management of the Catskill resorts. They loved their hotels. They appreciated their guests, and they treated the staff respectfully.

Catskill hotels, resorts, and bungalow colonies were heimish, a Yiddish word meaning homey, warm feeling, like time spent with family and friends you like. Many vacationers at the hotel met at Brown's annually, and some guests met their future spouses there. I became close friends with Mr. Tolkoff, my co-workers, and my employers, Charles and Lillian Brown. I spent four full seasons at Brown's in the 1960s, where I met many people who became my lifelong friends. Periodically returning to the hotel as master of ceremonies, where Jerry Lewis said he got his start, I later became the entertainment director at some of the East Coast's finest resorts, and I vacationed at Brown's Hotel with my wife, Sheila, the girl from Philadelphia whom I met in 1963 at my alma-matzoh.

Essen, Fressen, and Take a Lesson

During my career as an entertainer and an activities director in the Catskill Mountains, I learned that eating and sports were the three most popular activities. I know I left one out, but you can figure that one out for yourself. Located in Kiamesha Lake, the Concord Hotel was known for its grandeur, boasting five outstanding kosher kitchens, a spacious dining room, and an elegant theater with a seating capacity for over 2,000 guests. As the world's largest nightclub, the Concord's Imperial Room made it into the *Guinness Book of World Records*.

The Concord Hotel social staff members and I often took the guests on a tour of the facility. During my guided tours of the hotel, I always told a handful of jokes, mostly about food. One joke was about a lady who came up to me and asked, in private, if she could have the recipe for the incredible chocolate cake she had on her last visit. When I told her the secret recipes belonged to the head chef, the woman said she would pay $50 for the chef's recipe. Back in 1966, $50 was a sizable amount of money. I went to the chef and explained that this woman wanted the recipe for chocolate cake and would be willing to pay the tidy sum of $25. Surprisingly, the chef agreed. He took a few minutes to scribble something on a piece of paper, put it in an envelope, and handed it to me. I gave him $25. I contacted the woman to tell her that I had the recipe. She gave me $50, and I gave her the recipe. A half-hour later, she came back to me, irate. "Okay, Rick, I paid for the recipe. I got it, and I'm not going to ask for my money back, but really…" She handed me the recipe. The instructions read, "First, take 600 fresh eggs, 30 pounds of butter, and 20 gallons of milk…"

My friend Larry Best, who appeared in Jerry Lewis' 1960 movie *The Bellboy*, was an excellent comedian and a first-class dialectician. Larry began performing in the Catskills in the late 1930s. By the 1960s, he was legendary, telling most of his jokes with a Yiddish accent when performing in the Kosher hotels, which made the jokes sound even funnier. One of Larry's stories was about the Catskill food. "A man at the hotel walked up to the front desk. Complaining, he said. 'I don't mean to complain, but the food here is absolutely terrible. As a matter of fact, the food here is like poison.' He continued, 'And the worst thing is the portions are way too small.'"

Another popular joke was about a woman who came to breakfast and asked for extra rolls. The waiter accommodated her. The woman opened a cloth napkin, placed the rolls in it, and then tucked them into her pocketbook. She ordered extra rolls at lunch, put them in her napkin, and tucked them into her pocketbook. Again, at dinner, she ordered extra rolls, wrapped them in her napkin, and tucked them into her pocketbook. This went on for all three meals a day during her two-week stay. Finally, the maître d'hôtel realized what she was doing: She was stealing napkins.

Another one of my favorite stories was about the hotel guest who ordered steak. When the waiter brought it over, the customer looked very concerned and asked the waiter, "Why is your thumb on my steak?"

The waiter explained, "I didn't want it to slide off the plate and fall on the floor…again."

All joking aside, the food in the Catskills was exceptional, and the kosher cuisine became quite popular with guests of all backgrounds and religions.

True Catskill Mountain epicureans knew the chocolate egg cream was the most popular drink at any hotel coffee shop. Jerry Lewis often bragged about his days as a soda jerk. During an interview, I heard him say that he worked occasionally behind the counter at the Brown's Hotel Coffee Shop and that his chocolate egg creams were the best. Jerry was a dreamer.

Hotel owner Charles Brown with Jerry Lewis. Jerry is enjoying his coveted Chocolate Egg Cream!

Chris Lewis, Jerry's 4th son, was my guest on a nationally broadcast radio show I hosted on July 22, 1999, and he shared a story about Lillian Brown. Chris began, "Lillian, whom I called Aunt Lil, said to me the last time I saw her…in about 1987…'We tried to keep your father (young Jerry Lewis) out of the soda fountain because he kept messing everything up.'" Sounding amused, Chris continued, "She said he was…clowning around, throwing the ice cream up in the air and catching it in a cup, splashing everything. She said, 'We couldn't control him.'" I remarked that Jerry was like a tornado, and if you could harness the energy and make it work, that would be a good thing. However, early in his career, many people thought Jerry was crazy or a nut. Chris added, "Lillian was so funny. As sweet as she was, her quote to me was, 'We just thought he was an idiot.'"

When I was with Jerry on his yacht in San Diego, California, in 2007, he told me he had a surprise for me in the galley. Opening a small refrigerator, Jerry took out a bottle of Fox's U-Bet, the chocolate syrup most widely used in the Bronx, Brooklyn, and the Catskills for making egg creams. Jerry put a massive amount of chocolate syrup in a glass, added a dash of milk, and a squirt of seltzer. After he stirred it, he proudly served it to me. With effort, I took a gulp and thought he was trying to kill me. It was like trying to sip a chocolate bar through the straw. No research was needed to realize Jerry did not invent the "Egg Cream Assist." Jerry tried his best, but here's my chocolate egg cream recipe: "First, take 600 fresh eggs…" Oops, that's not right.

Start with a 12-ounce glass, about 7" tall. Fill it with an inch of Fox's U-Bet chocolate syrup, add an inch of chilled whole milk, and stir. Next, pour in chilled, unflavored seltzer water. Using a long teaspoon, slowly pour the seltzer down the spoon into the chocolate and milk mixture, stirring the concoction from the bottom up. Be careful not to let the foam overflow the top of the glass. The perfect egg cream has an inch to an inch and a half of thick foam on the top. Drink it with or without a straw. By the way, do not put ice or eggs in an egg cream.

Jerry's Future "Lies" in the Catskills

In a 1948 radio interview, Jerry Lewis claimed that six years earlier, in 1942, he began working at Brown's Hotel in Loch Sheldrake, New York, and was paid $30 per month. In an interview in 2000, produced and archived by the Television Academy, Jerry Lewis proudly boasted that when he began working at Brown's Hotel in 1942, he earned $9,000 as a busboy and an additional $1,000 as a tea boy; thus he made $1,000 more than his father for the summer season. If the Lewises combined salaries equaled $20,000, they could have rented a New York apartment for $600 per year, paid 19¢ a gallon for gas, and bought a 1941 Cadillac for $2,000, and there would be $18,000 left over to keep the tank filled. That's the good news. The bad news was that Brown's Hotel in Loch Sheldrake, New York, did not open its doors until the summer of 1944, and Jerry's entire story was bullshit.

In 1965, Mrs. Brown's grandson, Cliff Turiansky, was a busboy who became a waiter on the "gold coast" of the main dining room, which meant he served the hotel owners and the season guests seated at prime tables. For accuracy, I wanted to speak to someone who would know what a busboy and a waiter earned. Cliff, who worked his way up to an executive position at the hotel, said he earned $300 a week as a server, which was good money in those days. For Jerry to have made $10,000 during the summer season at Brown's Hotel in the 40s, Cliff explained, with his tongue firmly planted in his cheek, "Jerry must have been giving sexual favors."

According to Jerry, while his parents were performing out of town, he stayed with his grandmother, Sarah. Sarah died in 1937, when Jerry was 11. After that, his aunts cared for him when his parents were on the road. During the winter season of 1939-1940, Danny and Rae Lewis were employed by Charles and Lillian Brown at the Hotel Arthur in Lakewood, New Jersey. During the following winter season of 1940-1941, Jerry spent his winter break with his parents, who were once again employed by the Browns in Lakewood. The 14-year-old Jerry met and became friends with Mrs. Brown's 15-year-old daughter, Lonnie. Together, the two teens collaborated to develop an act in which she sang and worked the phonograph while Jerry lip-synced in costumes to various records. They occasionally performed their musical skits for the guests in hotel lobbies and at staff talent shows. While Lonnie was simply having fun, this experience inspired Jerry to develop an act after dropping out of school.

Over those two seasons in Lakewood, Jerry crafted his record pantomime act, performing wherever he could. With Lonnie's aid and support, Jerry developed his record mime act, which ultimately became his entry into show business. After Jerry's winter break ended, he returned to school in Irvington, New Jersey, and stayed with his Aunt Rose.

In the summer of 1942, the Browns were the managers of the Ambassador Hotel in upstate New York and gave 16-year-old Jerry Lewis a job as a busboy as a favor to his parents, who were also working there. It became apparent within days that Jerry was not cut out for this job, and he was reassigned to the athletic staff. However,

Jerry broke his arm almost immediately and was unable to work for six weeks. Because he shared a room with his parents, Jerry, who had dropped out of high school, was able to remain at the hotel.

Lillian Brown's daughter, Lonnie, told a different story. According to her, Jerry was a tea boy at the Hotel Arthur in Lakewood, New Jersey, and then he briefly worked on the athletic staff at the Ambassador Hotel in upstate New York before he broke his arm. Both concurred that he performed his 12-14 minute record mime act at some of the smaller hotels in Lakewood when he was 16.

It is important to note that by the time Charles and Lillian Brown opened Brown's Hotel for business in the summer of 1944, Jerry was already traveling as a record mime act and under contract to a New York theatrical agent, Abner J. Greshler.

Angel Lopez, owner of New York's Havana-Madrid nightclub, and Abby Greshler matched Jerry Lewis with Dean Martin. In 1954, ten years after the Browns bought their famous resort in the Catskills, Jerry appeared at Brown's Hotel in Loch Sheldrake to promote the Martin & Lewis film *Living It Up*. Excited about this event, the Browns renamed their Playhouse Theatre, a combination theater and recreation hall, the Martin & Lewis Playhouse. Both stars' names were boldly spelled out on the marquee in glowing neon lights. The media from New York City attended this gala Hollywood-style premiere. Everyone of importance was in attendance. That is, everyone except Dean Martin, who had no interest in attending this contrived event. At this point, Dean and

Jerry's relationship was strained, and Dean had no desire to share in Jerry's glory and hear the lie told again that this is where Jerry got his start.

The most successful hotels were the ones that were creative in their advertising. In the mid-1950s, Jerry Lewis became one of the Browns' most valuable advertising assets, although Jerry Lewis' career had little connection with Brown's Hotel or the Catskill Mountains. While Lillian had stars in her eyes, Charlie Brown had dollar signs in his. In 1952, Martin & Lewis hit their stride. Jerry liked Uncle Charlie and Aunt Lil, as he called them, and agreed to lend his name and likeness to their advertisements and promotions. As a result, the names of comedian Jerry Lewis and Brown's Hotel became welded together, contributing to the urban legend that Jerry got his start in the Catskills. Research into Jerry's background makes it apparent that all of these alleged associations with Brown's Hotel insulated him from any legal issues dating back to his assault on his principal. In other words, it gave him an alibi.

One day in 1965, Lillian Brown called me into her office and proudly told me that Jerry Lewis was to make a long-awaited appearance at her popular resort. Even though my Uncle Ernie had dissolved his business relationship with Jerry after the star's disastrous attempt at his own ABC-TV talk show, I kept in touch with Jerry and was eager to see him again. It had been many years since Jerry Lewis visited Brown's Hotel. Jerry had been there a decade earlier for the world premiere of the Martin & Lewis film *You're Never Too Young*, but Dean refused to go on that trip, and the comedy team did not speak to each other for months.

Weeks before his trip to the Catskills, Jerry Lewis was injured during the dress rehearsal for Andy Williams' TV variety show. While practicing a dance routine, Jerry fell on the slippery floor and cracked his head on the ground, sustaining a fine linear skull fracture and a concussion. Although suffering from impaired vision and problems with his equilibrium, he still fulfilled his commitment to appear at Brown's. However, Jerry was scheduled to perform at a 10 p.m. show, but he did not arrive at Brown's Hotel until 12:30 a.m., wearing a dark fedora, draped in an outlandish black cloak, and carrying a walking stick. He looked exactly as he did when he portrayed himself in the 1960 movie *The Bellboy*. The zany, lovable Jerry Lewis the hotel guests expected did not show up. The "Jerry" that did arrive at Brown's was arrogant, aloof, and indifferent to the many fans who only wanted to show him their admiration. His head injuries were not widely known. That might explain his cane; however, he picked up a bat and played baseball the next day.

Comedienne Totie Fields used to tell a story on the TV talk show circuit about her first encounter with Jerry Lewis. "He sent me a bouquet of flowers after my Las Vegas debut," she boasted. "A week later, I sent them back to him with a note reading, 'Your damn flowers died!'" It's a funny story, but that is not what happened at their first encounter. The truth is that Totie, who was performing at Brown's, and I awaited Jerry's homecoming together at the foot of the hotel's main driveway all evening. My job was to report his arrival to Mrs. Brown. For hours, we stood there thinking that every car approaching the hotel on lonely Route 52 would be his limousine.

Totie, who had not yet become famous, was excited about meeting Jerry Lewis. She asked my dad, who had his camera, to photograph her with Jerry. That Friday night, the Browns had ordered all the facilities in the hotel to remain open. When Jerry arrived, he wanted to go to the coffee shop, and we all followed him like peasants begging for alms from the nobility. Once in the restaurant, Totie managed to seat herself next to Jerry. My father jockeyed into position to snap a picture for her, but when Jerry noticed the camera, he turned his head away from the comedienne. Totie got a photograph but did not get a friendly word from Jerry until she became a celebrity.

On Saturday afternoon, Jerry Lewis donned dark glasses and sat in the hotel dining room to have lunch with Charles, Lillian, and their family. While Jerry was sitting at the table, the athletic staff formed an absurd security circle around him by holding hands with their backs to the star. The staff was instructed to protect Mr. Lewis in the event some crazed guest lost total control and asked for his autograph. If he had really wanted privacy, he could have had lunch in his hotel suite.

In his 1982 autobiography, *Jerry Lewis In Person*, Jerry expressed his feelings about returning to Brown's and the Catskills by writing, "All at once, looming up as the sun had just burst through a cloud, there was the sight of me returning as a sort of hometown hero, the big, international celebrity and 'King Shit of the Catskills.'" Well, that afternoon in Brown's dining room, "King Shit" was seated on his throne.

Jerry Lewis seemed uncomfortable being at Brown's. Maybe that was because his fabled springboard to fame from this hotel in the Catskills was just that…a fable. His actual ties to the Catskill Mountains were negligible. For years, Jerry told the story that at five, he got his first taste of the theater when he stayed with his parents at the President Hotel in Swan Lake, New York, where they were performing. With his father at his side, Jerry supposedly sang the doleful "Brother, Can You Spare a Dime?" which in 1933 came to be regarded as the anthem for the Great Depression. Questioned by Peter Bogdanovich in a 2008 interview, Jerry recanted everything he had said about that defining moment when, as a little boy, he knew he wanted to be a comedian and confessed, "Whatever I'm gonna tell you now is all bullshit. I have no idea what I'm talking about. I'm referring to whatever I read, I said."

After lunch on the Saturday of Jerry's visit to Brown's, we all trudged down to the softball field for a game: the Staff vs the Guests. Jerry played first base while I was on second, wearing my "Rick 'The Chest' Saphire" sweatshirt the athletic staff gave me to honor my scrawny, slender physique. The batter from the Guests' team was Herb Saphire, my father. In contrast to me, Dad was a brawny, muscular man who had been a former semi-professional baseball player.

Jerry Lewis and Sam Tolkoff tending to the injuries which ended the softball game

Photo by Herbert Saphire

Dad, from the Guests, slammed a hard grounder toward first base. Lewis, from the Staff, charged the ball, picked it up, and fired to "The Chest" at second. I grabbed the throw. At the same time, Dad, ignoring the fact that he was about to pulverize his only son, slid in hard, avoiding the tag. His legs tangled with mine, pushing me off base. The impact knocked the ball from my glove…SAFE, as the go-ahead run scored from third. As if I was not embarrassed enough because I accidentally let my Dad get the best of the bases, Jerry glared at me through his sunglasses and said for all to hear, "Gar nicht helfen" (Yiddish for "No help"). You could cut the tension with a knife. Maybe Lewis was thinking about the hotel softball game he wrote about in his autobiography when his father scored the go-ahead run as the young Jerome Levitch (Jerry Lewis) looked on. But I was the underdog this time, and my dad was getting the cheers.

Our game suddenly ended when two athletic staff members collided while trying to catch a fly ball. They collapsed to the ground, their faces covered with blood. Jerry rushed over to them, dropped to his knees, and opened the deep gash in the forehead of one of the boys. As the blood shot out, the athletic director, Sam Tolkoff, who had been tending the other boy, screamed, "Close that damn thing. Put pressure on it." Tolkoff muscled Jerry out of the way and administered the proper first aid.

Jerry looked as if he had fallen off his throne. Sheepishly, he returned to the hotel to prepare for the evening's show.

Sam Tolkoff was always a good sport. One rainy day, while performing my magic act in the hotel lobby for a few hundred guests, I needed an assistant for an illusion. When I called on Mr. T, the staff went wild. There

Sam Tolkoff with Rick Saphire at Brown's Hotel

was apprehension in his eyes when he saw a display of swords. I had him take a seat and placed a large box over his head. As I thrust the first of 15 blades into the sealed chest that encompassed his head, he began to shake. From inside the box, I heard his voice: "Saphire, get me the fuck out of here." I did the trick quickly and released my boss from his terror. In a conversation with him 30 years later, we were reminiscing, and Mr. T confessed, "Rick, I hated to admit it, but I was scared to death inside that box." After all those years, I apologized.

As far as Jerry Lewis was concerned, Sam Tolkoff did not have much admiration for the man whom he had known for many years. Mr. T talked about one day writing his autobiography and calling it *The Priest in Sneakers*, the nickname his students gave him. Sometime after Jerry Lewis heard Mr. T's moniker, the star's office contacted him to warn him never to use that title. Jerry claimed he had it copyrighted for his own use, even though a song, film, or book title cannot be copyrighted. Jerry's threat irked Sam Tolkoff. "Rick, because my life has always been sports, I have learned to judge a man's character by the way he acts on the ball field." Mr. T added, "When Jerry Lewis stood only ten feet away from me and threw the ball to me as hard as he could, I knew he was a mean bastard."

That night, Jerry was the headliner in the Brown's nightclub. After Martin & Lewis split up, it was renamed the Jerry Lewis Theater Club. Before the show, my father, who had known Jerry Lewis for years, was backstage snapping pictures of the performer as he posed with everyone. Jerry always loved cameras and kept volumes of photo albums containing shots of nearly every engagement throughout his career. While helping my father with a few lens adjustments, Jerry seemed to be at ease and relaxed.

I was the chief spotlight operator at Brown's when I was not performing stand-up comedy at some other hotels on my nights off. It was a fun job and made me feel a part of the show, albeit behind the scenes. I climbed the steps to the spotlight room with my buddy Cliff. Cliff, the son of Jerry Lewis' childhood friend, Lonnie, and I made a great team. We followed the dancers and acrobats without ever missing a cue. That night, Cliff and I flawlessly worked Jerry's show.

Jerry Lewis' 1965 performance met everyone's expectations, as he was charming and funny. After the show, Charles and Lillian Brown, various hotel VIPs, special hotel guests like my parents, and I sat in the otherwise empty theater to review and relive the evening. Jerry was amiable and asked my father to take a picture of him with the Browns. I then asked Jerry if I could get a picture with him. He looked at me squarely and said, "There will be no pictures for you."

I thought. "He must be joking." Several minutes later, I asked him again if we could take a picture. This time, his face assumed a grim expression, as if some painful memory had just triggered an anxiety attack.

I was taken aback and asked, "Why not?"

While my parents, employers, and friends listened, Jerry Lewis growled, "Someday, I'll tell you when you grow up."

It was beyond me why the man who was so engaging with everyone else went out of his way to be rude to me. Everyone in the room seemed shocked and embarrassed on my behalf. Jerry's behavior dampened the festivities, and I was on the verge of tears. However, when Jerry took a seat next to mine, I saw my father pivoting around us with his camera. At that moment, all I wanted was the satisfaction of that picture, and I got it. The photograph speaks for itself. Jerry Lewis looks towards me with a smirk as his head rests on his fist with his middle finger fully extended.

Shortly after my mother's death in 1982, I found a carbon copy of a 1964 letter she had sent to Jerry Lewis in my defense. I also found Jerry's two-page typewritten response, espousing his self-importance and alluding to a problem he had with my father. However, he offered no details about what happened. In his reply to my mother, Jerry compared my father's enthusiasm for my career to "the man who killed his friend with a gun (although it was truly an accident) nonetheless killed him."

It is hard to imagine Jerry equating a father's love to murder. But then again, my research uncovered a bizarre memo Jerry wrote a memo to himself about one of his employees, Dick Jarrard. He titled the memo "Man Against Himself," which is also the title of a book about suicide and self-harm written in 1938 by American psychiatrist Karl A. Menninger. In the memo, Jerry wrote, "Dick isn't any different from me or any other human I must stab him and hurt [him] deeply if I am to keep us together. The hurt will be something we will laugh at years from now if I handle it honestly and correctly…JL." Equally as masochistic in tone, Jerry ended his letter to my mother by admitting that he intentionally hurt me to get back at my father for his behavior backstage. It has been decades since Jerry wrote his disconcerting letter, and I am still not laughing. Is it possible Jerry was really getting even with his own father? Was this a case of misplaced aggression?

I believe Jerry was resentful of the relationship I had with the Browns and their family because the work I did at Brown's Hotel was work Jerry bragged about doing himself yet never did. Even I got drawn into Jerry's lies about Brown's. When he talked about me in *Teen Life Magazine* in 1963, Jerry said, "Right now, he's knocking 'em dead at Brown's Hotel in Loch Sheldrake in upstate New York, where I started my career." Over the years, I realized the dates and events Jerry Lewis talked about did not align, and Jerry could not have gotten his start at Brown's.

In the late 1970s, when I returned to Brown's as the hotel's Master of Ceremonies, I met musician Sam Bidner, a Jerry Lewis disciple, who was working at the hotel with his band. Sam and I had several things in common, most notably Jerry Lewis. Sam's association with Jerry dates back to the Martin & Lewis heydays when he was a band leader at New York City's Latin Quarter. In addition, Sam played saxophone and flute for Dean and Jerry on *The Colgate Comedy Hour*. After the

The REAL Jerry Lewis Story

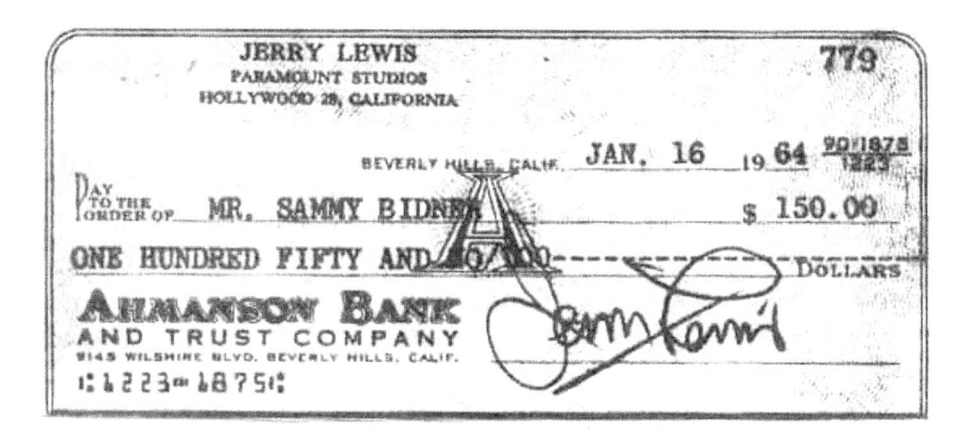

breakup with Dean, Sam continued to travel with Jerry around the world as part of the Lewis entourage.

Sam was famously known as Jerry's "supplier." Yes, he got Jerry the "stuff" whenever Jerry needed it. The "stuff" was Indian nuts. Jerry's cravings for the little, smooth, bean-like morsels were legendary. Sam Bidner would get them from his source and deliver them to the star wherever he was. One of Jerry's telegrams to Bidner made it to Earle Wilson's nationally syndicated newspaper column. "Jerry Lewis wired Latin Quarter musician Sam Bidner, 'Airmail 20 pounds of Indian nuts. Lives are at stake.'" Jerry paid Sammy by check.

This very entertaining man reminded me of a Jewish Rocky Graziano. Sam, who was slightly "punchy," had a raspy voice. He spoke fast and was sometimes hard to understand, and he took advantage of that. One night at Brown's Hotel, while Sam and his quartet played dance music at a cocktail party, a woman approached the bandstand and told Sam how much she enjoyed his music. He removed the saxophone mouthpiece from his mouth and said to the woman, "Oh, fuck you very much." She misunderstood his words, smiled, and said, "Thank you."

Sam Bidner was frequently the target of Lewis' infamous tie-cutting, lapel-shredding, and other impractical jokes. While sailing on Jerry's yacht, the Pussycat, the predictably unpredictable movie star threw Sam's clothes overboard. Wearing only his swimming trunks, Sam had to go into town to purchase a new suit, which Lewis bought. Another time, Jerry called Sam, who was playing sax for the Broadway musical *Once Upon a Mattress* starring Carol Burnett, to ask Sam to take a short 45-minute car ride to the Tappan Zee Bridge between showtimes. Once there, Jerry was supposed to arrange for a limousine to take Sam back to the theatre. "The son of a bitch hijacked me," Sam wailed. "I was sure my career on Broadway was finished. Jerry then called the theatre and told the guy I was sick, and I'd be away for a few days. When the guy realized he was talking to Jerry Lewis, it was like God called him." Jerry refused to let Sam out of the car until they reached his destination, Brown's Hotel in the Catskills for one of Jerry's rare appearances.

Their 2-hour ride was anything but peaceful. After securing Sam's job for him, Jerry attempted to snatch Sam's coveted saxophone mouthpiece from his pocket. A brawl ensued. They tumbled around in the back seat of the limousine. Still grappling, the two men rolled onto the ground when the driver opened the car door. Sam received teeth wounds to his arm, which matched Jerry's bite. After Jerry Lewis' performance at Brown's, Sam went to the hospital for a tetanus shot. I mentioned this incident to Jerry while spending a day with him on his yacht in San Diego in 2006. When I got to the part where Jerry bit Sam in the arm, leaving teeth marks, Jerry said, "Yeah, he wanted me to sign it."

One afternoon, while Sam Bidner was visiting Jerry's hotel suite, Jerry gestured for Sam to enter the bathroom. To Sam's surprise, the comedian asked him to help him with a pair of handcuffs. Without resistance, Sam permitted Jerry to handcuff him to a pipe in the bathroom shower. As Jerry left the bathroom, laughter turned to terror. Jerry left the claustrophobic musician helpless. Sam was so terrified that he began to cry as he yelled for help. Jerry left to go shopping for a few hours while Sam was shackled to the pipe. Some people tolerated Jerry's antics because they admired him or because he represented a status or a payday. Others found Jerry Lewis amusing and liked him. For Sam Bidner, it was all of the above.

Sam Bidner was on the stage in Las Vegas that memorable night in 1976 when Frank Sinatra briefly reunited Dean Martin and Jerry Lewis as the telethon audience watched in awe. He described the decades he spent traversing the globe with Jerry Lewis as an exciting time. Although Sam took a lot of abuse, the rewards compensated for it. "For 20 years, I rode in limos," he explained. "I traveled to and stayed at the finest hotels, and there was plenty of work."

A few years later, Jerry Lewis was appearing at Atlantic City's Resorts International. My wife and I saw the show and then went backstage to meet Sam Bidner. When we arrived, Sam poked his head out of the band room and said, "I'll be out in a minute."

I brought along a bunch of 3-D stereo photos my father had taken on his visit to Beverly Hills in 1953. Several photos showed a young Jerry Lewis, and I knew Sam would enjoy seeing them. Sam knew about the tension between Jerry and me, which began at Brown's in 1965 when he refused to pose for a picture with me. Like Sinatra reuniting Martin and Lewis, Sam hoped to reunite Saphire and Lewis. So, he purposely delayed coming out of the dressing room, knowing Jerry, who was coming off stage, would bump into me. Sam's timing was right on cue, but the result was not what he expected.

As we waited backstage for Sam, I sensed Jerry approaching. The smell of Jerry's favorite cologne, Alfred Dunhill of London, always preceded him by 15 seconds. As I had nothing pleasant to say to Jerry, I hoped to avoid seeing him. But there he was, standing in front of me, for the first time in years. He looked me squarely in the eyes. Instinctively, I acknowledged his presence.

Jerry replied, "Hi, Ricky Saphire. You've grown some."

"It's been a long time, Jerry."

His entourage moved in a bit closer to hear what was happening. Jerry looked down at my stereo viewer and the 3-D slides in my hand. Casually, I said, "If you've got a minute, you might enjoy some pictures I brought to show Sam Bidner." The art of 3-D stereo photography, a fad during the 40s and early 50s, had quickly faded (no pun intended).

As I handed Jerry the old stereo viewer and slides, he made a remark, "Did you hear? Lindbergh landed in Paris," and I chuckled. Jerry Lewis studied the photos and identified the people in them. While going through the slides, he accidentally dropped one, and we both bent down to pick it up, stopping halfway. We were nose to nose. Everybody backstage was watching Saphire vs Lewis. Had there been more time, they might have placed wagers on who would finally relent to pick it up.

After an uncomfortably long pause of three long seconds, Jerry handed me the slide with a grim expression, an expression I remembered seeing in 1965. I looked away for a moment to break the tension and noticed what my wife was holding. There we were, the four of us: Sheila, Rick, Jerry, and my CAMERA. The temptation was too great to resist, so I asked Jerry, "Would it be all right if Sheila took a picture of us together?"

Sarcastically, Jerry sneered, "Your minute's up."

To appear disinterested and aloof, Jerry raised an eyebrow, flicked his head back, did a 180-degree turn, and strutted away, looking much like the cartoon character Wiffle Piffle with his swaying lanky arms and a funny walk. Except for Sam Bidner, the others seemed shocked at Jerry's rudeness. I would have been more surprised if Jerry had been accommodating. Jerry was a moody man, although not all of his moods were bad. His angry, childish persona worked well in his movies and on television with Dean Martin. Little did the audience know that was the REAL Jerry Lewis.

For years, I had heard that the French adore Jerry Lewis. When I asked Sam why the French loved Jerry so much, Sam replied, "The French love Jerry Lewis because they don't understand a word he's saying."

The longevity of Sam Bidner's relationship with Jerry was easy to explain. Sam truly liked Jerry, who provided him with a great deal of employment. So, Sam endured the offensive treatment and cutting remarks, as many of Jerry's followers did. Remarks were not the only thing Jerry cut. Jerry would admire a man's tie, feel the fabric, remove a pair of scissors from his pocket, and cut the man's tie off below the knot. To make amends, Jerry would replace it with a more expensive one, never considering its sentimental value.

One day, Sam experienced a moment of sweet revenge for all the ties he lost. Encouraged by another musician, Bidner picked up a large pair of sheers lying on a dressing room table. He proceeded to vanish into Jerry's dressing room. Driven by years of abuse, Sam sauntered up to the entertainer, withdrew the cold metal blades held in his trembling hand, brought the sharp instrument up to Jerry Lewis' throat, and…cut off his tie. Lewis stared emotionless at his attacker and said, "It's about time."

Jerry Lewis' humor could be biting and sadistic. While vacationing at Brown's, Jerry used an office typewriter to poke fun at the menu by ridiculing the selections of rich, traditional Jewish dishes and kosher foods. It was a tasteless attempt to be funny. Jerry sent copies to his cronies, adding a line at the end that stated, "...all the rest of the stuff that knocked off more Jews than Hitler." After Lillian Brown packed a box full of Jewish delicacies for Jerry to enjoy on his trip to his next engagement, Sam Tolkoff overheard the unappreciative star scoff, "I don't want this 'mocky' food (an offensive term for Jewish)." Although Jerry Lewis (nee Jerome Levitch) was born Jewish, he mocked his religion. At the 1996 Muscular Dystrophy Telethon, Jerry often referred to himself as a "Jew," but found it necessary to joke about one of his staff members as having once worked for Eva Braun, Hitler's girlfriend during the reign of the Third Reich. The scars of World War II were still fresh in the minds of many, and using Hitler and the Holocaust as a basis for humor was not well-received. Jerry's lack of good judgment followed him throughout his life and career.

A short time after Brown's Hotel in Loch Sheldrake closed its doors in November 1988, Arnold Graham, a representative of the Charles Rapp Theatrical Agency in New York, did a mitzvah (good deed) and secured a position for Lillian Brown as a greeter at the nearby Concord Hotel. The Concord had at one time been keen competition for Brown's, but seeing Mrs. Brown, who was in her 90s, seated at the front table in the enormous dining room gave many of the guests a warm feeling. Mrs. Brown's husband, Charlie, had passed away, and her family had grown up and moved on their own. She felt loved and at home in the Catskill surroundings, except for one sad state of affairs. Her beloved Jerry Lewis found a reason to end his relationship with his Aunt Lil and refused to talk to her.

When I saw Mrs. Brown at the Concord Hotel, she looked as stately as ever. Her red hair was neatly pulled back into a French twist, her nails were manicured, her makeup was perfect, and her clothes were suitably fashionable. Mrs. Brown asked me what she could do to get back into Jerry's good graces. At the time, Jerry and I were not on speaking terms, either. Unable to give her a solution, she asked me if I thought it would help if she sent him a bag of his favorite snack, Indian nuts. Considering his alienation of affection, I did not think that would have any effect. The question is, "Why did Jerry Lewis abandon his Aunt Lil and turn his back on her forever?"

Between the 1950s and 1980s, Jerry Lewis came to Brown's Hotel in the Catskills a handful of times. Insiders knew that after Charlie Brown died, Jerry charged his Aunt Lil the hefty sum of $50,000 for a one-night show on the stage of the Jerry Lewis Theatre Club. Having Jerry Lewis appear at Brown's that night did little to draw in guests, but Mrs. Brown was starstruck, and Jerry, stuck on Jerry Lewis, insisted on bringing his musicians and staff with him, which imposed an additional financial burden on the struggling hotel. After the performance, Jerry received his more-than-substantial fee, especially for a Catskill Mountain resort, even on the busiest holiday weekend. However, the check Mrs. Brown gave Jerry bounced. Jerry ran with the story, insisting Lillian Brown purposely gave him a bad check, and that was why he never spoke to her. I know that because Jerry Lewis told me that himself.

The REAL Jerry Lewis Story

In 1995, Mrs. Brown called me to ask if I would take her on a date. Intrigued, I said, "Sure. Where would you like to go?" Mrs. Brown wanted to go to Manhattan to see Jerry Lewis on Broadway in *Damn Yankees* and offered to buy our tickets.

Mrs. Brown added, "I would just like to see Jerry backstage, either before or after the show. I just want some acknowledgment from him." Even though Jerry and I had not been in touch for quite some time, I faxed him at the theater and did not expect a reply.

It was my birthday when the phone rang. My wife answered it and handed it to me with a peculiar smile. She whispered, "It's your friend, Jerry Lewis." I was more than mildly surprised since we had not spoken for ten years.

"Hello Jerry, how are you?"

He had received my fax, and his response was classic Jerry Lewis, "Rick, mind your fucking business when it comes to me and Lillian Brown. It's nothing but trouble." After assuring him that I was not involved in any controversy, I repeated what I had written in my fax, stating that Lillian Brown would like to see the show and say hello to him. Jerry cautioned me, "Just don't get involved, Rick." Although he was quiet, he didn't hang up, and I could tell he was waiting for my response.

I broke the silence, interjecting, "Jerry, I heard about the check, but I have to tell you, Mrs. Brown was not aware that the money was not in the account."

© 2024 Rick Saphire

Jerry erupted, "That's bullshit. Others who performed there that summer got paid, but she stiffed me because it's family, and when it's family, you can get away with it."

Realizing I was getting nowhere, I closed with, "Okay, Jerry. Stay well, and if you change your mind, you have my number." And so ended our contentious conversation.

Years later, theatrical agent Arnold Graham confirmed that several top-name acts performed during the final season at Brown's Hotel, and yes, the other acts received their pay because they booked through Arnold Graham's office at the Charles Rapp Agency, and their wages were guaranteed. Jerry Lewis had a different deal. To save the commission fee, Jerry booked directly into the hotel, never considering that all of the hotels in the region were beginning a fast fade-out.

The evening after Jerry's telephone tirade, I called Lillian Brown at The Concord to say I had spoken to Jerry. When she asked what he had said, I hesitated, "Mrs. Brown, I would rather not tell you because I don't want to hurt your feelings."

In classic Lillian Brown fashion, she replied, "Ricky, you've known me most of your life. You must know by now that you cannot hurt my feelings." After I relayed Jerry's story to her, she explained, "Jerry eventually got most of the money that was owed to him for his show, but that is not why he isn't talking to me anymore. He knows the hotel went bankrupt, but that is not why he snubbed me." Mrs. Brown disclosed information about why Jerry

Lewis, who was then in his 60s, requested to use her Florida address for a legal matter. Understanding full well what Jerry was trying to do, Mrs. Brown continued, "I thought it over briefly and said, 'No, Jerry, I'm not looking for trouble, and neither should you. I don't think you should enter such an important agreement with a lie.' He slammed the phone in my ear, and I never heard from him again."

Brown's Hotel profited in several ways from its association with Jerry Lewis throughout the years. Jerry and his parents also benefited from the association with Charles and Lillian Brown. There might not have been the Jerry Lewis the world knows and appreciates today if it were not for the Browns and Lillian's daughter, Lonnie, who inspired Jerome Levitch and helped create Jerry Lewis' record mime act. But, all that history was reduced to one last comment on the subject when Lillian Brown said, "Ricky, if you talk to Jerry Lewis again, you can tell him to kiss my ass."

The REAL Jerry Lewis Story

I've Heard That Song Before

Jerry Lewis recorded the following lyrics set to music in April of 1951. The recording was meant for only one person to hear as Jerry dedicated this song "To Patti on Our Sixth Anniversary":

They call me a comic, they call me a clown,
But even a clown can feel.
When I take off the grease paint and put the mask down,
I return to a world that's real.
And that's where an angel waits when day is through.
If you've never seen an angel, I'll describe one to you.

One night, two precious stars came falling from the sky,
And they became the eyes of Patti.
A sunbeam came along to shine for just a while
Then turned into a smile for Patti.
And to complete this work of art
Out of love and faith, they made her heart.
And now the job is done.
I thank the Lord above for giving me my lovely Patti.

Later that same year, Dean Martin and Jerry Lewis were on location at the military base at Fort Benning (renamed Fort Moore in 2023) in Georgia to film parts of their movie *Jumping Jacks*. While staying at the Ralston Hotel in Columbus, Georgia, Jerry wrote the following letter to Patti. Sounding distraught, Jerry Lewis penned the emotionally charged letter postmarked December 12, 1951:

Tuesday

Sweetheart:

I just got in from work, 8 a.m. to 6 p.m., 10 hours out in the coldest climate I've ever known. My hands are still so raw I can hardly write, but if I don't, I'll flip. I just don't want you to think I'm lonely and miserable just because of this place. That's not so. It's just that I can't go away from you anymore. I don't care if we argue morning to night, but from here in, no matter where it is, you'll be with me. I just don't seem to get along right being away from you.

Holy mackerel, I'm torching more now than in New Haven. Oh well, I guess you're my lovely lady for the next 96 years. Oh, by the way, I've picked up your option for 50 more years, and when we celebrate our 57th, I'll pick up the other 46 years. That's if you want me to.

When I sit down to write you, I get so goddam mad 'cause I can't put on paper what I feel in my heart. (How do you like my penmanship?) Wow, it's cold!!

All I know is when I look at your picture, I get all nervous and all choked up inside. Honest, Patsy, I'm so in love with you. I don't know what to do. Then, when I just sit and think, I get all kinds of crazy thoughts, like maybe you don't love me, and that you don't want to hurt me. Sometimes, I could cry from the pain I get. I guess I'm silly, but I can't help it.

I need you so badly. If you stopped loving me, I know my heart would stop. Please love me always, and I'll do all I can to make you happy.

Kiss my boys for me. I'm getting misty. I love you, Mommy. You're my angel. I better stop before I blow up. I'm your fella "Till the day I die."

"Always"
Jer-

Author's note: When Jerry recorded this romantic anniversary song for his wife Patti, he was having an affair with his girlfriend model, Lynn Dixon, who was pregnant with his baby. Both of them were cheating on their respective spouses.

Several months after Patti Lewis received her husband's desperate, heartfelt letter, Lynn Dixon gave birth to Jerry's daughter, Suzan.

The REAL Jerry Lewis Story

Relatively Speaking

Suzan "Lewis" Minoret
Photo by Rick Saphire

Throughout my 60-year association with Jerry Lewis, many people approached me, claiming to be one of his relatives, a former classmate, or a business acquaintance. However, in almost all of these cases, it just wasn't possible. For instance, a man once told me that his father had gone to school with Jerry Lewis and was Jerry's best friend. But, as it turned out, the man's father was many years older than Jerry and attended a different school. Despite this, I politely smiled and left him to enjoy his father's legend.

Like many other people in Jerry Lewis' life, our relationship had its ups and downs. Despite any difficulties that arose between us, I felt a sense of allegiance towards him and often ran interference. On an afternoon in 2007, my phone rang. A child-like voice asked to speak with someone who could put her in touch with Jerry Lewis. She identified herself as Suzan Minoret, Jerry Lewis' daughter. My skeptical inner voice said, "Here we go again," but my outward voice was far more polite. I explained to her that Mr. Lewis had six sons (one adopted) and one adopted daughter, as far as I knew. Then, I asked her if she claimed to be any of the previously mentioned children. She laughed and said,

"No." Suzan explained that in the late 1940s, her mother was introduced to Jerry Lewis by comedian Milton Berle at New York City's Copacabana Night Club, where the team of Dean Martin & Jerry Lewis was appearing in person. This 55-year-old woman cited specific dates, locations, and names that the most ardent Jerry Lewis fan would not know. It bought her another 10 minutes. Intrigued, I listened to her story.

During our conversation, Suzan told me about her mother, a former professional model known as Lynn Dixon. Lynn married Hy Uchitel, whose family owned several upscale restaurants, and she became instrumental in promoting the French cuisine at the Voisin on *Joe Franklin's Memory Lane* TV show. I had known Joe Franklin for decades, and he was a very influential New York television and radio talk show host. A quick call to Joe could be all the verification I needed.

Growing up, Suzan said she attended exclusive schools, lived in luxurious quarters, and met many influential people. After telling her I needed time to digest her information, I asked for her phone number and address. To my surprise, she revealed she was currently living in her car. I took her cellphone number and told her I would call her back.

Beginning in the early 1960s, Joe Franklin often included me on his daily TV show as "a comedy magician and Jerry Lewis' protégé." Joe, a highly respected member of the broadcast community, became one of my best friends in the entertainment business. I called Joe the following morning. After exchanging some pleasantries, I offhandedly asked, "Joe, do you know anything about a young lady named Suzan Minoret?"

Without skipping a beat, Joe Franklin replied, "Oh yes, that's Jerry Lewis' daughter." He mentioned that he knew her mother, whom he described as an attractive and charming woman. Joe then asked if I had ever met Suzan. When I replied that I had only spoken to her once on the phone, he said with a smile in his voice, "When you see her in person, you won't have any doubts about who her father is."

My next phone call was to my good friend and client, Gary Lewis. Gary, Jerry Lewis' eldest son, is also the world-famous rock'n' roll legend and lead singer of Gary Lewis & the Playboys. When I informed Gary that a woman had contacted me claiming to be his sister, he casually responded, "Oh, another one?" I went on to report that Suzan said she met him at one of his concerts, and Gary stopped in his tracks. "Yes, I do remember a woman named Suzan introducing herself to me as my sister, and I was shocked. She looked exactly like my dad in drag." Gary went on to say that he had only spoken with her briefly because he had to take the stage. He then said three critical words, "I believed her."

Over the next few weeks, Suzan used the library's computers, scanners, and copy machines to send me photos and memorabilia. I spent several hours on the phone listening to her fascinating stories about her affluent upbringing as a child and teenager. Suzan also sent me biographical materials about her background and family via email. In conversation, Suzan revealed that, for professional reasons, her mother had changed her original name from Esther Linsky to Lynn Dixon. Suzan described her mother as looking like the actress Lana Turner, whereas she described herself as looking like Lana's sister, "Stomach" Turner.

In the late 1940s, life was not easy for Suzan's mother. Lynn Dixon married Milton Kleinman, a young man studying to become a lawyer with a promising future. However, Milton was drafted into the military, and when his tour of duty ended, he reenlisted, to Lynn's dismay. With her husband rarely home to help raise their son, Lynn moved back home with her mother. Lonely and longing for companionship, the glamorous blonde began to frequent local nightspots. At the Copacabana, New York City's famous nightclub, Lynn met and became friends with comedian Milton Berle. In May 1949, Berle introduced Lynn Dixon Kleinman to the duo of Martin & Lewis. Lynn was attracted to the young monkey-like comic, not the suave Italian singer. And so began a more than two-year-long romance between Jerry Lewis and Lynn Dixon.

Before Jerry became a celebrity, he was young, gawky, skinny, and undesirable. After Jerry became a celebrity, he was young, gawky, skinny, and quite desirable. With fame came temptation, and reports of Jerry's infidelity made the news. Jerry often cheated on his wife Patti Palmer, the mother of his children. Their oldest son, Gary, recalled how he would go on vacations with only his mother. As an adult, he realized that these trips coincided with his parents' separations. In 1948, Hollywood columnist Jimmy Fidler reported, "Mary

Hatcher, the Paramount starlet, will marry nightclub star Jerry Lewis when his divorce is final." Jerry Lewis sustained his flings by promising to marry his girlfriends as soon as his divorce was finalized. There is no telling exactly when Jerry's relationship with singer and actress Mary Hatcher began or ended, but she did appear on Martin & Lewis' radio program in 1949. Several other articles in 1948 suggest that Patti and Jerry were breaking up, but their divorce did not occur until 1983, over 30 years later.

In 1949, the duo of Dean Martin & Jerry Lewis were introduced to movie-goers in a motion picture based on the radio show *My Friend Irma*, starring Marie Wilson. The following year, 1950, Martin & Lewis were featured in the movie sequel, *My Friend Irma Goes West*. Jerry's girlfriend, Lynn Dixon, was present on the Paramount set in Hollywood, California, which was just a few miles from where Patti was home with Jerry's sons.

In 1951, Dean Martin & Jerry Lewis were back at the Copacabana in New York City for the month of May. The Copa had rooms upstairs where the entertainers could change clothes and relax between shows. When Jerry performed there, he would often turn to the band and say, "Don't play so loud. There are gangsters sleeping upstairs." The audience found it amusing, but the band knew it was true. The rooms upstairs also provided a convenient location for Jerry and Lynn to carry on their affair. Within show business circles, Jerry and Lynn's relationship was common knowledge. While her husband Milton was away on maneuvers in the military, Lynn and Jerry were on undercover maneuvers in Manhattan.

Suzan's mother told her that she and Jerry were in love. During one night of intimacy in the bedroom above the Copa, their passion got out of control. As soon as Jerry realized he might have just placed an order with the stork, he became quite agitated. Jerry might have blamed himself for poor timing, or he might have felt seduced. After all, Lynn's part-time marriage was falling apart, and she had little to lose and much to gain. Regardless of the situation, the young comedian at 25 and the glamorous model in her 30s were going to be parents of a "lovechild." Lynn Dixon Kleinman effectively robbed the cradle and filled it, all at the same time.

When Lynn's husband came home on leave from the service, she and Milton Kleinman acted like a married couple. However, Lynn's calculations proved she was carrying Jerry's baby, not her husband's. Although Jerry and Lynn talked about leaving their respective spouses and marrying each other before the birth of their child, that never came to fruition. By the time their daughter was born, Jerry and Lynn's affair had ended. On February 3, 1952, while her husband was away on active duty, Esther "Lynn Dixon" Kleinman gave birth to Jerry Lewis' daughter.

While Lynn was in the maternity ward at Women's Hospital in New York City, she received a surprise visit from Milton. However, it was not her husband Milton Kleinman who visited her, but her friend Milton Berle, who had first introduced her to Jerry Lewis. During his visit with Lynn, they discussed possible names for her newborn baby. To cheer up the new mother, Berle sang, "If you knew Susie, like I know Susie..." Although it is unclear what else they talked about, Uncle Miltie's song inspired Lynn to name her daughter Suzan.

Esther "Lynn Dixon" Kleinman faced a difficult decision before leaving the hospital. She needed to choose who would be listed as the father on her daughter's birth certificate. If she put Jerry Lewis' name, it could lead to many complications. The truth had the potential to destroy Jerry's marriage to Patti and her marriage to Milton. Theatrical contracts often had a morals clause, and an accusation of infidelity and a paternity suit could cast a shadow over Jerry Lewis' image and career. Back in 1952, DNA paternity testing was not available. With one swipe of the pen, Lynn committed paternity fraud, naming Milton Kleinman as the father of her newborn. This ensured Suzan would have Milton Kleinman's military benefits, support, and surname.

Sometime after Suzan was born, Lynn and Milton divorced. The courts granted Lynn custody of their son and her daughter. At this point, Milton Kleinman had no reason to think he was not Suzan's biological father.

Raising two children as a single parent was financially and personally challenging for Lynn, who accepted monetary help from both Milton Kleinman and Jerry Lewis. Periodically, Lynn sent Jerry pictures of their little daughter, and periodically, he sent her a check.

In 1952, when Suzan was only three months old, a published report surfaced, "Mr. and Mrs. Jerry Lewis expect to adopt a baby girl in two weeks." Several weeks later, follow-up reports stated that the Lewises' adoption plans were shelved. Then, the Associated Press reported that Patti and Jerry Lewis had adopted a baby girl, Sally May, in December 1953. "She's wonderful," said Lewis. However, this proved to be yet another failed adoption attempt. These on-again-off-again adoption reports continued for nearly two years. Research indicates that Jerry and Patti were negotiating with Lynn to adopt Jerry's own daughter, and Patti wanted to name the little girl after her baby sister, Anna May, who had passed away.

When Suzan was two years old, her mother married Hy Uchitel, a wealthy, well-connected businessman, and Lynn felt she entered New York society, achieving financial security for the first time. Hy, who reportedly could not have children, welcomed Lynn and her children into his family.

After Lynn's marriage to Hy, Jerry maintained a distance from his daughter. Lynn could now afford a nanny to assist with raising her children. As Hy's wife, Lynn achieved popularity and established herself as a promoter for the Uchitels' highly successful, high-profile enterprises. According to Suzan, Hy was so fond of her that he offered to adopt her. However, her "father," Milton Kleinman, would not give his consent. To circumvent Milton's refusal, Lynn called her daughter Suzan Uchitel. Occasionally, Lynn would arrange for Jerry to see his daughter even though Suzan did not know why. How frustrating it must have been for Jerry Lewis to be the biological father of a little girl he could not call his own.

Numerous news articles and reports indicated that Hy and his brother had ties to the underworld. Hy and Morris, also known as Maurice, were Holocaust survivors. Losing their family to Nazis made them close, and Morris did not want anything to interfere with Hy's happiness. Therefore, he made it clear to Jerry, in no uncertain terms, "Stay away from the little girl and her mother." Pursuing a relationship with either of them could be detrimental to Jerry's career as well as to his health- and to his knees. Due to the Uchitel brothers' connections, Jerry Lewis considered this a serious threat, which haunted him throughout his life. Although Jerry never publicly admitted Suzan was his daughter, he also never denied it.

While Suzan shared many stories about her friends, childhood, schooling, and relationships with her parents with me, François shared information about their life as a couple. Suzan met François Minoret in 1968, just after her 16th birthday. It was not long before their relationship got serious, and François asked Suzan's father, who he mistakenly thought was Hy, for her hand in marriage, and Hy advised him to talk to Lynn. Suzan's mother did not approve of her daughter marrying a Frenchman who worked on a cruise ship. To discourage the relationship, Suzan was sent to school in Switzerland.

Over the next several months, the couple kept the flames of their romance burning by exchanging letters through the mail. François then left his job at sea and moved to Paris where he found work and living quarters. One day, François unexpectedly received a big box in the mail from Suzan. To his shock, when he opened it, he found it filled with Suzan's belongings. He called her in the United States right away, and she explained, "My parents don't want us to get married, so I sent you all my things." Suzan divulged that she had worked as a roller-skating waitress and saved her pay. She also confessed that she received additional money from Hy under the pretext of needing it for school, which was a lie. Outlining her plans to run away to France, François warned her not to come. "No, it's not possible. Even if you have a flight ticket, don't come to Paris because you are only 17. You cannot come here. If you come here, Hy Uchitel will send the police, and I'll have problems. It's impossible. We cannot do that. You have to talk to your dad and your mom."

Even though François wanted to marry Suzan, he could not do so without her parents' consent. Once Lynn and Hy realized the depth of Suzan's love for François, they approved of their marriage. Lynn and Hy went so far as to arrange for the couple's wedding to take place in Palm Beach, Florida. At the time, François believed Hy Uchitel was Suzan's father, and he was unaware of Milton Kleinman, who believed he was Suzan's father. Curiously, when François met Suzan's brother, he noticed they did not look at all alike.

Following their wedding in 1970, Suzan and her husband moved to France and settled in Paris. They were happy and soon expecting their first son, Oliver. Meanwhile, Lynn and Hy got divorced, and they both remarried.

In 1976, Lynn called Suzan in France to say she had breast cancer and asked Suzan to come to Los Angeles to see her. During this visit, Lynn revealed the secret she had hidden from her daughter for 26 years, "Your father is not Milton Kleinman." The news confused and shocked Suzan. Then, when Lynn told her, "Your father is Jerry Lewis," Suzan was speechless.

Learning that her mother was unfaithful to her father was quite a shock, but learning that her biological father was a world-renowned superstar was traumatic. According to François, Suzan began acting troubled after Lynn revealed the truth about Suzan's real father. In response to this, her family encouraged Suzan to have another child, and she named her second son Jerry after her famous dad. Suzan resolved to meet the man who gave her life, Jerry Lewis.

Although Suzan's French family was thrilled with this revelation, everyone agreed to keep it a secret from the children. Nevertheless, Suzan's young son overheard the truth about his grandfather being France's beloved funnyman, and he boasted to his friends, who did not believe him. Suzan dreamed of the day her famous father would call her on the telephone, although there was no indication he even had her phone number.

Suzan desperately wanted to meet and bond with Jerry. In her mind, she was not meeting the international comedian idolized in France but Jerry Lewis, her father. In 1980, Jerry, his entourage, and his mistress du jour were in Paris. When François received information from one of his friends that Jerry was staying at the Paris Hilton Hotel, he told Suzan, who decided to go there with her infant son, Jerry. When Suzan told the concierge she was a member of Jerry Lewis' family, the woman told her that Mr. Lewis was out but would be back soon. Suzan waited eagerly for her father's return to introduce herself and her child to him. Finally, she saw Jerry enter the lobby. She approached him and introduced herself: "Hi, I'm your daughter, Suzan." Jerry was momentarily speechless as she told him her mother was Lynn Dixon. Realizing Suzan was his daughter, Jerry invited her to come to his suite to talk. Once up there, they spent a few hours getting to know each other.

Suzan found it amusing that Jerry spent most of their time together lying on the floor on his back, talking about himself. He explained to her that this was his way of relieving his chronic back pain. Excusing himself frequently to meet with his girlfriend, members of the media, and his manager Joe Stabile, Suzan could see them in the suite's living room each time Jerry opened the bedroom door. During this father-and-daughter bonding, Jerry surprised Suzan by asking her to phone her mother, and he called Lynn overseas. Although Suzan only heard his half of the conversation, it seemed as if her parents had a pleasant reunion. Throughout Jerry's career, he publicly lamented about wanting to have a daughter. This was Suzan's first opportunity to share her life with her father, and Jerry's first opportunity to share his life with Suzan, the daughter he always wanted.

At the end of their meeting, Jerry asked Suzan to stay in touch and promised to meet her again before leaving France. He also reassured her that he would be available if she ever needed his help. This comforting statement marked the end of their visit. It had been a perfect day.

Her French family was overjoyed at the news that their Suzan was the daughter of France's favorite funnyman and encouraged her to contact him again. When she phoned Jerry the next day, his manager, Joe Stabile, took the call, and Suzan asked to speak to her father. Joe told her, "You won't be able to reach him anymore." Feeling she and her father had bonded, she faulted Joe Stabile for this separation and headed to the Hilton. In keeping with protocol, she phoned Jerry's suite from the lobby. Again, Jerry's manager answered. Joe told her to stay where she was; he would be right down to meet her. To Suzan's shock and dismay, Joe Stabile, looking tense, firmly reiterated that Jerry no longer wanted to see her. The excuse was, "You look so much like Jerry that anyone who saw you two together would know who you are. We have to protect his reputation." Suzan left the hotel devastated and dejected. She finally had the father she always wanted, but only for a day.

What a paradox! Jerry was concerned somebody might look at Suzan and guess she was his illegitimate child. Yet, it didn't matter to Jerry that anyone seeing him with his lover might guess he was committing adultery. Jerry

Lewis had a wife and six children at home and had openly brought his paramour to France. Jerry cared little about people's thoughts regarding his activities, except in Suzan's case. Suzan's resemblance to him may not have been the real problem. The real issue was that Jerry's reunion with Suzan and Lynn churned up too many memories and fears of the warnings to "stay away from the little girl and her mother." This threat had no expiration date.

Additionally, Jerry Lewis, perceived as the champion of children, repeatedly proclaimed on various broadcasts how he wanted a daughter. He went so far as to ask the public to "will" him a baby girl. What would the public think of him if they knew the truth? Even after their meeting, Jerry Lewis could not acknowledge Suzan as his daughter without admitting this deception as his 26-year-old daughter had just visited him at the Hilton. An anonymous phone call to Jerry's hotel issuing a death threat against him further heightened his concerns. It may never be known whether the danger, which caused Jerry to hire a personal bodyguard, was connected with Suzan's visit. Under the circumstances, Jerry and his inner circle were not about to take any chances.

Jerry Lewis was afraid of people and trusted almost no one. Without warning, he could strike out at someone who never harmed him. He always traveled surrounded by a group of perceived allies. At one time, Jerry Lewis hired a detective whose job, among other duties, included checking the backgrounds of Jerry's female escorts. Retired police officer John Loiacono, affectionately known as John the Cop, remarked to me about Jerry Lewis, "When you fuck so many people, you get paranoid." So, I believe the Uchitel threat, among others, laid heavily on Jerry's mind.

The Minorets lived in France for years before François left his job in Paris. Suzan advocated for them to move to the States and pressured Hy into giving her husband a job in Florida. Offered a managerial position at one of Hy's restaurants, François, Suzan, and their two sons left the City of Light and took up residency in Miami, Florida, where they lived for a year. When Hy's restaurant closed due to a fire, François lost his job and was left stranded with no income and no way to support his family. After a contentious confrontation with Hy, Suzan's former stepfather relented and paid François his back wages. François moved his family back to France.

In 1982, two years after Suzan spent that one special afternoon with her real father, the Minorets vacationed in Florida. As fate would have it, Jerry Lewis was appearing nearby at Walden Books at the Omni Shopping Center in Miami, where he spent 30 minutes signing copies of *Jerry Lewis in Person*, written by Jerry Lewis with Herb Gluck. In this autobiography, it is interesting to note that Jerry Lewis effectively eradicated my uncle, Ernest D. Glucksman, from his book and his life, although Uncle Ernie had been Jerry's manager, executive producer, friend, and mentor for 14 years, guiding Jerry Lewis to fame and fortune.

Here in Miami, Suzan had an opportunity to see her father again. She bought one of Jerry's books and mustered up enough courage to have it autographed and took a picture with him. If this encounter had happened a few years earlier, she would not have known she was face to face with her father. Either Jerry did not recognize Suzan as his daughter or refused to acknowledge her. When Suzan and her family returned to France, something within her snapped. She purchased a plane ticket to the United States, dropped her son off at school, boarded a flight back to New York, and left her husband and their two children behind.

Having heard her gripping stories, I looked forward to meeting Suzan in person. Coincidentally, I had an extended booking for Gary Lewis & the Playboys in Florida, so this was the perfect opportunity to meet her. When I saw Suzan, Joe Franklin's comments echoed in my head. She was a dead-ringer for her father, Jerry Lewis. Gary Lewis' description also resonated: She looked like Jerry in drag.

Aside from Suzan's striking resemblance to Jerry, what I noticed the first time I saw her was that she looked haggard, and her wiry, salt-and-pepper hair was unusually long. She had been living in her car without air-conditioning in the Florida heat. During lunch, she rallied, and we talked. According to Suzan, on and off after her divorce, she and her male companion stayed with friends or relatives, survived on the streets, rented rooms at boarding houses, and lived in air-conditioned storage units. It was a heartfelt, hard-luck story. She said neither she nor her friend could hold a job due to their physical disabilities.

Because this seemingly witty, bright woman had such an unorthodox lifestyle, I assumed she was simply down on her luck. I told her I was willing to explore her potential. Still, I could not go to Jerry Lewis and say, "Jerry, I'm sure you remember Suzan, your long-lost, homeless daughter who is currently out of work, out of luck, out of money, and living on the streets of Florida. That would not play well in Las Vegas." I initially thought I could find her work on the lecture circuit telling her "riches to rags to riches" story. Of course, to make her story ring true, she would need to pull herself together and put sleeping in her car behind her. This was my primary goal, with the residual effect that Suzan would get the recognition she wanted from Jerry Lewis.

During the two-week booking for Gary Lewis & the Playboys, Gary, his wife Donna, and I often saw Suzan at our hotel. At first, Gary was apprehensive about her intentions. However, Suzan, who was very personable, asked no favors from Gary. After a time, she ingratiated herself with all of us. To my surprise, Gary invited her to his concert, and to nobody's surprise, she accepted. For Suzan, this was her chance to be part of the Lewis clan.

While riding in the band bus to the venue, Gary announced to the Playboys that he had a special guest coming to the concert, ending with, "It's my sister, Suzan."

One of the musicians countered, "I didn't know you had a sister."

Gary responded, "Yes, we've known about her for years, and you'll get to meet her tonight." As I turned to look at Gary, I had never seen him so pleased with himself. Making that statement gave Gary great satisfaction.

After the concert and standing ovations, Gary, Donna, the band, the show bookers, Arnold Graham representing the prestigious Rapp Talent Agency, Suzan, and I met in the now-empty theatre for a casual get-together. Once Gary introduced Suzan to the group, she became the center of attention. Calling Suzan Gary's sister confused those who thought they knew the Lewis family history. Most of them only knew about the baby girl Jerry Lewis at age 66 and his second wife adopted in 1992. Gary then explained that Suzan, age 56, was his half-sister.

Suzan had initially contacted me with the sole goal of getting in touch with her biological father. All she wanted was for Jerry Lewis to acknowledge her as his daughter. Having an allegiance to Gary, as my friend and client, I would only assist Suzan if Gary was on board, and he was. Because of our long, shared family history, I felt obliged to let Jerry know what was happening.

Since I didn't know when I would see Suzan again after I left Florida, I had her pose for a series of headshots to be used for potential publicity. In the pictures, she looked tired and careworn. Despite her appearance, I suggested she record a short video for Jerry. Her video script read, "Hi, Jerry. This is Suzan. I want to wish you a very happy birthday, and I want to tell you that I cherish the moments we had together back in Paris in 1980. I wish that our relationship could have continued back then, but I guess it just wasn't meant to be at that time. But, I hope that now it can be different. Love, your daughter, Suzan." Jerry received the video but did not respond.

At the end of the concert tour, Gary, Donna, Suzan, and I had one final luncheon together before going our separate ways. Never one to miss a chance to do something dramatic, I invited two special guests to join us. Bruce Turiansky, the grandson of Charles and Lillian Brown and one-time manager of the renowned Brown's Hotel, and his mother, Lonnie, who was living in Florida. I consider Lonnie Brown Rowley, daughter of Lillian Brown, one of the most influential people in Jerry's career, and I affectionately dubbed her "the girl who invented Jerry Lewis." As a teenager, she lived at her parents' hotel in Lakewood, New Jersey, where Jerry's parents were performing. When Jerry popped into Lonnie's room with a message for her, he saw her lip-syncing to recordings and mimicked her, which was the beginning of Jerry's record mime act. Sitting at the table, Lonnie looked at Suzan and whispered to me, "She's Jerry's clone."

Before returning home to New Jersey, I reiterated that Jerry would not embrace Suzan as his daughter in her present situation. I explained that she needed to go to work and get her life together so her father could be proud of her. She agreed. In conversation, I suggested she might become a spokesperson for people who are homeless and disabled by first molding herself into a successful role model. At this point, Suzan thought it was a good idea.

Once home from Florida, Suzan and I kept in touch via cell phone, laying the groundwork for what I envisioned would be a speaking tour. Over the next few weeks, she sent me volumes of biographical materials. I was impressed with her charmed life growing up. Suzan attended the finest private French school in Manhattan, met countless luminaries, dined in the most elegant restaurants, and hobnobbed with the city's social elites.

By watching Jerry Lewis on TV, Lynn made him part of her daughter's world, and Suzan enjoyed seeing his performances. In 1963, Jerry Lewis signed a five-year contract with ABC to do a two-hour, live weekly TV show. This was the most lucrative contract in television history to date. The series was canceled after the first broadcast and only ran for 14 weeks. During the high-profile debut of Jerry's live Saturday night show, the cameras panned to where Patti, pregnant with their sixth child, sat with their young boys, who waved on cue. Jerry Lewis expressed his hope of getting a daughter to call his own. As a talisman, the studio cameras were bedecked in pink ribbons, symbolizing femininity. Quipping that his five sons in the balcony were his "Jewish Boys Town" (even though they were all raised Catholic), he led viewers to chant along to his "Think Pink" song. Between each stanza of the lyrics, which mentioned Jerry's sons and how he wanted his wife to give him a daughter, the chant "think pink" was repeated over and over again, as if Hera, the queen of the ancient Greek goddess of childbirth, would hear him and answer his plea.

While Jerry prodded an unresponsive audience to sing "Think Pink," Patti looked uncomfortable, and their sons looked bored. Meanwhile, the sponsors were hanging themselves in a closet. As Jerry's family watched from the balcony, his 11-year-old biological daughter, Suzan, remembers sitting at home with her mother, viewing this same TV broadcast. Imagine the irony. Although it is the male chromosome that determines the sex of a child, Jerry put the onus on Patti. There is evidence that Patti, who was hoping to give Jerry their first daughter, knew of Suzan's existence. Jerry knew he had a daughter. Sitting at home, Lynn knew she was the mother of Jerry Lewis' daughter, and at the time, Suzan, Jerry Lewis' biological daughter, had no clue the man with whom she was chanting, "Think Pink," was her father.

© 2024 Rick Saphire

The Suzan Lewis Story

The more I knew about Jerry's daughter, Suzan, the more impressed I was with her abilities rather than her disabilities, which she claimed resulted from an accident. From my vantage point, I saw no disabilities precluding her from earning a living or living a more traditional lifestyle. Her only obvious disability was her trouble walking and the occasional use of a cane.

Her internet access was limited because of her living conditions, so she used the public library's computers for her email communications. She wanted to improve herself, and I offered her my assistance. I outlined a salable lecture for her, which included discussing her lifestyle and her impressive background, peppered with humor, which would be expected of Jerry Lewis' daughter. At one point, I told her I would do all I could to help her because I liked her and would hate to see her become "a 60-year-old Jewish bag lady."

On a Sunday at 5:30 a.m., my business phone rang. It was Suzan calling, terrified. While sleeping in her car in a bank parking lot, where she thought she would be safe, she was confronted by a Florida police officer who was about to arrest her and her companion on vagrancy charges. She pleaded with me to talk to him. He explained they were breaking the law and would be arrested or put in a shelter if they didn't find a place to live. When I explained to the officer that I was arranging for her to move up North, he agreed to let them off with a warning, but they were not to sleep on the bank's lot again.

I was able to find housing in Philadelphia for Suzan and her companion. When my family and friends heard about Suzan's plight and desire to make a new start, they donated clothing, furniture, services, and money. Suzan sold her old car in Florida and purchased train tickets, one for herself and one for her friend. When she called to say their train had arrived in Philadelphia, Suzan, who had grown up surrounded by famous people, told me she had made a new friend on the train, President Bill Clinton's former Secretary of State. I thought she was kidding, but when I got out of the car to help her with her luggage, Suzan introduced me to Madeline Albright.

As I drove toward my brother-in-law's home, where Suzan and her companion would be staying, I felt relieved that she would no longer be homeless. Despite being disabled himself, Ned Crane willingly welcomed Suzan and her friend into his house. The only obligation the newcomers had was to contribute a small preset fee toward the household each month. Suzan and François had kept in touch after she left her husband and their sons and returned to the United States. I later learned from François that even after their divorce, she would ask him for money, and he would send it to her.

Meanwhile, Suzan had assured me she wanted to earn an income beyond the benefits she was receiving. Because Suzan was fluent in French, she could have been a translator. Eager to explore an opportunity in this field, she agreed to go to an interview but decided, at the last minute, not to go. She could have been a hostess with her food service background, but she did not want to do that. Her sights were set on speaking engagements and being acknowledged as Jerry's kid. In the meantime, Suzan also wanted her biography written and asked if I would do it. I looked forward to working with her, aware that any degree of success would take time, development, and commitment, and there were no guarantees.

Throughout my career as a celebrity manager, I have always joked that I am a lazy manager because I only represent people who are already famous. Suzan became the exception. No one in the public knew who she was, and even when we told them, they did not believe her. Her story was fascinating, her likeness to her father was remarkable, and she was charming. When I agreed to represent her, I told her the same thing I told my other clients: My only guarantee is that I will do my best.

While Suzan rehearsed her scripts and delivery, I contacted venues where she might be invited to appear.

At this early stage of development, Suzan's 12-minute act consisted of a short comedy monologue. Then, as a tribute to her father, she lip-synced Mario Lanza's "Be My Love" in a comedic fashion reminiscent of her father's record act. She concluded her performance with a heartfelt plea for the audience to help people who are homeless and disabled. My association with Suzan was challenging. I had to work with her to develop an acceptable persona while putting together a comedy act for someone with zero experience. Additionally, my family and I were also providing shelter for her and her companion.

The primary obstacle I faced in getting her bookings was that people were unwilling to believe Jerry Lewis did have a biological daughter who had been homeless. Even though Suzan had made a few successful appearances, she still needed more media exposure and recognition. I called one of my trusted contacts, Shelby Loosch, a well-known gossip columnist at *Globe*

Magazine. Shelby's 90-minute phone interview with Suzan became an impressive two-page spread, bringing Suzan into national prominence on May 19, 2008. On the heels of the *Globe* article, I arranged for Suzan to make a few local appearances. However, the question remained, "What proof could I offer the public that Suzan was really Jerry Lewis' daughter?"

Jerry Lewis had a dilemma as he publicly lamented not having a daughter, yet he and Lynn Dixon did have one. How could Jerry acknowledge Suzan without admitting he knew about her all along? He could not feign ignorance about Suzan since too many knew the truth. A public acknowledgment would not bode well with the Muscular Dystrophy Association since they had developed Jerry Lewis' image as a public figure who was a devoted family man and champion of children. Looming in the back of Jerry's mind was also Maurice Uchitel's threat to "leave Suzan and her mother alone." Jerry took the only recourse he had: Neither admit nor deny Suzan was his child.

When *Inside Edition*, a syndicated entertainment news program, contacted me to do a story on Suzan, I knew it would make for interesting press, and it could promote her and her cause. Before having her on the program, I suggested *Inside Edition* contact Jerry Lewis about the plan. Had he objected, I would have pulled her appearance. When *Inside Edition* reached out to Jerry for comment and verification, Claudia Stabile, the widow of Joe Stabile, one of Jerry's former managers, said, "Mr. Lewis has no comment." Since Jerry was never shy about voicing his favorable or unfavorable opinions, I interpreted Jerry's silence as giving his approval.

This was a great opportunity, and I drove Suzan to the studio in Manhattan to record her spot. *Inside Edition* put together a well-edited segment with Suzan discussing her early life and her desires for the future, interspersed with video clips of her dad featuring an uncanny likeness between them. Suzan was charming and witty, and her spot was so well-received that she was asked to make another appearance with her brother, Gary Lewis.

Suzan and half brother Gary Lewis

To the public, Suzan's claim that Jerry Lewis was her father was simply that, Suzan's claim. If Gary appeared with Suzan, it would bolster her credibility. When I approached Gary, he did some soul-searching. By aligning himself with Suzan, he risked alienating himself from his father, but Gary agreed to go on the program. The producers, however, added the stipulation that a certified DNA test be performed between Suzan and Gary, and the results be announced live on the air. Even though this would give Suzan the credibility we needed, I stepped on the brakes. None of us doubted Suzan was Jerry Lewis' daughter, but research indicated there was still a chance the test could result in a false negative.

If only Jerry Lewis had embraced Suzan, even privately, she would not need *Inside Edition*. Gary Lewis opted to help Suzan, asserting, "Everybody deserves to know where they came from and who they are." Gary offered to take the DNA test because Suzan was needy, and this could potentially help her. Nevertheless, I was still worried about Gary's relationship with his family and Suzan's future. While discussing my trepidations with her, I came up with an idea. "Suzan, why don't you just call your father?"

In October 2008, Suzan called Jerry Lewis. His current wife answered the phone, and she and Suzan had a brief conversation resembling the staccato script from *Dragnet*. According to Suzan, when she asked to speak with her father, Mrs. Lewis played interference. After a brief but guarded exchange, Suzan asked, "Now, may I please speak to my father?"

Jerry's wife replied, "But Suzan, how do we know it's true?"

Suzan countered, "If you ever get to meet me, you'll know it's true." The conversation ended there, and she did not get to speak to her father.

After Suzan relayed their conversation, it persuaded me to approve the test. Confident science would prove, once and for all, that Suzan was Jerry Lewis' daughter, I

"Cousin" Bruce Morrow did a lot to promote Gary Lewis' music in the rockin' 1960s. In the 2000s, he helped Gary's half sister to establish herself in the public eye.

permitted *Inside Edition* to administer a DNA test and reveal the results in March 2009. Arrangements were made for Suzan, a camera crew, and me to visit the offices of Boston Paternity in Manhattan, where her DNA was collected. At the same time, in upstate New York, representatives from Boston Paternity and a separate *Inside Edition* camera crew visited the home of Gary and Donna Lewis to collect samples of his DNA. A few weeks later, the results of the highly publicized tests were revealed on national television. The findings were proof-positive. Suzan and Gary Lewis share DNA from the same father.

After this evidence was made public, there was an uptick in offers for Gary and Suzan to appear together. They went on Howard Stern's radio talk show, where he asked them both thoughtful and insightful questions. Often caustic in his interviews, Howard Stern was unusually kind to Suzan. Gary and Suzan did a radio talk show tour for 15 stations. One of my all-time favorites, the popular New York DJ Bruce Morrow, known to his fans as Cousin Brucie, conducted an excellent live interview with them in his Manhattan studio. Cousin Brucie was a considerable force in the music industry in the early '60s and was partly responsible for the rise in popularity of Gary Lewis & the Playboys. Because Bruce knew Gary at the beginning of Gary's career, his interview took on greater meaning. Bruce, who usually avoids discussing politics or anything controversial, asked intimate questions in a caring manner.

Still eager to connect with her father, Suzan wanted to attend one of Jerry's speaking engagements. On November 22, 2009, I took her to "An Evening with Jerry Lewis," hosted by Peter Bogdanovich for the Museum of the Moving Image in New York City. My assistant, Wendy Klarman Weiss, and my friend, Mark Haltzman, attended the show with us. We were joined by my friend and client, entertainer Sammy Petrillo, who was well-known in the '50s as "the other Jerry Lewis." I also invited the man who knew of Suzan's identity from the beginning, television and radio icon Joe Franklin. I got our tickets and would have been satisfied sitting anywhere in the theatre. However, when one of the ushers noticed Suzan using a cane, he asked us to follow him, and he escorted us to seats in the front row. This thoughtful gesture was nearly a disaster for the show. After Suzan, Sammy, and I were seated, someone on Jerry's team spotted her in the audience and informed Jerry where we were sitting.

After the show's start was delayed for about 20 minutes for unknown reasons, a woman from backstage approached us and told us we would have to move our seats. When I asked her, "Why?" the woman had no answer but insisted we move to the back of the theatre. Seated behind us, Wendy, my assistant, offered to exchange seats with Suzan so she would not be in the front row. "That's not enough," the woman declared. Sammy Petrillo became irate, took out his cell phone, and called his lawyer friend, who advised us to stay where we were. When we steadfastly refused to move to the back of the room, the woman excused herself. Suzan looked distraught. Another 15 minutes went by before she reappeared. Flanked by two sizable men, and a few back-up security guards, the woman addressed us, "Mr. Lewis demands that you move to the rear of the theatre, or you will have to leave." Then she added that the show would not go on if we did not comply.

Sammy addressed the woman. "My attorney said, 'The ticket we purchased for this show is a license that is in effect till the show is over.' We were ushered to these seats, and we are going to stay here." The woman and her posse left. The audience became agitated. They had no idea why the show was delayed, and in reality, neither did we; however, it was apparent that we were at the center of the issue.

When the woman returned for the third time, she had tears in her eyes. Sammy immediately reacted, "If you want us to leave, you'll have to call the police."

The woman surprised us by profusely apologizing, saying the show would go on, and we could remain where we were. I thanked her and said, "You must be facing some tough issues backstage." She smiled knowingly and left. A few minutes later, Peter Bogdanovich introduced Jerry Lewis and thus commenced a somewhat contentious interview. The program went on without a hitch as Suzan sat about 25 feet from her father.

Wendy recalled that Jerry Lewis never once looked in Suzan's direction, effectively ignoring a third of the audience. That was a good thing since Suzan had fallen asleep; I had to nudge her awake twice. Wendy also remembered seeing a thin, somber man in dark glasses with arms folded across his chest glaring at us for a long time. He was leaning against the wall, looking very self-important, reminiscent of *Mayberry*'s bumbling deputy, Barney Fife. The man, who was Jerry's friend at the time, was actor and comedian Richard Belzer. We wondered if Belzer was sent out to impersonate a security guard.

Jerry Lewis had a well-documented reputation for cutting a performance short. Sometimes, he was a no-show. He would intentionally argue with producers and the stage crew as if he were looking for an excuse not to perform. During our tour in Berlin, Germany, after his "rehearsal from Hell," Jerry, visibly shaken, confided in me that he suffered from stage fright. Then, he added, "It's been getting worse as I've been getting older." Knowing Suzan was in the audience must have exacerbated his anxieties since he did not know if she was ill-intentioned or not. Years ago, Jerry had been warned, even threatened, to stay away from her, yet there she was right in front of him.

Sitting on my other side was Sammy Petrillo, the man Jerry blackballed decades earlier by pressuring agents not to book "the Jerry Lewis lookalike." Although Sammy, who was only present to enjoy the show, had long since forgiven Jerry, the memories of what he tried to do to Sammy likely still rankled in Jerry's mind. Whatever happened backstage to convince Jerry he had to go on with the show remains a mystery. I assumed that he was sternly held to his contract.

Before going to the show, Suzan and I agreed we would only discuss her true identity once the show was over. As I left the theatre with my small group, we were stopped in the lobby by curious people asking us why the show was delayed. Rochelle Slovin, who had apologized earlier, reappeared and apologized again and hugged Suzan. In the interim, she must have learned who Suzan was. Joe Franklin wove his way through the crowd to say goodnight to us. As he left the theatre, Joe waved goodbye and commented, "I guess Jerry knew his daughter was in the audience."

Just as we thought the evening was over, we went outside, and Suzan came face-to-face with Peter Bogdanovich. He had a solemn expression as he looked intently at Suzan. Offering her hand to Bogdanovich,

The REAL Jerry Lewis Story

Suzan introduced herself. "Hi," she said. "My name is Suzan. I'm Jerry Lewis' daughter."

Peter Bogdanovich peered into her face, scrutinizing it, but remained expressionless. Suddenly, he understood. "Oh?" he remarked. "That's what it was all about."

Peter Bogdanovich meets Suzan Lewis Minoret

It became evident to me that Jerry Lewis would never have anything to do with Suzan. Although she got more press, and I continued to focus on scripting her for what she could say as a spokesperson and inspiration for homeless people and people with disabilities, it wasn't long before Suzan became disheartened as the grandeur she and her friend envisioned for her was turning into work. Although the book she had asked me to write as payment for all I was doing for her was underway, she lost interest in it. She and her companion thought her story was so valuable that they hustled it to multiple writers. Several of them contacted me asking about her credibility because they had spent time with Suzan working on her book, and then she disappeared.

Suzan and her companion had lived in my brother-in-law's house in Philadelphia for well over a year, but unbeknownst to me, they had stopped contributing to the household after the first few months. Ned, a trusting soul, did not report it, permitting them to stay with him because he did not have the heart to ask them to leave. In previous years, Suzan and her companion had resided with friends and relatives and lived in rooming houses, storage units, and her car. The end was always the same. Nevertheless, when Ned finally told me they had not paid him, I presumed that Suzan did not have the funds, so I asked her if she would be my paid assistant for a function where I was providing entertainment. I suggested she could use her remuneration to cover her back rent. She refused my offer, saying she was too busy. After I told her that her free ride was over, she remarked to Ned, "I knew it would eventually come to this."

Once Suzan and her companion moved out of Ned's house, I discovered that during the months she and her friend "could not afford" to contribute to the household, they were making monthly payments to rent a private storage unit some distance away where they kept an unknown quantity of personal effects. Many evenings, when they were not at Ned's house, they were at the storage facility. Ned quipped that they would leave his house after dark and roam the streets by night, only to return the next morning by sunrise to sleep all day, like vampires. Nothing had changed since Florida.

When Suzan and her companion vacated Ned's house, the items our friends and family donated to her had yet to be worn, sold, or removed from the bags. One dresser drawer was filled with hundreds of used soda bottle caps. Like some eerie museum, the personal photos that decorated her bedroom were left hanging on the walls.

My expertise has always been in the field of entertainment rather than in psychology. What I learned from this experience was how little I understood about the plight of the homeless. From the time she was a child, Suzan was blessed with golden opportunities with family and friends who were willing and eager to help her make something of her life; I was merely one of those people. It is doubtful that Jerry Lewis was responsible for her lifestyle nor could he have remedied it.

In the end, I came to the disturbing realization that when Suzan left Ned's house to head for the streets of Philadelphia, she was actually heading home.

The REAL Jerry Lewis Story

Imitation, the Highest Form of Effrontery

Sammy Pertillo & Duke Mitchell

The Legend of Jerry Lewis

Jerry Lewis was an immense talent, but this multi-faceted entertainer did not subscribe to the maxim, "Imitation is the highest form of flattery," especially regarding his skills. Simply put, Jerry's stage, TV, film, and recording personas were a compilation of many other retired and current performers of his day. Yet, Jerry Lewis reviled and often stifled performers who tried to emulate him.

Imitation was the heart and soul of Jerry Lewis' act. Going back to his beginnings, Jerry started his show business career as a record mime who made his living by comedically impersonating and exaggerating the gestures and mannerisms of other entertainers. He played the works of recording artists and mouthed their lyrics in funny costumes. Without making a sound, he contorted his face and body to generate laughter from what, in most cases, was a serious piece. As a record mime, Jerry almost always received complimentary reviews, even from the harshest critics. His characterizations were silent caricatures of other talented artists. In an interview, Jerry bragged that Frank Sinatra's mother enjoyed watching the young Jerry Lewis do an over-the-top impersonation of her famous son. Eventually, Frank Sinatra himself became one of Jerry's biggest fans and a friend.

In developing his act, Jerry's manager, Abby Greshler, instructed him to secretly attend shows featuring the comedy team of Dick and Gene Wesson. Once Jerry learned the Wesson Brothers' material, he became a Dick Wesson clone, imitating his movements, facial expressions, and his trademark squeaky voice. Undoubtedly, the prototype for Dean Martin & Jerry Lewis' act was the Wesson Brothers. They also openly impersonated other artists. Dean Martin liked to do his impression of Cary Grant, while Jerry often imitated Barry Fitzgerald from *Going My Way*. Many of Dean Martin & Jerry Lewis' motion pictures were rewrites of earlier movies and Broadway shows. Their 1954 comedy film *Scared Stiff* was a remake of the 1940 comedy *Ghost Breakers*, starring Paulette Goddard and Bob Hope, produced and released by Paramount.

Shortly after Dean Martin & Jerry Lewis broke up, Jerry recorded his only Top 10 hit record, the old tune "Rock-A-Bye Your Baby with a Dixie Melody." Made famous by Al

Jolson, one of the greatest entertainers, Jerry imitated Jolson's voice and singing style throughout the recording. Danny Lewis, Jerry's father, was known as an Al Jolson impersonator, so the question is, "Was Jerry copying his father's singing style or Al Jolson's?"

The delightful 1937 film *Nothing Sacred*, starring Carole Lombard and Fredric March, was rewritten for Broadway and opened in 1953 as *Hazel Flagg*. In 1954, the plot was revised, changing the female protagonist to a male role for Jerry Lewis, who portrayed the main character, Homer Flagg, in the film *Living It Up*. The 1960 musical comedy film *Cinderfella* was a twist on *Cinderella*, starring Jerry Lewis as Fella. Jerry Lewis' 1963 film, *The Nutty Professor*, was a double steal. The film's plot was a direct takeoff on Robert Louis Stevenson's 1886 novel *Dr. Jekyll and Mr. Hyde*, and its title was an adaptation of the earlier 1961 Disney comedy hit, *The Absent-Minded Professor*.

The Belle of Fontainebleau

Jerry Lewis received widespread acclaim for his multifaceted involvement in the creation of the movie *The Bellboy* released by Paramount Pictures in 1960. With no dialogue, the main character is portrayed as if in a silent movie. Jerry is credited with writing, directing, and starring in this comedy shot at the Fontainebleau Hotel in Miami Beach, Florida. This motion picture earned Jerry a reputation of a genius, a title he never refuted. While the film was in production, Jerry received a letter from comedy legend Stan Laurel of Laurel & Hardy movie fame suggesting the film's title be renamed, *The Belle of*

Fontainebleau, but Jerry decided against this recommendation. Interestingly, Stan Laurel was astute enough to recognize the similarities between Jerry's production and the 1918 silent Paramount release titled *The Bell Boy*, which was written, directed, and starred silent comedy legend Roscoe "Fatty" Arbuckle. Is it possible that Fatty Arbuckle stole Jerry Lewis' idea eight years before Jerry was born?

While the Jerry Lewis version of *The Bellboy* has some interesting and creative comedic moments, the 1918 version is a nonstop potpourri of sight gags, acrobatics, and slapstick. The original 26-minute film stars the overweight yet very agile and graceful Roscoe Arbuckle and features the deadpan comedian Buster Keaton. In those silent-era days, film stars were the innovators. Buster Keaton often opted to do his scenes, even the dangerous slapstick ones, without the use of a double or stand-in.

In Jerry Lewis' 1960 version of *The Bellboy*, he paid homage to Stan Laurel by featuring comedy writer Billy Richmond, a Stan Laurel look-alike, doing his impression of the famous film star, and Jerry's non-speaking main character was named Stanley.

With the advent of the 1960s video cassettes and DVDs and the 1990s Internet, silent black and white films like Fatty Arbuckle's *The Bell Boy* became outdated and were remanded to the past. Collectors of silent movies could only watch these silent treasures via 16mm or 35mm film prints, which were quite rare. So, Jerry's secret was safe, and Stan Laurel was certainly above letting the "Fat" out of the bag.

When Jerry filmed *The Bellboy*, he put a closed-circuit television camera next to a motion picture camera, permitting him to see what a scene would look like on the TV monitors before the film was developed. The crew nicknamed this setup "Jerry's toy," which became associated with the video assist method of filming. Although Jerry Lewis often claimed he invented the video assist, he did not invent the motion picture camera nor the closed circuit television camera, making the system unable to be patented.

The REAL Jerry Lewis Story

In the mid-1950s, my sister Joan and I watched a film at home starring Dean Martin and Jerry Lewis. At least, that's what we thought. During this movie, my sister commented, "Dean Martin doesn't look like himself." A few minutes later, I asked her, "Is that really Jerry Lewis?"

Joan and I had already met Jerry and knew what he looked like on and off screen. Joan grabbed a *TV Guide* to look up the movie. We were watching *The Boys from Brooklyn*, starring Duke Mitchell and Sammy Petrillo. Duke Mitchell, a handsome guy with a singing style like Billy Daniels, was not a Dean Martin imitator; however, his partner, Sammy Petrillo, was a dead-ringer for Jerry Lewis. Joan and I found the film delightful and amusing. I enjoyed it even more because one of my favorite scary movie stars, Bela Lugosi, played a mad scientist, and the movie featured a funny gorilla. From my childlike point of view, this was as good as watching Martin & Lewis.

Jerry Lewis knew Sammy Petrillo because they had appeared on *The Colgate Comedy Hour* together. How ironic that the bulk of Jerry Lewis' body of work had come from other performers, yet he went ballistic over the thought that someone was impersonating him. As one of the stars of *Bela Lugosi Meets a Brooklyn Gorilla*, Sammy Petrillo was now in Jerry's gunsight. Paramount producer Hal Wallis had every right to be concerned about this motion picture since it unashamedly mimicked a Martin & Lewis-style movie. After Wallis' negotiations to prevent the film's release failed, the movie hit the theaters in 1952 with limited circulation. Although the movie's title was temporarily changed to *The Boys From Brooklyn* when it was first released to television, it is available on the Internet under its original title, *Bela Lugosi Meets a Brooklyn Gorilla*.

While representing a few of my clients at a celebrity collectibles show in the 1980s, I spied a movie poster for the Duke Mitchell and Sammy Petrillo movie. Sammy Petrillo was sitting at a table in front of this display. I was eager to meet and tell him how much I enjoyed his movie as a kid.

Genuinely pleased to meet one of his fans, Sammy was conversational and gracious. When I mentioned having known Jerry Lewis most of my life, our conversation turned to the only movie the Duke Mitchell & Sammy Petrillo comedy team ever made. Sammy's recollection of his encounters with Jerry Lewis was unsettling.

Shortly after the release of the Mitchell & Petrillo movie, Jerry contacted Sammy with an offer to help his movie career. The plan was for Sammy to fly from the East Coast to Hollywood, where Jerry would introduce him to a theatrical agent. Sammy was thrilled, not because he wanted a career as a Jerry Lewis impersonator, but because he hoped this agent would advance his comedy career as Jerry promised. When Sammy met this agent and manager who was close friends with Jerry, the agent talked a good story and presented Sammy Petrillo with an exclusive two-year contract. At 21, Sammy felt this was the break he had been hoping for, and it had been made possible by a man he admired, Jerry Lewis. The back story is that this was an unscrupulous theatrical representative who colluded with Jerry Lewis to blacklist Sammy Petrillo from show business. The agent tied Sammy to a two-year exclusive contract but never got him a lick of work.

After meeting Sammy Petrillo, I began representing him for autograph shows and other personal appearances, and we became good friends. At that time, I was also managing Jerry Lewis as well as his son, Gary Lewis. At least 50 years had passed since Jerry blackballed Sammy, and I asked Sammy if he wanted to send a message to Jerry. Sammy, who held no grudges, made a charmingly funny video, "It's about time you stopped stealing my act." Done in good taste and good humor, I showed Jerry the video when I visited him on his boat in San Diego on July 31, 2007. It had been over five decades since Jerry last saw Sammy, and they no longer resembled each other. Jerry watched the video in pensive silence and then asked to see it again. This time, when the three-minute video ended, he did not say a word.

Jerry and I had had differences of opinion in the past, but none was as serious as our disagreement regarding Gary Lewis co-hosting the Atlanta 2007 MDA telethon. Everything was set for Gary's three-hour appearance in Atlanta, but then, Jerry withdrew his backing without explanation and instructed Gary and his band to perform at the MDA telethon in Las Vegas. When Jerry recanted, it created friction between Jerry and Gary and tension between Jerry and me.

Eddie Deezen from "Grease"

Hopelessly Devoted

The 1978 movie *Grease* captured the essence of the 1950s, showcasing the music, dances, and styles of that era. The film was named *Grease* after the oily products men used to make their hair manageable and shiny. Television commercials urged men to stop using "that greasy kid stuff" and start using Vitalis Hair Tonic. The 1950s saw a significant focus on men's hairstyles, ranging from the military-inspired crew cut to the iconic Elvis Presley style of long, slicked-back hair and sideburns. The movie *Grease* starred a popular 1970s TV personality, John Travolta. Along with Travolta, there were a myriad of young character types, including a teenager named Eddie Deezen. Eddie was a carbon copy of young Jerry Lewis from two decades earlier. Eddie Deezen used his naturally high-pitched voice, his thin frame, and his compelling comedic style to garner much attention in this film.

When I spoke to Eddie Deezen, I asked him if the director of *Grease* wanted him to portray a character similar to Jerry Lewis, and Eddie answered, saying Jerry's name was never brought up. Although Jerry Lewis was Eddie's idol, he never tried to impersonate him. Eddie Deezen's portrayal of the nerdy Eugene Felsnic contained elements of the classic Jerry Lewis, but it wasn't by design.

Toward the end of my conversation with Eddie, he said those magic words, "By the way, Rick, I do have a personal Jerry Lewis story I would like to share with you." I expected the worst, but in this case, it wasn't the worst, just a little bit sad. Jerry was appearing at a store to sign autographed copies of the DVD version of *The Jazz Singer*, starring Jerry Lewis. I knew this show quite well because my uncle Ernie, who was the show's producer, had also adapted the original story for television and was very proud of this one-hour TV special. After Eddie purchased five copies of the DVD, he approached Jerry's table to have him sign them. Jerry looked at Eddie and seemed taken aback. "He might've recognized me from *Grease*," commented Eddie, "but he never said anything to me. He just became very serious." Eddie went on to explain that when he told Jerry how much he had admired him, Jerry looked up with a surly expression. Describing his short encounter with his hero, Eddie remarked, "Then, I told Jerry how much he influenced my life. Jerry blankly glanced at me with silent hostility, and he signed my DVDs." After Eddie told Jerry that his favorite Martin & Lewis movie was *The Stooge*, Jerry looked at him and muttered a "thank you." Eddie was so heartbroken by this experience that, as he left the store, he gave his five autographed DVDs to some random shoppers. In a TV interview, Eddie describes this encounter with Jerry Lewis, "It was like meeting Santa Claus and getting kicked in the balls." I told Eddie Deezen that his experience with Jerry Lewis was just another example of Jerry's disdain for people who remind him of himself.

In another broadcast interview, Eddie shared his thoughts on how it felt to have his first motion picture turn out to be one of the most popular musical comedies of all time. He drew a parallel between his experience and the extras featured in a battle scene from the classic film *Gone With the Wind*, where hundreds of extras are lying on the ground, depicting the fallen soldiers. Eddie jokingly suggested that each of those individuals probably spent the rest of their lives proudly recounting their roles in *Gone With the Wind*, which starred Clark

The REAL Jerry Lewis Story

Gable and Vivien Leigh. Similarly, Eddie Deezen can boast how his film debut was in *Grease* alongside John Travolta and Olivia Newton-John.

The musical comedy team of Martin & Lewis and the characters Jerry Lewis portrayed have inspired several talented impersonators. Angelo Capone has a love and feel for Jerry's characters and performs impressions of some of Jerry's best mime routines, like the "Typewriter"and "Chairman of the Board." Angelo admitted to me that he once met Jerry but was afraid to tell him he was a professional Jerry Lewis impersonator because it was no secret that Jerry took offense to imitators. Tony Lewis, who is from Australia, is another Jerry Lewis impersonator. Adept at hiding his accent, Tony performs and looks incredibly like Jerry without trying. His partner, Tom Stevens, who is from Las Vegas, is reminiscent, in sight and sound, of Dean Martin. Stevens & Lewis do a convincing impression of Martin & Lewis. After ten years, the team of Dean Martin & Jerry Lewis had sadly passed their prime, and their impersonators were better than they were.

The Day the Clone Tried

I would be remiss if I did not mention a movie about a German-Jewish entertainer who captivates both adults and children with his performances. This compelling World War II psychological drama features a Jewish-American actor and film producer. While wearing clown makeup that does not conceal his cleft chin, he elicits laughter through silent, exaggerated facial expressions for the audience. In his performance, the actor utilizes his expertise as a skilled mime. The star of this film is none other than World War II veteran and film producer Kirk Douglas. Released in 1953, *The Juggler* is a post-World War II movie about a circus performer who lost his wife and children to the Holocaust but suffered "survivor's guilt." In the powerful final scene, Douglas cries dramatically in a riveting close-up while still wearing clown makeup as tears streak down his face. Kirk Douglas created the role of the clown who cried.

Variations of a theme are not uncommon in Hollywood films. In the early 1970s, Jerry Lewis was cast in a motion picture with a theme that had previously been addressed. *The Day the Clown Cried* is a retooling of *The Juggler*.

Jerry Lewis bequeathed his copies of the unfinished reels of *The Day the Clown Cried*, plus other works, to the Library of Congress. For decades, Jerry made a mystery out of why he refused to release this film depicting the Nazi-era concentration camps, promising that he would never permit it to see the light of day, at least not during his lifetime.

In the late 1970s, Sam Bidner gave me a handwritten letter he received from Patti Lewis. Dated June 4, 1972, she wrote, "Jerry has had a lot of aggravation from the producer. He'll finally finish the picture this week and will be home. We'll sure be glad to see him. It's so darn lonely." Patti's letter reveals interesting insights because it was written when Jerry was in Germany working on *The Day the Clown Cried*. Since Jerry was facing difficulties with the producer, he was obviously not the producer of the film as he often claimed, and, as such, he did not have the authority to either distribute or withhold it from distribution. The veil of mystery Jerry created about this movie has garnered significant attention over the decades, likely more interest and controversy than it would have received had it been released. As a final note, the film was never completed during his lifetime.

The Real Gary Lewis Story

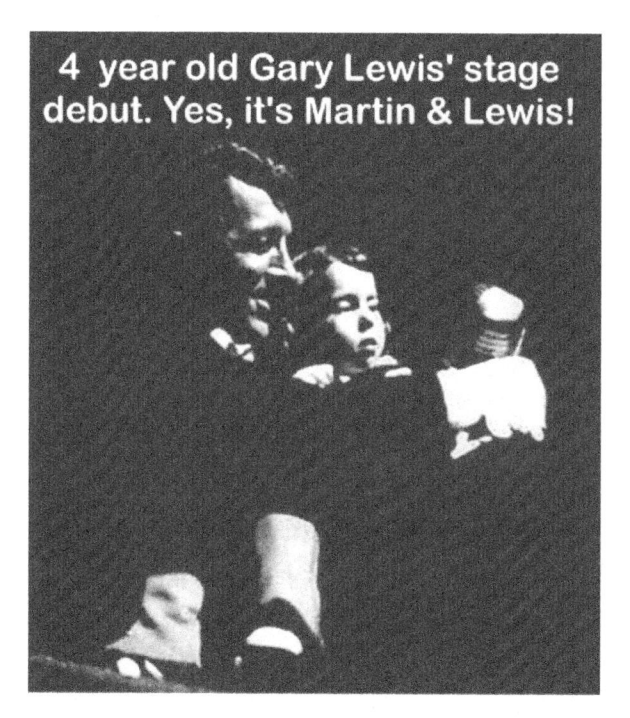

4 year old Gary Lewis' stage debut. Yes, it's Martin & Lewis!

Some entertainers claim they were born on the stage, but *Cash Box Magazine*'s 1965 Singer of the Year, Gary Lewis, was born at Beth Israel Hospital in New York City on July 31, 1945. On this rainy Tuesday, his mother arrived at the hospital at 8 AM (Eastern War Time), and Gary, originally named Cary, debuted at 4 p.m. Cary's parents, Jerome and Esther Levitch, and his grandparents, Rachel and Daniel Levitch, were all professional entertainers. Married only three months, Jerome could not accompany his bride Esther and their infant son Cary home from the hospital because he and his first professional show business partner were the featured act at the Chanticleer, a well-known nightclub in Baltimore, Maryland. Billed as Marty Drake and Jerry Lewis, they were the headliners hired to perform as a musical comedy team. Some reports indicate Jerry showed up briefly at the hospital after the baby was born and then returned to Baltimore to complete his theatrical engagement. When Jerry's wife and son were discharged, they took a taxi home to a small apartment at 10 Lehigh Avenue in Newark, New Jersey. Coincidentally, the Saphire family lived on Bergen Street, just around the corner and down the block from the Levitch family. Because children conceived or born out of wedlock in the mid-20th century were branded as illegitimate, their first child's birthday was often misreported as 1946.

Married couples typically link their newborn to their heritage by giving the baby the family's last name. However, Levitch, the family's legal name, is nowhere on Gary's birth certificate. Contrary to many media accounts, recording artist Gary Lewis was not born in 1946, and his birth name was not Cary Harold Lee Levitch. Born in 1945, his parents named their son Cary Harold Lee Lewis. Yes, he was born Cary Lewis, even though no one in his family was named Lewis. Gary confided in me that he has no idea why his birth certificate is filled with intentional inaccuracies. The only thing for certain is that Gary Lewis was born.

When Gary was 13, he had his first credited role in a motion picture, the musical-comedy *Rock-a-Bye Baby*, starring his father, Jerry Lewis. Six years before becoming the lead singer of Gary Lewis & the Playboys, he portrayed Jerry's character as a child in a flashback. As the scene ends, Gary, portraying Clayton Poole as a child, sings a song and harmonizes with Jerry, portraying Clayton Poole as an adult. Over the years, Gary appeared in movies and on television with his famous father.

The REAL Jerry Lewis Story

Many artists performed a take-off on Al Jolson's sentimental hit song "Sonny Boy" from the 1928 movie *The Singing Fool*. In 1941, the Andrews Sisters released a recording in which the first half was traditionally sung, and the second half was humorous. Adding a comedic twist to the song "Sonny Boy" in the 1940s, the Wesson Brothers incorporated it into one of their many hilarious routines. The short-lived singing-comedy team of Marty Drake and Jerry Lewis borrowed Wesson Brother's routine and performed their version of "Sonny Boy" at the Chanticleer nightclub in Baltimore during the summer of 1945. Twelve years later, after Martin & Lewis split up, Jerry made his second solo TV appearance and performed yet another take-off of "Sonny Boy," this time with his son, Gary, and his father, Danny Lewis. As long as the cameras were rolling and Jerry was in control, there was some harmony between father and son.

Jerry Lewis and his father often had issues. It was Danny's birthday, and Jerry and Gary drove to his parents' apartment to deliver his dad's surprise present, a brand-new car. Jerry honked the horn and Danny looked out of the window. Jerry yelled, "Happy birthday, Dad," as Gary pointed to the car. Looking down at his gift, Danny shouted to his son, "What? No convertible?" Either Jerry did not have a sense of humor or Danny was not very appreciative. Either way, Jerry and Gary drove off, and, no, Jerry did not give his father a car. Another time, Danny asked Jerry if he would buy tickets so he and Rae could go to Hawaii. Jerry said, "Sure, Dad, if it's one-way." Jerry was equally as talented at being an entertainer as he was at being vengeful.

© 2024 Rick Saphire

The REAL Jerry Lewis Story

Being the son of comedian Jerry Lewis was not always an asset to Gary Lewis. Often beaten by his father as an "educational tool," Gary grew up in what he referred to as "hell" while surrounded by the heavenly trappings of Hollywood.

Jerry Lewis was an immensely talented and equally troubled individual. Ghosts that haunted Jerry since his unhappy childhood manifested themselves in compulsions, which caused him to lash out and, emotionally and physically, hurt people who loved him and needed him the most. His wife Patti was also a target of Jerry's anger and a victim of his bizarre behavior. Before his untimely death, Jerry's youngest son, Joseph, wrote in his memoirs, "As 'Jerry's kids' became popular, his own children were at home and afraid of the man who many people thought was the greatest humanitarian on the planet."

The REAL Jerry Lewis Story

Comedian Jerry Lewis did not like competition. To be more exact, comedian Jerry Lewis despised competition, even from his own family. As a teenager, Gary Lewis inadvertently alienated his father by topping Jerry on the record charts time after time. After Gary Lewis & the Playboys became superstars to the 1960s generation of young music lovers, Gary's relationship with his father became even more strained, and they never got back on track. Gary and his father rarely spoke during the final decade of Jerry Lewis' life. Five years before his death, the "King of Comedy" disinherited all the children he raised with his first wife Patti Lewis, making Jerry's "will" seem more like a "won't."

Mouseketeer Doreen Tracey attends Gary Lewis' 11th birthday party.

Gary Lewis remembers some lighthearted moments from his childhood. When Jerry did something kind for Gary, predictably, he went over the top. At ten years old, Gary developed his first crush on a girl named Doreen, who had a remarkably big set of ears. Actually, the hat she wore on TV had the big ears. As a youngster, Doreen Tracey was a talented singer and dancer and a regular member of an elite group of kids known as the Mouseketeers. *The Mickey Mouse Club* had been a moderately successful radio program in the 1930s and 1940s. Then, in 1954, *The*

Mickey Mouse Club made its television premiere, coinciding with the grand opening of the Disney theme park, Disneyland, and both were instant hits. Gary once told me he couldn't fall asleep as a kid because Doreen was on his mind. Mouseketeer Annette Funicello had not yet developed into a superstar. When Jerry got wind of Gary's infatuation with Doreen Tracey, he picked up the phone, called the Disney corporate office, and secretly arranged for her to attend Gary's 11th birthday party. Jerry, being Jerry, also invited every one of the Mouseketeers to attend.

In 2010, I ran the 45th reunion of my graduating class from Livingston High School in New Jersey. I wanted to give my former classmates something to remember, so I

Gary Lewis and his one time crush Mouseketeer Doreen Tracey meet for the first time since his 11th birthday

invited Gary Lewis. Most of the alumni were fans of his music and grew up watching the original Mickey Mouse Club. To surprise everyone attending, I also invited my friend and client, Mouseketeer Doreen Tracey. Together, they entertained the crowd by answering questions and telling anecdotes. Doreen had the entire reunion on their feet, some with tears in their eyes, singing along to the *Mickey Mouse Club* theme. Unfortunately, examples of the lighter side of Gary's relationship with Jerry were rare.

In 1979, I worked as the comedy emcee in the Catskills at Brown's Hotel. I spent a lot of time chatting with my buddy Sam Bidner, who led one of the dance bands at the hotel. Sam had been a saxophone and flute player with Jerry Lewis' show band dating back to the 1940s and had many great stories. One tale dates back to 1939 when 13-year-old Jerome Levitch was preparing for his bar mitzvah. According to Sam, while Danny and Rae were on the road entertaining, their son had to live with relatives and was studying his haftarah, a portion of the Bible for the service. When a Jewish child reaches the age of 13, there is a religious ceremony commemorating the coming of age. On the day of this coveted event, Jerome's parents were working and did not attend this service, which left an indelible emotional scar on Jerry Lewis that never healed.

Fast-forward to 1958: Thirteen-year-old Gary Lewis was instructed to go into his father's portrait studio in their Bel Air home. Jerry Lewis told his son to put on the clothing laid out for him. There, Gary found a suit and tie; a yarmulke, the Jewish skullcap worn to show reverence for God; and a tallis, a fringed prayer shawl worn by Jewish men at prayer. Gary was not given any explanation for this photoshoot, but he followed his father's orders. Holding a book, Gary posed for several pictures his father took using his sophisticated, professional photographic equipment. In the memoirs of Gary's youngest brother, the late Joseph Lewis, he attested to Sam's story when he wrote, "My oldest brother Gary was confirmed, but my father's parents (who were Jewish) wanted him to have a bar mitzvah. Well, neither of my parents wanted this, so my dad, being the photographic whiz, shot photos of my brother in bar mitzvah clothes and yarmulke, holding a Torah [he held a book], and showed them to his parents. They went to their graves thinking he had been bar mitzvahed." A child other than Gary Lewis might have figured out what was going on, but in his case, it made no sense since he and his brothers were raised Catholic. Sam Bidner said that Jerry sent Gary's pictures to his parents as a mean-spirited practical joke. Along with the portrait of Gary, Jerry included a note to his parents, Danny and Rae Levitch, "Sorry, you both missed your grandson's bar mitzvah."

Decades later, I was with Gary at one of his appearances and asked if he remembered that photoshoot. Gary stared at me and asked, "Rick, what the hell was that all about? My dad made me get dressed up in a Jewish outfit, but when I asked him what we were doing, he had no answers for me." Although Gary would have never knowingly been so mean to his grandparents or anybody, he was in the middle of a very un-funny practical joke produced and directed by Jerry Lewis.

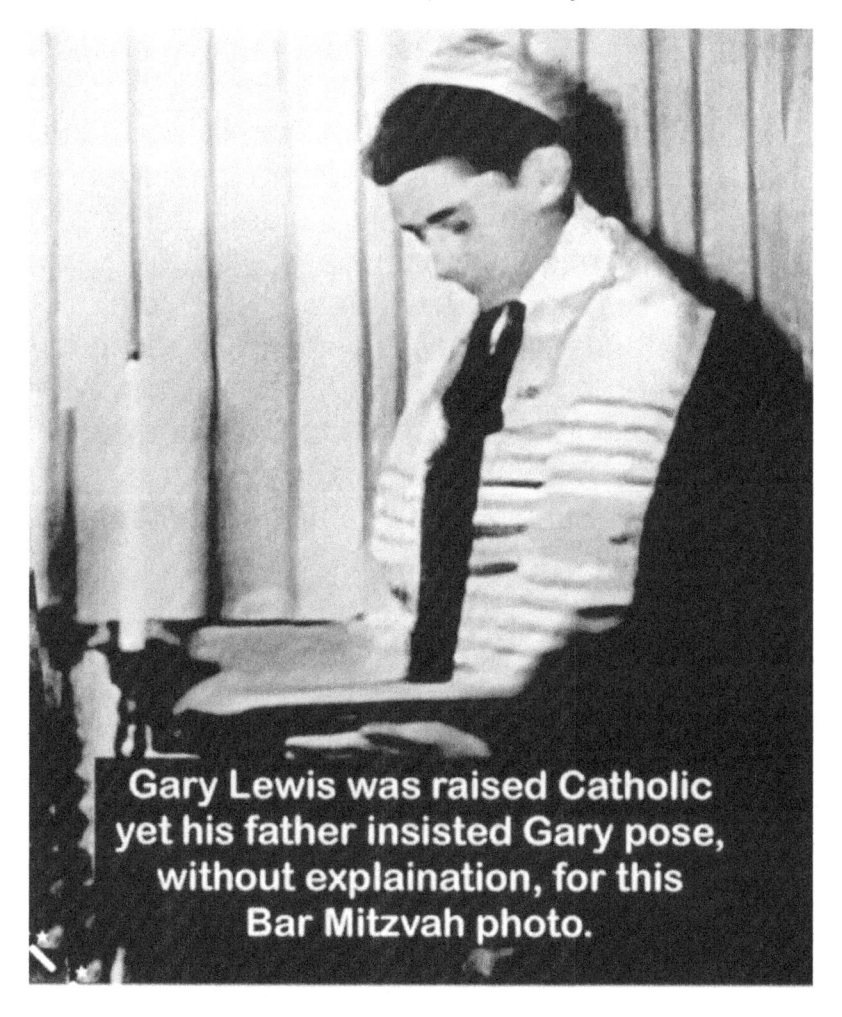

> Gary Lewis was raised Catholic yet his father insisted Gary pose, without explaination, for this Bar Mitzvah photo.

In 1959, Jerry Lewis presented a 60-minute modernized version of the often-revived story of *The Jazz Singer.* In this made-for-TV version, co-written and produced by my uncle, Ernest D. Glucksman, Jerry portrayed a nightclub comedian and singer whose father is a cantor in the synagogue. Hailing from a long line of cantors, his character is expected to be next in line. In this telecast, many characters' names were changed to reflect real people from Jerry Lewis' past. The cantor, despondent because his only son is not following family tradition, picks up a framed photograph of the family and slides out the portrait, revealing a hidden photo of his son's bar mitzvah picture beneath it. Only insiders and friends of the Lewis family might realize the boy in the picture is Gary Lewis. This photograph was one of the pictures from Gary's father's photo session, and I noticed it while watching a rebroadcast of *The Jazz Singer*. When I shared this story with Gary, who had been unaware of his unpaid, uncredited, and unauthorized appearance on this TV show, he finally knew the facts behind the bar mitzvah mystery.

During a June 2014 SiriusXM broadcast interview with Maria Menounos at the Friar's Club, Jerry stated he had never met comedian Joan Rivers. However, in 1968, he met Joan Rivers and appeared with her in front of a studio audience on her syndicated, televised program, *That Show*. The topic of discussion was "Children in Show Business." Jerry Lewis, whose parents were in show business, was on the program with Joan Rivers and the respected child psychologist Dr. Stephen Beltz.

Around the time of the 1968 broadcast of *That Show*, Gary was honorably discharged, having served in the U.S. Army for two years. Most parents would have been proud of their son's service record, but Jerry Lewis twisted the facts. Here was a chance for Jerry to proudly announce to the national viewers that Corporal Specialist 4th Class Gary Lewis had completed his tour of duty and was released a few months early to start college. The truth could have helped Gary who intended to resume his musical career. Had Jerry asked Gary's fans to support his son's comeback, he might have improved his own public image. But that's not what happened.

When asked if Jerry, whose parents had been in show business, wanted his son to enter the entertainment field, he said he would support whatever career his son chose. After commending Gary for making it on his own, Jerry expounded on his parenting skills. Jerry pontificated that his children were strictly disciplined while under his care and offered love, hugs, and spankings until they reached 21. The "King of Comedy" boasted that he had used this method of disciplining Gary from the time his son was four years old. Jerry proudly detailed how he beat 14-year-old Gary with a wide leather belt, one lashing for each of five poor grades on his military school's report card. Gloating that the strikes raised welts on his son's bare bottom, Jerry added, with a maniacal look, how he tuned his intercom to the teenager's bedroom, hoping to hear Gary cry. Dr. Beltz, who took exception to Jerry's violent tactics, explained that there is a better way to make children learn the rules, using love and understanding. On national TV, Jerry Lewis argued vehemently against the doctor's theory.

In Jerry's most disturbing TV appearance, he admitted to the national TV audience, "I really hit him. I hit him because I was angry." With visible welts appearing on Gary's bottom, Jerry told his son to march to his room, where he was to remain until Jerry told him he could leave. I wonder if the president of the MDA caught this display of "affection" towards "Jerry's kid."

At the time of the 1968 Joan Rivers program, corporal punishment was still legal in most states with certain restrictions. Controlled spanking was a common practice to "teach the child a lesson." Smacking a child with an open hand in an area of the body that would not cause severe damage was acceptable. Hitting a child with a closed fist could be considered an act of violence, but striking a child with a weapon that could cause physical damage to the child's body could be regarded as criminal abuse. It was disturbing when Jerry Lewis admitted in this interview that he beat Gary out of anger. Can a person who is lashing out in a rage truly practice self-control? Gary Lewis knows the answer to that question.

In my discussions with Gary, he cited incidents of physical and emotional abuse meted out by his father. While lying in bed, Jerry entered Gary's bedroom and pressed his fingernails into his son's forehead, leaving crescent-shaped indentations in his skin that were visible in the mirror. After one such episode, his father returned to Gary's bedroom with a tearful apology. Such physical abuse usually heals after a short period, leaving no visible scar. It's the psychological scars, those invisible scars, that Gary endured for a lifetime. Fortunately, in Gary Lewis' case, his music, the love of entertaining, the enthusiastic ovations that his on-stage performances generate, and the support of his loving wife, Donna, have all gone a long way to ease the pain.

Jerry Lewis was a dictator at home. Lamenting that Jerry was only an attentive dad when the cameras were on, Gary remarked, "We were props for his photo-ops. We kids could be kids when Dad was out of the house." Patti would warn them over the intercom when Jerry was coming home so the children could take cover. "We lived in fear. We never knew which Jerry Lewis would be coming through the door. There was no telling if Dad would be in a good or evil mood."

As Jerry Lewis' wife, Patti always felt pressured to keep herself looking good. "Mom had beautiful long Italian hair," Gary recalled, "but Dad made her cut it off so guys wouldn't find her as attractive." His father was so possessive of his wife that he refused to let Patti dance with another man. Jerry told Patti at a party, "If I don't dance, you don't dance." Since Jerry never danced, Patti didn't either.

Regarding his wife, Jerry Lewis had a double standard. While Patti had to avoid contact with men, Jerry played the field. One day, Gary saw his father in a compromising situation with a woman who was not his mother, and his father responded, "Oh my God! I'm caught." The topic was dropped because Gary could not hurt either of his parents, especially his mother, by telling her what he had seen.

Gary was not the only family member to catch Jerry, who was the supposed image of a devoted family man, in a compromising position. One time, after Joseph caught his father with a woman other than Patti, Jerry bought his son's silence for $1,000. Joseph writes, "In 1979, Jerry once again attempted to resurrect his movie career by writing and directing *Hardly Working*, which he spent nearly two years in Florida creating. During the filming,

The REAL Jerry Lewis Story

Jerry met...a disco dancer with whom he began to have an affair. After denying tabloid reports to his family, Jerry continued the affair. During a visit to Florida by Patti and Joseph, Jerry was caught red-handed by his wife and youngest son. When Patti and Joseph returned from dinner one night to Jerry's condominium, Joseph saw a woman leave as they approached. Entering the living room, Patti was shocked to find the bedroom in disarray. A picture of Patti and Jerry, which earlier had been hanging on the wall, was hidden in a closet. Smoke lingered in the air despite Jerry's claims of having been asleep for two hours. Patti and Jerry separated weeks later."

Both Joseph and Gary independently agreed their father was a tyrant. Despite all the tensions, hurt, and animosities, time and again, Gary dreamed of a better relationship with his father, hoping the next time would be better than the last, but it was never different. Nevertheless, Gary always defended his father in the press, often adding credibility to the lies Jerry Lewis told the media. Whenever Gary got close to his father, he felt Jerry had an ulterior motive. Case in point: the bar mitzvah photo. Gary spent his whole life longing for that positive change. But, it was always the same. Jerry Lewis was forever egocentric and forever driven.

In 1963, at 18, Gary began turning his hobby of playing drums into what he hoped would become a viable business for himself and a few of his friends. By entertaining at local events and college parties with his rock 'n' roll band, Gary aimed to lessen his dependency on his intrusive father. While making money was on

Gary's mind, fame was not a part of his dream. Approaching this venture in a level-headed manner, Gary knew he would need some quality portable amplification equipment and a new set of drums. His current drum set had been a gift from his parents some years earlier, and he had used them when he took drum lessons from his dad's good friend, Buddy Rich. To make his band a reality, he needed guidance from someone with knowledge and experience in the music business. Enter Gary Lewis' first manager, agent, investor, and former big band vocalist, Patti Palmer, aka Patti Lewis, aka Mom.

During the height of the World War II Big Band Era, Patti Palmer was the featured vocalist with the Ted Fio Rito and Jimmy Dorsey orchestras. Patti's schooling gave her an exceptional education in all facets of the music world, and she was quite accomplished in playing several instruments, including saxophone, accordion, and vibes. Patti was also a recording artist and a star of her own musical radio show. In 1956, Patti Lewis convinced her husband, Jerry Lewis, to invest his money into a recording session and take the resulting record and tapes to the major record companies. Patti's idea worked like a charm. Jerry's treatment of "Rock-a-Bye Your Baby with a Dixie Melody" hit the Top 10 on the national music charts, resulting in a lucrative recording contract with Decca Records, one of music history's most celebrated record labels, which added a new dimension to Jerry Lewis' fame. Finally, Jerry received recognition for his non-comedic singing, just like his father and his former partner, Dean Martin.

The REAL Jerry Lewis Story

As the driving force behind the success of Gary & the Playboys, Patti kept the band under wraps in the beginning and omitted Gary's last name until his group caught on. Jerry Lewis, who was at a high point in his movie-making career, was not to know about Patti and Gary's secret project, at least not until they had some positive reviews. Jerry spent a significant amount of time away from home, fully engrossed in his work, juggling multiple projects simultaneously from 1963 to 1964. In late 1963, Jerry faced the failure of his high-profile ABC-TV talk show and the success of his high-profile film, *The Nutty Professor*. During this same time, Gary was working hard to develop a unique sound while still playing popular songs from other bands. Although he did not yet have his own original tunes, the band sounded good to Gary and Patti, and in 1964, Gary & the Playboys had their first gig. Using her influence, Patti Palmer Lewis got the band a booking at Disneyland, but there was a caveat: Gary's last name was not to be used in advertising the band. Gary wanted to succeed on his own, and Patti supported that idea. Without Jerry's knowledge, Patti financed the band. In March 1964, Gary & the Playboys debuted at Disneyland. The band was instantaneously popular with the teenage audience and the management at Disney. Liberty Records music producer Thomas Leslie "Snuff" Garrett saw and heard the band at the Disney theme park, and a short time later, he and Patti signed a recording contract. Patti's name was on the legal agreement because Gary Lewis was still a minor.

As Gary Lewis explained to Dave Kane in 2023 on the *Kane & Company* radio show, Thomas Wesley "Snuff"

Garrett, who basically ran Liberty Records, was instrumental in the success of countless bands. Snuff Garrett knew how to pick hit songs, how to produce them, and when to release them. Taking a strategic approach to the music industry, Snuff would wait until the excitement of Gary's new release settled down, and then he would release the band's next recording. According to Gary, music arranger Leon Russell was heard instrumentally in his songs. Gary, who enjoyed collaborating with other professionals, thought Leon was brilliant, creative, and innovative.

Things moved quickly for Gary & the Playboys, and Jerry Lewis was made aware of the newest family member to enter the entertainment business. "This Diamond Ring" became *Billboard*'s #1 hit record, pushing the Beatles out of first place. In 1965, respected columnist and author James Bacon reported that Gary Lewis was the United States' answer to the Beatles. Once the band was on the charts, Jerry got Gary and the group some quality TV appearances. What nobody predicted was that the band, now officially called Gary Lewis & the Playboys, would catapult Gary to a chart-busting vocalist who would surpass Jerry Lewis as a recording artist.

The history of Gary Lewis & the Playboys is an amazing story of a rock 'n' roll group that battled music's "British Invasion," which began in 1965. In quick succession, Gary Lewis' songs all soared to the Top 10 list with six additional hits that year: "Count Me In," "She's Just My Style," "Save Your Heart for Me," Everybody Loves a Clown," "Sure Gonna Miss Her," and "Green Grass." These were only the first seven recordings Gary Lewis &

the Playboys released. It took Dean Martin 17 years to accumulate his first seven Top 10 hits.

While some musicians change their charts or vocal arrangements, Gary always felt that his live music should sound exactly as it does on his original recordings; otherwise, his fans could be disappointed. As his representative, I have often been asked if it is really Gary Lewis and his musicians who are heard on his Liberty hits, and the answer is a resounding "Yes." The iconic recordings of The Beatles were sweetened with additional musicians. When it came to Gary's voice-doubling to create a fuller sound, especially on stereo recordings, an additional background singer was sometimes used, but Gary was always closest to the microphone to ensure that his voice would be the dominant one heard.

Gary was the band's drummer and lead singer for the first year and a half. However, during live appearances, the drums and the cymbals blocked Gary's view of the crowd, and the stage lights glared in his eyes, making it difficult for him to get a sense of the audience's reaction, and his fans could not see him. Plus, he had too much energy to sit in the back and play drums. After hiring a drummer, Gary grabbed his guitar by the neck and began moving about the stage, interacting with his fans.

The British bands often sported long hair and wore avant-garde outfits, bouncing about the stage as they made childish gestures. These groups frequently resorted to silly choreography designed to make them unique and sell their songs, and sell them they did. In contrast, Gary Lewis' group was clean-cut and conservatively dressed, usually in a tie and jacket. Their music was infectious, their lyrics were tasteful and easily understood, and they also sold many records. Gary Lewis dispelled the old show business adage, "You gotta have a gimmick." His band's gimmick was the fact that they didn't have one.

Gary Lewis & the Playboys made an indelible mark on the history of music in the United States and around the world as they accrued eight Gold Singles (one million sales minimum per record), 17 Top 40 Hits, four Gold Albums, and until they lost count, over 45 million records sold worldwide. The group's popularity soared largely due to DJ Dick Biondi from radio station KRLA in Pasadena on the West Coast and DJ Bruce Morrow, known as "Cousin Brucie," from radio station WABC in New York on the East Coast. That all happened between 1965 and 1966.

Gary Lewis & the Playboys' songs climbed the charts, and Gary became established as a rock 'n' roll star. Jerry Lewis admitted he had little to do with his son's rise to fame, crediting Gary with making it on his own. However, Jerry never gave any credit to his wife, Patti. Jerry occasionally promoted his son and tried to hitch his wagon to Gary's star.

As Gary's successes grew, he appeared with the band on countless TV programs appealing to the rock 'n' roll generation. Whereas the 1955 teenagers adored Dean Martin and Jerry Lewis, the 1965 teenagers adored Gary Lewis and found Jerry's antics corny. By performing with

Gary on the TV show *Hullabaloo*, Jerry hoped to grab a piece of Gary's audience, but that appearance only magnified their generational divide. Jerry, who had a burning desire to be a popular recording artist, developed a deep resentment toward his son's success.

Gary's career continued on an uphill trajectory until one day in January of 1967 when he had an "Elvis moment" as he was drafted into the United States Military. Gary commented in a statement to the press, "If Elvis could do it, so can I." Without putting forth an effort to escape the draft, which so many young men did during the Vietnam era, Gary put the band's appearances on hiatus. His goal was to fulfill his duties to his country and then come home and pick up his hugely successful music career from where he left off. Gary Lewis did not realize that the music industry had moved forward in his absence. By the time he returned home to the USA, rock 'n' roll had transitioned into rock. While Elvis Presley had his famous 1968 comeback special, Gary Lewis & the Playboys had their comeback in 1980.

Martin & Lewis' film *At War With the Army* was released in 1950. In the early 1970s, Jerry WAS at war with the Army for real. In 1971, Jerry Lewis went on a media blitz to vent his anger about his son Gary being drafted and serving in Vietnam. In an article published in the *Miami Herald* on May 30, 1971, Jerry said his son Gary had told him that while having a meal in the mess hall, he saw two of his army buddies, Bert Lazarus and Jimmy O'Connell, blown up in front of him. In various articles, Jerry claimed this tragic act of war was the key incident that caused the young rock 'n' roll star to come home as a different person. Describing his eldest son as depressed with no desire to work, devoid of any feelings or emotions, Jerry lamented, "He just didn't give a damn about anything," Jerry Lewis said his son would have been better off had he been killed in Vietnam.

Jerry's rage went as far as to threaten to exterminate the politicians in Washington, D.C. In this passionate newspaper interview, the elder Lewis threatened to leave the United States and move his family to Switzerland to protect his other sons from being drafted into the Vietnam War as Gary had been. Yes, it was a compelling and politically charged story in 1971, giving Jerry Lewis much-desired media attention in his stalled career. Taking advantage of the Nation's divisiveness regarding the Vietnam conflict, these media interviews generated sympathy for Jerry Lewis. It may be argued that this was a forgivable reaction of a father who saw his son torn apart by the ravages of the war. There was also an unexpected secondary effect: Jerry's story about his son turned Army Specialist 4th Class Corporal Gary Lewis into a Vietnam War hero for serving. Gary's newfound status came at a price.

I often received calls from veterans' organizations asking Gary to accept awards for his military service, but Gary instructed me to decline the requests politely. Was Gary Lewis so traumatized by the war that he could not even face accepting an honor from those who fought with him in Vietnam? No!

Gary was traumatized by his father, who went to the media with those war stories. Despite what Jerry Lewis reported to the press, Gary never saw anyone killed in a mess hall or anywhere. Gary was not familiar with the names of the "victims" his father gave to the media, and he did not come home depressed. The truth is that Gary Lewis never saw action in Vietnam because he never set foot in Vietnam. It was as if Jerry Lewis was writing a screenplay and trying it out on the media. Jerry Lewis invented the whole damn story.

Jerry mentioned on Joan Rivers' show in 1968 that Gary had been stationed in Korea, and he knew his son had been honorably discharged from the Army two months early to attend college. When Gary Lewis & the Playboys appeared on NBC's *The Jerry Lewis Show* in 1969, Gary commented on the air that he had recently returned from Korea. Jerry and some members of the press evidently suffered, among other ailments, from selective amnesia. Three years after the band appeared on Jerry's show, Jerry Lewis created a storm of controversy by giving the phony "Vietnam" newspaper interview. Some fans and historians may ask why Gary did not set the record straight many years ago, which brings to mind another adage, "Blood is thicker than water." Gary shouldered the burden of Jerry Lewis' fabrications because he could not bring himself to expose his father as a liar to the world. When asked why he thought his father intentionally misled the public about his service record, Gary replied, "I don't know what drives the insane."

Any depression or anxiety Gary Lewis suffered as an adult was unrelated to his two-year tour of duty for Uncle Sam but related to the terror he faced daily when his father was at home. Gary was more at risk in his bedroom at home than he was serving in the Army. As a stickler for discipline, Jerry Lewis sent his firstborn son to a prestigious Hollywood military academy, the Black-Foxe Institute, five days a week, in full uniform, starting at the age of six until his graduation at 17.

In many families, parents help their children with their schoolwork. When asked if Jerry ever helped Gary with his homework or offered to help him study for a test or to prepare a project, Gary's answer came swiftly and without reservation: "Of course not. He didn't want us to know he didn't know anything. That's a fact, not an opinion." Helping Gary with his studies would have been more productive than taking a belt to his backside.

Determined, Gary Lewis kept the ghosts of his past from controlling his future. In 1970, the 1965 *Cash Box* Singer of the Year Award recipient reorganized his band, performing his ever-popular songs for soldiers at military bases in the USA. However, when Gary attempted to resume his musical career as a recording artist, he found the studios only welcomed newcomers, British groups, and psychedelic stylists, which was not his style. Several years later, the nostalgia craze began, making the timing right for Gary Lewis & the Playboys to take to the road again. Since the 1980s, Gary and his ensemble of top-quality musicians have entertained audiences around the globe. In the 2000s, I was privileged to coordinate a five-concert tour of the Philippines for the band, and the capacity houses and standing ovations throughout his 90-minute concerts were proof that Gary Lewis & the Playboys remain an international class act.

Gary Lewis survived the torments, pain, and embarrassment that came with being a child of Jerry Lewis. With the help of his loving mother, he harnessed his skills as a musical performer. Since 1964, he has provided quality entertainment to millions worldwide. Traveling the globe with him as his theatrical representative, I saw his adoring fans on their feet at his concerts, cheering for his unique brand of classic rock 'n' roll.

Patti Palmer Lewis with Gary Lewis. Two music legends

In 2009, this consummate professional became the only family member to help his estranged half-sister gain her desired acknowledgment. On the nationally syndicated TV news show *Inside Edition*, he courageously submitted to a DNA test proving that Suzan "Lewis" Minoret, born in 1952, was, in fact, his half-sister and Jerry Lewis' only biological daughter. He should have received a humanitarian award for this display of kindness, but he was satisfied with helping Suzan verify who she was. By offering this woman his DNA, Gary Lewis jeopardized his reputation and relationships with his siblings and father. Although Suzan said she never wanted anything from her biological father except for him to acknowledge her, Jerry Lewis ignored her. Gary's DNA test was broadcast, giving Suzan the much-desired recognition she wanted: proof that Jerry Lewis was her birth father.

The word humanitarian is often used in reference to Jerry Lewis, and there is no doubt that Jerry was a dedicated fundraiser who gave a good deal of his time improving the quality of life for "Jerry's kids," the victims of Muscular Dystrophy, and their families. Gary Lewis is a talented musician, a U.S. Army veteran, and an all-around great guy. For what he did for his sister Suzan, he is a certified humanitarian.

The Real Joseph Lewis Story: Think Pink Baby

Joseph Lewis, Jerry's youngest child, died in 2009. As a result, he did not have the opportunity to contribute to this book and cannot speak for himself directly. However, through his memoirs, Joseph clearly describes his feelings about his father, his family, and the world.

Joseph Christopher Lewis, Patti and Jerry Lewis' youngest son, passed away at the age of 45. His death was attributed to acute morphine intoxication; however, it is unclear whether it was intentional or accidental. Despite his love for his mother Patti and admiration for his oldest brother Gary, who was 19 years his senior, Joseph lived a troubled life. Before he was born, Joseph was a victim of a unique form of child abuse, which I have dubbed "pre-partum" depression.

Not only was Jerry expecting another baby with his wife Patti in 1963, but he was also starting his highly publicized ABC television program to be broadcast every Saturday night. Everybody was curious to see what Jerry would do to fill two hours with live entertainment. During the show, Jerry faced mounting technical problems, and he was ill-prepared for most of them. However, he was well-prepared for the sing-along directed at his pregnant wife. Millions of viewers in the US watched as Jerry pointed to Patti and their sons in the balcony while he sang a jingle composed by his longtime friend and songwriter Lil Mattis:

"Think Pink"
Six months and then my dreams all come alive,
A small carbon copy of Mom will arrive.
If it's another boy will I survive?
With all the things I bought her,
I'm sure we'll have a daughter.
THINK PINK.
That's the only way to do it.
THINK PINK...

Jerry, who usually had a keen sense of comedy, missed the mark on this one. There was nothing funny about it, and he lost his audience.

During this period of time, Jerry hosted private Hollywood "Think Pink" parties and distributed "Think Pink" souvenirs Margie Little, Jimmy Durante's wife, threw Patti a "Think Pink" baby shower luncheon.

> We're having a shower
> To get in the mood
> To welcome a baby
> To the Lewis brood.
>
> Five sons are a blessing,
> But they don't wear curls
> And Patti and Jerry
> Also like girls.
>
> So be informal
> Or wear mink,
> All we ask is
> **THINK PINK!**
>
> (For Mrs. Jerry Lewis)
>
> *But we certainly hope YOU can make it.*
>
> Time 2:00 P.M. (luncheon)
> Date Sunday, December 8th
> Place 511 N. Beverly Drive
> Beverly Hills, California
>
> GIVEN BY: Mrs. Jimmy Durante
>
> R.S.V.P.
> Mrs. Durante - CR 1-9540
> Miss Taini, *secretary* - 876-3196
> *after 7:00 P.M.*

Despite the hopes and prayers that Patti would finally give Jerry a baby girl, they were outvoted. God had His way, and on January 7, 1964, Joseph Christopher Lewis came into the world, letting down his father and the entire country through no fault of his own. Imagine being a little boy whose father is one of the world's most beloved entertainers. Before your birth, your celebrity father told millions of people on national television how he was hoping and praying that when his baby was born, he would finally get the daughter he always wanted. Imagine, too, that your father asked the entire country and people worldwide to pray that you would be a female.

As an adult, Joseph aspired to be a writer and drafted a retrospective record of his life. Psychologists often recommend writing therapy to help those with depression and anxiety by having them transfer their thoughts onto paper. A memoir is generally a personal account of someone's life experiences. However, in Joseph's case, his unique writing style creates a sense of detachment from the subject matter, as if written about him rather than by him. As a result, the notes he wrote in his memoirs read like a biography rather than an autobiography. All of what Joseph wrote is believable, and much of it is unsettling.

In his memoirs, Joseph wrote that Patti wanted to have a sixth baby, but the 40-year-old Jerry Lewis did not want his wife to have another child and admits, "I don't know what my father's reaction was to the news of a new baby, but he was quick to take advantage of the situation. For the kid he told his wife he didn't want, he made the public think it was the media event of the century."

During his formative years, Joseph was often asked if he was the "Think Pink Baby" and was teased with comments like, "Weren't you supposed to be a girl?" This led to struggles with low self-esteem and a lack of friends

Joseph Lewis and mom Patti

as he grew up. Joseph also feared his father and suffered at his hands. As if someone else was speaking, Joseph wrote in his memoirs, "Jerry continued to take out his anger against his family, who, despite all of the pain they endured, still supported the man who mentally and physically abused them. When Jerry was around his children, they were forced to act like dogs and obey cruel commands given by their father. The only attention the family received was when Jerry was angered with them. This virulent anger could be set off by virtually anything, and his children were forced to hide from him whenever they could." Joseph continued, "The most hard hit in the family was Joseph, who, at a young age, began to have panic attacks and would hide for hours in closets in order to avoid his father…Because of the great fear Joseph had of his father, this transferred into other areas of his life, and he grew up lonely with few friends in the world." In describing his home life, Joesph's own words were, "Jerry's rages were terrifying and unpredictable…and he would discipline his children with a thick leather and metal belt." Jerry Lewis corroborated this allegation, openly bragging on television about how he exercised corporal punishment on his boys.

While filming his comeback movie, *Hardly Working*, Jerry spent almost two years in Florida, away from his family. Around this time, the tabloids began publishing articles about Jerry's affairs, which he vehemently denied to the press and his family. However, when Joseph and Patti visited Jerry in Florida in 1979, they "caught him with his pants down." Writing in the third person, Joseph described the situation: "When Patti and Joseph returned from dinner one night to Jerry's condominium, Joseph saw a woman leave as they approached. Entering the living room, Patti was shocked to find the bedroom in disarray. A picture of Patti and Jerry, which earlier had been hanging on the wall, was [now] hidden in a closet. Smoke lingered in the air despite Jerry's claims of having been asleep for two hours." Patti was no stranger to dealing with her husband's extramarital affairs and disliked his philandering, yet she tolerated them because she had her children to think about, and she valued her comfortable lifestyle. Devastated that her photo with Jerry had been stashed away in a closet proved to be her breaking point, and Patti filed for separation from her husband a few weeks later.

Joseph wrote, "During Patti and Jerry's divorce, Jerry filed for Chapter 11 bankruptcy to thwart Patti's attempt to get her share of his wealth. Patti was left with little money and was forced to move into a small house." Days after the divorce was final, Jerry remarried, and the couple left for a one-month honeymoon in Europe. Only a teenager at the time, Joseph confessed, "After finding several types of drugs left behind by Jerry in his office, Joseph began to experiment with drugs. Nights filled with marijuana, LSD, and Quaaludes were not uncommon for Joseph, who looked to relieve the pain from the abuse and neglect given to him by his father." Joseph claimed this began his addiction, and when his parents split up, he was so shattered that he required psychological treatment. Although Joseph later realized drugs were not the answer, it was too late; he was already addicted.

Finding steady employment was challenging for Joseph, who found little solace in life except for his love of writing, photography, and collecting baseball cards. Joseph was often out of work because his drug habit interfered with his job. Approached by the National Enquirer, the leading gossip tabloid at the time, he was offered substantial money for a tell-all article about his father and agreed to give them his story. When the sensational article hit the newsstands, it widened the wide rift between father and son. Jerry was so furious that he threatened Joseph's life, and Joseph was so scared that he went into hiding, and no one knew his whereabouts.

Before the days of the Internet, CompuServe was a sophisticated text-only bulletin board service that enabled people to communicate. Hidden behind a keyboard and computer screen, people could make up their own personas. Men could pretend to be women, the poor could pretend to be wealthy, and the unimportant could pretend to be very important. Joseph's father pretended to be a lovable, charming, and funny character on the screen, and now Joseph, lonely and looking to connect with others, immersed himself in a similar world of make-believe. Intending to embark on a new career venture, Joseph purchased three computers in as many months and acquired some computer skills. It was not long before his computers became an addiction, replacing his drugs. Joseph felt as though he had lost the ability to interact with real people. Once he bought a CompuServe Telecommunications kit he began bingeing on typing to strangers, entering into new and dangerous ways of socializing. Via computer modem, he met countless other computer users around the world and made cyber friends. Using the computer to search for romance and someone to be, his online relationships began taking over his life. Joseph spent 16 hours a day typing to total strangers, talking about love and sex. Through these cyber-connections, he had numerous misadventures, which often put him in peril and caused him mental anguish.

Over time, he met someone special through CompuServe. Nobody in his family knew where he was when he disappeared into the arms of Kimberlee Marshall, a sweet young woman from Michigan. Romance blossomed, and Joseph and Kim got married. In the beginning, they were happy and had two sons, Bobby and Dan. For the three years Joseph was with Kimberlee and her family, he was at peace with himself.

In his writings, Joseph described his relationship with his father as a nightmare and reflected on their contentious interactions. He was grateful for having known Kimberlee's father, Bob, who taught him valuable life lessons, like what it meant to be a real man, something his own father never did. Joseph found his first steady job, had a loving family, and finally felt complete. His first son was born in 1990, and he opened his own business. The couple's second child was born in 1991. Despite Joseph's best efforts, he fell back into drug use, which ended his marriage. When Joseph left his home, his loving wife, and his young sons, he gifted all of his possessions and his memoirs to Kimberlee, who shared his writings with me so that I could share Joseph Lewis' words, thoughts, and voice with you.

Both Kim and Joe remarried. Joe's second wife, Cheri, gave birth to his third son, Zach. Jerry Lewis never met either of Joseph's wives or his grandchildren who longed to meet their famous grandfather, and Jerry did not provide for any of them in his will. In Joseph's memoirs, he lamented that as a child, all he ever wanted was for his father to take him fishing, but Joseph, like his father, also missed the boat.

It's interesting to see how much Jerry Lewis' story mirrors Joseph's. Both felt abandoned by their parents due to the demands of show business. However, the impact was not entirely the same. While Jerry's father was never accused of being physically abusive to him, Jerry proudly admitted he was that way to his sons. Although Joseph never beat his children, he beat himself up for 45 years.

The REAL Jerry Lewis Story

Rick and Jerry Together Again

Since the beginning of my career as a celebrity representative, I have always told those interested in listening that I am a lazy manager. That's because I only represent people who are already famous. In my early days, I represented my childhood heroes. My first client was a man who had not made a movie in 25 years. His name was George Robert Phillips McFarland, better known to his millions of fans as Spanky McFarland, the child star of Hal Roach's *Our Gang* comedies, syndicated on television as *The Little Rascals*. Back in the 1970s, the nostalgia craze swept the country. Buffalo Bob Smith had a *Howdy Doody* revival, and Spanky and I rode the wave, appearing at colleges and universities throughout the United States.

Another of my childhood heroes was the one and only Soupy Sales, the television comedian known for his avant-garde humor and taking pies in the face. In the 1960s, I frequently took the bus from Livingston, New Jersey, to New York City, where I walked from Port Authority to WNEW-TV Channel 5. I was permitted to go into the viewing room to watch the live performance of *The Soupy Sales Show*. After the broadcast, I often talked with Soupy. In one of our conversations, I learned that Soupy had lived in a house in Beverly Hills, once owned by my uncle, Ernie Glucksman.

Author Rick Saphire with his long time friend and client Soupy Sales

During the height of its popularity in 1965, *The Soupy Sales Show* was suspended for a short period because of something Soupy said on his live broadcast. There were a couple of different stories about what happened. Soupy told one to the media and another privately to me. The public version was that when he was on the air, he told the kids to take those green papers with the pictures of men with beards on them from Daddy's wallet and send them to him at the station. In return, Soupy would send them a postcard from Puerto Rico. As a result of the joke, the show was suspended for a short time.

In a private conversation, Soupy told me another version of what happened. He said, "I told an open-ended joke on the air: 'I took my girl to a baseball game,' he quipped. 'I kissed her between the strikes...'" The rest of the joke was not articulated but resided in the minds of the adult listeners. According to what Soupy told me, the station found this joke offensive and knocked him off the air. Due to the onslaught of requests Channel 5 received from fans, saying, "We don't care what he did. Just bring back Soupy Sales," the New York kiddie show was back within ten days. Readers are free to believe either or neither of these tales.

Part of Soupy Sales' success was that children watched the show because Soupy was a funny man-child and never broke character. His goofy puppets and pies in the face delighted them. The parents watched the show because Soupy would rattle off one-liners like a machine gun, which often contained double-entendres only the adults appreciated. For teenagers, this show was the best of both worlds. *The Simpsons* was not the first television show created to appeal to children and adults on multiple levels.

On my first date with Valerie Benson, a girl from my hometown, I surprised her with a visit to New York City to meet Soupy Sales in person. Like many teenagers, Valerie was one of his fans. Our date was quite a success, especially since she got a kiss from Soupy.

Thirty years later, I represented Soupy Sales for personal appearances, interviews, and autograph shows. During the time I was securing these bookings for him, he suffered from ailments that necessitated his being on medication, which slowed his thought processes, speech, and walking, but not his spirit. When his fans approached Soupy as he sat at his autograph table, they were sometimes taken aback by his frailty. However, he always extended his hand, and in a loud whisper, he offered a pleasant word or a joke. Soupy Sales' fans loved him, and he loved his fans.

When I booked Soupy into a four-day celebrity autograph show in Atlanta, he traveled there with his wife, Trudy Carson, a performer in her own right. Trudy was a Radio City Rockette, who also appeared on Broadway and performed on several television programs, including *The Jackie Gleason Show* as one of the famous June Taylor dancers.

When I met them for breakfast in Atlanta, I asked, "How did you sleep last night?"

Soupy looked at me momentarily and said, "Rick, I slept like a baby. I cried all night and peed in bed."

The REAL Jerry Lewis Story

Sometime after the Atlanta appearance, my wife and I met Soupy and Trudy at New York City's legendary jazz club, Birdland, where another one of my heroes, Lew Anderson, was performing. Aside from being a fabulous musician and a prominent band leader on the New York City circuit, he was best known by millions of children around the United States as TV's Clarabell the Clown on *Howdy Doody*. Lew Anderson was featured in one of the most emotional moments ever on television.

Premiering in 1947, many children grew up watching NBC's *Howdy Doody*. Beginning in 1948, Clarabell became a regular on the show. In 1955, Lew Anderson took over the role of the mischievous, seltzer-squirting, silent clown who only "spoke" through his horn. After 13 years of continuous broadcasting, the original series went off the air in 1960 with a special closing episode. Clarabell carried signs and displayed placards promising a big surprise throughout the one-hour broadcast. In its final minute, the camera slowly zoomed in on Clarabell's tearful eyes, filling the entire screen. The set was silent. Clarabell looked into the camera and spoke for the first and only time, saying, "Goodbye, kids." September 24, 1960, was the day the clown cried.

After Lew's performance at Birdland, Trudy and Soupy discussed his health and mentioned part of Soupy's problem might be a form of neuromuscular disease. I asked if they had contacted the Muscular Dystrophy Association, and they hadn't. When I offered to contact Jerry Lewis on their behalf to see if he could suggest help, both Soupy and Trudy agreed.

© 2024 Rick Saphire

It had been years since Jerry Lewis had called me to bend my ear about how angry he was at his 92-year-old Aunt Lil, whom I knew as Mrs. Lillian Brown of Brown's Hotel. I wondered if Jerry would respond if I contacted him about Soupy. And if he did, what would his response be? I took a shot. Confident Jerry Lewis would receive my message, I faxed him a letter, and then I put it out of my mind.

A few days later, I received a call from my friend and client, comedian Charlie Callas, who told me he had received a call from Jerry Lewis asking about me. Jokingly, I quipped, "Well, Charlie, did you have anything good to say about me?" Charlie told me he was unsure but thought Jerry was going to call me, and I was sure it would be about Soupy.

Not more than an hour passed before the phone rang. The person on the other end said, "Is this Ricky? This is Jerry Lewis." I wondered why he had to tell me his last name because I would recognize his voice. This was our reunion, and Jerry had a lot to say. "First of all, Ricky, Let's talk about Soupy. Where is he living?" I told Jerry he was living with his wife Trudy in Manhattan. Jerry continued, "Well, if it's okay, I'm going to have somebody from New York contact Soupy by phone, and we'll see if we can get him some medical attention. If there is any connection to neuromuscular involvement, the MDA will do whatever they can to help Soupy. Can you please give him my love?"

"I think you just did that," I replied.

He did not acknowledge my comment but said, "Now, Ricky, Let's talk about us." If this was the Old West, and I was wearing a holster with my trusty six-gun, I might have been ready to draw. But Jerry's voice sounded like the old Jerry Lewis, as I remembered him in 1962 when we were friends. Then Jerry said, "Ricky, I noticed on your letterhead that you have Soupy Sales, Charlie Callas, Rip Taylor, and others. How would you like to put Jerry Lewis on there?"

"Jerry," I replied, "that's quite a compliment. Of course, I would love to, but only under one condition. I would like it to be legitimate. I would want actually to represent you."

"That's fine, but my name will have to go first on your letterhead." I couldn't help but wonder if Jerry would have wanted top billing if I had been representing Dean Martin. Jerry was right; his name would be at the top.

We agreed to talk over the rest of the details in a few days. As our conversation ended, I remarked, "You know, Jerry, I've been training for the position as your representative since 1953." We both laughed.

After several conversations with Jerry, I realized why he wanted to reestablish a relationship with me. He had become nostalgic, and I was a reminder of an exciting, successful, and productive era in Jerry's life and career. Although Jerry knew we could never recreate those days, he was sentimental about them and Uncle Ernie, who piloted many of Jerry's great successes. Those fond memories were dear to him, and I was a conduit to his past. Jerry occasionally sent me photographs of himself with my uncle, and he always complimented Ernie in our conversations. Jerry once sent me a picture with a handwritten note saying, "Ricky, here's Ernie. Love, JL."

Although Jerry could be difficult, he could also be solicitous and thoughtful. Jerry Lewis unselfishly arranged for Soupy Sales to receive medical treatment, which extended and improved his quality of life.

Show Business Is Like No Business

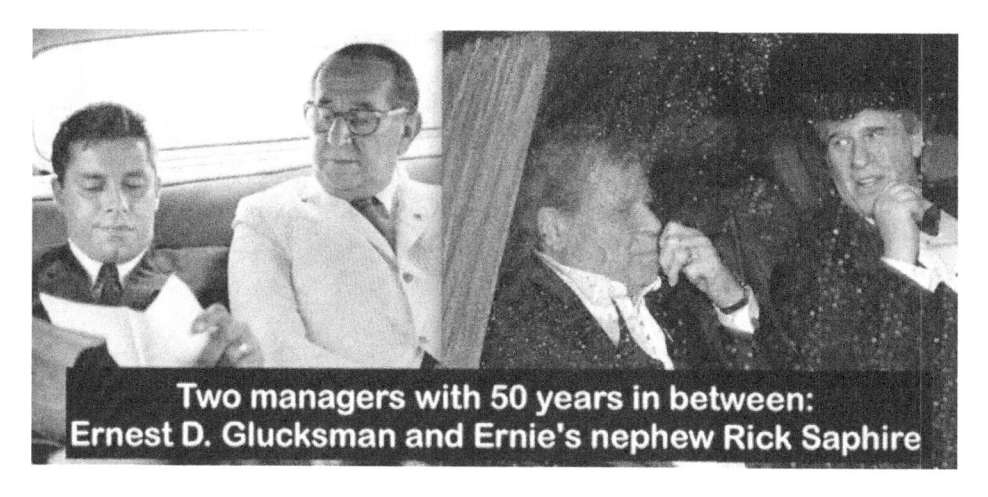

Two managers with 50 years in between: Ernest D. Glucksman and Ernie's nephew Rick Saphire

Joe Stabile, who was the brother of orchestra leader Dick Stabile, had been a musician with the Dick Stabile Orchestra and accompanied Martin & Lewis during their halcyon years. When my uncle, Ernie Glucksman, left the pack in the mid-1960s, Joe Stabile became Jerry's personal manager. His demeanor reminded me of my uncle's, which was no surprise. As Uncle Ernie often commented, "Jerry Lewis needed an affable person to protect him from the public and, at the same time, to protect the public from Jerry Lewis."

For a year before the debut of *Jerry Lewis Live!*, the program was touted as being like none other, hosted by the unrivaled comedian Jerry Lewis. Convinced that he would rise to the occasion, Jerry refused to plan and rehearse the first of the two-hour-long televised shows, which he was contracted to do weekly for five years. It was an artistic disaster. Although his handlers saw it coming, like watching an avalanche, there was nothing they could do. Jerry Lewis was hellbent on having his way. As a result, many people were hurt by his bomb, and the show was canceled after its premiere. Jerry Lewis made a speech at the last broadcast of this ABC debacle on December 21, 1963. In earnest, Jerry said, "There is a very, very lovely expression that my very dear friend and my manager, Mr. Glucksman, taught me. It's a Hebrew expression, saying, 'Gam zu le-tovah.' That means from all bad comes good." In the closing credits, Ernest D. Glucksman, Jerry's manager, was the executive producer, and Joe E. Stabile was the music coordinator.

Although Jerry Lewis could be charming and amusing, he could also be vindictive and unforgiving if he imagined that someone offended, wronged, or disagreed with him. Since Jerry rarely bothered to trust and verify, his actions against an alleged offender were often swift, arbitrary, and misplaced. Published in 1982, Jerry's first autobiography, *Jerry Lewis In Person*, written with Herb Gluck, intentionally omitted any reference to Ernie Glucksman, who served as executive producer and director for all of Martin & Lewis' appearances on *The Comedy Hour* from 1950 through 1955. When Martin and Lewis broke up in 1956, Ernie remained with Jerry as his personal manager. Ernie produced many of Jerry's films, such as *The Nutty Professor*, and was the associate producer of others, such as *The Bellboy*. My uncle produced all the TV shows starring Jerry Lewis until 1964. Once Uncle Ernie left Jerry Lewis, Jerry took credit for all his successes, omitting Ernie's name from interviews and publications, including *Dean & Me, A Love Story*, published in 2005, ten years after Dean Martin's death. Jerry made Ernest D. Glucksman, his former mentor, friend, and manager, disappear, rewriting history as he wanted it to be rather than presenting facts as they really were.

In 1990, Jerry had Joe Stabile call me from Las Vegas to ask if I still had my Martin & Lewis memorabilia collection and if I would be willing to part with any of it. Joe explained that after Patti divorced Jerry, he no longer had access to the materials in his house. Although Jerry had rented a warehouse in California where he stored most of his memorabilia, he was living in Nevada. Through a series of oversights, the rent on this unit went unpaid, and the facility liquidated its contents to satisfy the monies owed. In retrospect, Jerry might have mistakenly thought I had access to materials like his 1950s guilt-ridden letters to Patti and many salacious photographs, including shocking pictures of Dean Martin and Jerry Lewis posing together naked in a shower.

Joe arranged for show tickets after I agreed to meet Jerry in Atlantic City, where he was performing. After the show, I met Joe who asked how much I wanted for the items on my inventoried list. As I handed the paper to Joe, I remarked, "I don't want any money. I would just like Jerry to explain this letter."

Joe looked at the copy of the 25-year-old letter Jerry had written to my mother, in which he blamed my father for his deliberately rude behavior toward me at Brown's in 1965. "Let me bring this back to him," he offered. "Wait here." Fifteen minutes later, I learned that Jerry pulled a vanishing act. Jerry Lewis was not a magician, but he should have been because he had an uncanny talent for making people vanish. That included his friends, his staff, and yes, even himself.

When Joe returned, he apologetically said that Jerry could not see me because he had to leave unexpectedly and handed me my list and the copy of my mother's letter. I felt certain that Jerry backed away from our meeting because he did not want to discuss the things he had written to my mother years earlier. I had spent hours compiling my list and traveling to the shore, but I was happy to see one of my favorite performers, Bobby Rydell, who shared the bill with Jerry. While Bobby was terrific as usual, Jerry Lewis did virtually the same nightclub act I had seen him do at the Palace Theatre 34 years earlier. After I said goodbye to Joe Stabile, I headed home.

I always thought very highly of Joe Stabile for being a dedicated manager and doing what was in Jerry's best interest. In 1997, I sent a letter to Jerry Lewis' office regarding a book I had written, *Jerry Lewis in a Nutshell*. When Jerry's manager called to tell me that Jerry was interested in seeing a working copy of it, I agreed, adding that I would like Jerry to write the foreword. During my conversation with Joe, I once again brought up the incident at Brown's Hotel in the Catskills in 1965 when Jerry refused to pose for a picture with me. True to form, Joe explained that I had just gotten in the way of Jerry's bad mood that day, and he assured me Jerry was not that kind of person. In all candor, I knew Joe was only doing his job and felt he did not even know about the incident; this was a well-rehearsed, second-hand apology. Throughout his life, Jerry Lewis rarely justified or apologized for his verbal attacks or misconduct, whether intentional or accidental.

After Joe gave me the mailing information, I sent a working copy of *Jerry Lewis in a Nutshell* to Jerry, and he responded to the manuscript…a decade later. I did not publish that working manuscript because I did not feel the story was complete. I put the book on hold, and it was finally published under a new title years later. You're reading it now.

When Joe Stabile died in 2004, the *Las Vegas Review-Journal* published his obituary, inaccurately stating, "When Martin and Lewis split in 1956, Stabile became Lewis' manager." The newspaper acknowledged my correction and suggested that I contact the family, who intentionally provided the media with incorrect information as per Jerry Lewis' instructions. It was a particularly cruel trick for Jerry to play on my late uncle, who had a major impact on his career and fame, as well as on Dean Martin's success. The truth is Ernie Glucksman, who became Martin & Lewis' executive producer and director in 1950, became Jerry Lewis' personal manager in 1956 and remained in that position until 1964. Uncle Ernie used to say he would stop managing Jerry Lewis when he didn't like him anymore. In the aftermath of the 1963 *Jerry Lewis Live!* disaster, Jerry Lewis was a liability, and Uncle Ernie and Jerry Lewis parted ways. My uncle came home one day and told my Aunt Judy, "I'm through with Jerry Lewis. I don't like him anymore." When Ernie Glucksman left Jerry Lewis, Joe Stabile, who was a musician in the band, became his manager. Claudia Stabile, Joe's wife, kept things together when her husband became ill, and she was given the title of Jerry's manager.

I faxed Jerry regarding Soupy Sales' medical issues, and he called to talk about Soupy and said he wanted to discuss our relationship. In a follow-up conversation, Jerry surprised me by offering me the position of his manager, which Claudia, Joe's widow, already held.

As someone who had a history of an on-again-off-again relationship with Jerry Lewis, I had to consider this carefully before accepting the offer to manage him. Although he would undoubtedly be my most prestigious client, he would not be my only one. Given Jerry's unpredictable temperament, I felt that I could handle his appearances, but I also knew that I could walk away from him if I needed to. Having Jerry Lewis' name on my letterhead, even if only for a brief period, would elevate the status of Rick Saphire Celebrity Management, and it could be financially rewarding. However, I also knew about his numerous health problems.

Despite all my concerns, I felt a kinship with Jerry Lewis because of our long history and family ties. Jerry was kind to me in my youth and greatly advanced my early career. I witnessed his unstable temperament firsthand, but I still liked Jerry, so I thought for

Judy Glucksman and two of Jerry Lewis' managers

a moment and made my decision.

Once I accepted his offer, I began securing bookings for Jerry Lewis as his manager. Within two weeks, Jerry called me, sounding troubled. "Ricky, I have a political problem."

I asked, "Is it Claudia?"

"Claudia doesn't like to do any traveling, and she's not really an agent," Jerry replied, "but she has been helpful."

Although titles are essential in business, Jerry was obviously in a bind. "If it's the job title you're worried about," I responded, "I don't care about it. I can use 'personal representative.'"

Jerry thought for a moment. Being a consummate professional, he asked, "What the fuck is a 'personal representative'?"

I retorted, "What the fuck is a 'personal manager'?"

When we stopped laughing, Jerry added, "Okay. Use 'personal representative' here, and use 'personal manager' in Europe." That was fine with me because Jerry was far more popular in Europe than in the United States at this stage of his career.

My title as Jerry Lewis' "personal representative" was unique, as was my professional position with him. Unlike those who previously managed Jerry, I was not on his payroll. I never asked him for an exclusive agreement because that would have put too much pressure on me and distracted me from my other clients.

Within a few weeks, I began generating bookings for Jerry Lewis, which is the benefit of representing people who are already famous. The first personal appearance I secured for Jerry was at the Hollywood Collectors' Show. When I spoke to Jerry in September, he was not up to a stage performance, but he was up to signing autographs, especially since he could profit as much at this two-day celebrity event as he could doing a club date. Once I got the okay from Jerry, I contacted the show's promoter, Ray Courts. I had worked with Ray previously bringing many celebrities to his shows, and we had a good track record. When I asked Ray if he wanted to include Jerry Lewis in his October celebrity line-up, he told me he had to think it over. Three seconds later, Ray said, "Absolutely. Yes." I informed Ray that Jerry might be hooked up to oxygen due to his lung problems, and we would need ample security. Experienced in this type of situation, Ray extended his full cooperation. When I told Jerry that the show was confirmed, he was as pleased as I was.

A day later, Jerry called to say he had to cancel his appearance at the Hollywood Collectors' Show because his doctors recommended he voluntarily check into the hospital to get weaned off the steroid medication that saved his life. I immediately canceled the booking with Ray Courts, who was disappointed about the show but more concerned about Jerry's health.

About two weeks later, Jerry sent me a letter with a printed advertisement announcing his appearance at another such show which also had to be canceled. His note read, "Who dropped the ball?" I explained to Jerry that the promoter posted the news online moments after he approved his appearance. The paper Jerry sent me was a printout of the website's main page advertising the show. Jerry was stunned, unaware of how quickly information on the Internet could reach an audience worldwide. "You mean in the one day that it was a booking," Jerry queried, "this information made it around the world?"

The simple answer was, "Yes."

During the first year of our reestablished relationship, Jerry and I spoke on the phone several times a week, reminiscing about the old days, sharing bad jokes, and discussing family matters. Aside from a few paid interviews, I could not accept offers for Jerry because he was in the hospital for several months. Once Jerry was on the mend, he was eager to make appearances. Sponsored by the International Press Academy (IPA) in California in January 2005, Jerry was invited to attend a banquet where he would be presented with the Nikola Tesla Satellite Award for recognition of pioneers in the filmmaking technology industry. Jerry was to be honored for the invention and use of the video assist system, and I also arranged for Jerry's wife and his younger daughter to be in attendance.

While in my hotel room, I heard the bulletin on CNN Live that Johnny Carson, the longest-running host of NBC's

Tonight Show, had died. Knowing Johnny Carson was one of Jerry's friends, I called Jerry's suite to break the news to him, and he was audibly shaken at the loss. The call ended. A few seconds later, I heard Jerry's voice in a phone-in interview discussing Carson's death on CNN.

Meanwhile, I reflected on the piece I had written about Jerry and the video assist, published in the souvenir booklet for the event. I wondered if Jerry had really invented the system, as he often boasted, or if he simply found an additional use for the closed circuit video camera (CCTV), developed in 1942 by Walter Bruch and used during the Second World War. Jerry did not hold a U.S. patent on such a system; however, others did.

In late 2005 Jerry Lewis sent several photos of himself with my uncle, Ernie Glucksman. Uncle Ernie served as Jerry's producer, director, and manager. Jerry also included this note.

Furthermore, had Jerry invented the video assist system, he would have monetized it.

While awaiting the banquet, I asked Jerry Lewis what went wrong between my uncle and him. "Someone gave me erroneous information about Ernie," Jerry admitted, "and I believed it." Although he alluded to something untoward, Jerry never offered details, which was his typical reaction to an uncomfortable situation, especially if he could be held responsible. Acknowledging that he had wrongly accused my uncle of an offense gave me a little satisfaction, which was the most I could expect from Jerry Lewis.

Following a Hollywood-style photo-op in the lavish lobby, Jerry, his guests, and I waited for the elevator to take us upstairs to the IPA banquet. A reporter, who had flown in from France to get an interview with the "King of Comedy," approached me and, in her best English, introduced herself as a writer from a French newspaper. "Pardon. I would like to speak to Monsieur Jerry Lewis."

Inches from Jerry, I turned toward him and said, "Mr. Lewis, this young lady is a reporter from France who would like to speak to you for a moment." For the first time as Jerry Lewis' representative, I found myself in an untenable position of being his apologist.

With a testy look, Mr. Lewis faced the woman. She cheerfully introduced herself to him and briefly explained how excited she was to be here to do an assignment on him. Jerry sneered, "Yeah. You and everybody else." As if this was a scene from a movie, the elevator doors opened. Without a word, Jerry turned his back on the French reporter, and he and his companions vanished into the elevator as the doors shut.

I stayed behind to talk to the reporter, who was on the verge of tears, and asked if she was attending the banquet. "Yes," she replied, "that's one reason I'm here from France." I told her there would likely be an opportunity during the banquet for her to ask Jerry Lewis questions. This incident made it obvious that the love and admiration the French had for Jerry Lewis were unrequited.

Jerry Lewis' treatment of this reporter reminded me of what I witnessed during the 1950s and 1960s. In those bygone days, however, Jerry Lewis had a strong fanbase, and he was a payday for many people. In other words, he could get away with it. Some in the media admired his caustic behavior or found it funny, while others detested it. By 2005, Jerry's career consisted of hosting the annual Muscular Dystrophy Association telethons, interviews, and award ceremonies honoring his past body of work. Jerry Lewis never mastered the skills of graciousness, diplomacy, and self-control. Surrounding himself with admirers who praised him unconditionally, Jerry saw no need to change his ways.

As Jerry Lewis' theatrical representative, I only considered offers that could be meaningful to his future and give Jerry new opportunities to entertain, not just reminisce, and one of those offers came from German producer Beate Wedekind.

The REAL Jerry Lewis Story

Marketing Jerry Lewis

Jerry and I arrive at The Golden Camera Awards in Berlin, Germany

As a representative for well-known celebrities, I have rarely had to solicit work for them. My phone rings with offers; some are viable, and others are not. In securing an appearance for my clients, promoters often use seven little words that drive me crazy: "It will be good for his career." That's the code for "We want the appearance for free." My job is to negotiate solid offers for my clients, and marketing Jerry Lewis presented a unique set of challenges.

An honest salesperson wants to be certain that a product lives up to its sales pitch. With Jerry Lewis, there was no need for a sales pitch. The name "Jerry Lewis" instantly conjured up that lovable, irrepressible clown who was full of talent and wasn't ashamed to share it with his audience. However, during the second half of Jerry's career, he was none of the above. This, of course, was not all Jerry Lewis' fault. He had become a beloved character in his early 20s and was able to sustain it through his early 40s. However, physically and emotionally, it was impossible to portray that same character when he was in his 50s, 60s, 70s, and 80s. My job was to secure appropriate venues for him where his original audience could celebrate their memories of the superstar without him trying to replicate what he originally did on the screen.

One afternoon, I received a call from Berlin, Germany. Beate Wedekind, the prestigious Golden Camera (Goldene Kamera) awards executive producer, introduced herself. Beate wanted Jerry Lewis to appear at this popular annual event televised throughout Europe. This program is similar to the Emmy Awards in the United States. I listened to her offer and found it intriguing. Considering the travel involved, I thought Beate's first offer would be unacceptable to Jerry. Thanking Beate, I agreed to present it to Mr. Lewis and get back to her. When I spoke about it to Jerry that afternoon, he told me he knew Beate from a previous engagement some years earlier. As predicted, Jerry would agree to the appearance if the stakes were higher and sent his regards to Beate. When I relayed the messages, Beate said, "Rick, I want you to tell me what, in your opinion, Jerry would accept without our having to go back and forth on this. I want to get it booked." I gave her a number I knew Jerry would not turn down, and she agreed. Then, I called Jerry to confirm the deal. Before long, Jerry, his entourage, and I were bound for Germany.

Jerry Lewis flew out of Las Vegas with his friend actor Jac Flanders, his assistant/valet Jeff Lowe, and his son Anthony. I flew out of Philadelphia and was the first to arrive. Once at the Berlin airport, I was greeted by a young lady who explained she would be our interpreter and travel with us during our one-week stay in Germany. After we got my luggage, she escorted me to a waiting limousine with a uniformed driver and plain-clothes security guard. I was taken aback. I did not expect such royal treatment for myself, but I did not question it.

En route to the hotel, the interpreter, the limo driver, and the security guard pointed out historical areas. It struck me that when they identified the points of interest, they were apologetic and extremely self-conscious about World War II. It was 2005, yet they mentioned how thankful they were that in 1945 the Americans defeated Hitler's regime and handed their beloved country back to the German people.

When we got to the hotel, I met Beate, who was just as charming in person as she was during our many phone conversations leading up to our excursion to Germany. A few hours later, I returned to the airport to meet Jerry's flight.

While checking into the hotel, I noticed an attractive woman walking toward me. She said, "Hello, you're Rick Saphire."

Jokingly, I quipped, "I already know that."

By her accent, I knew she was an American, and by her beautiful smile and sparkling eyes, I realized she was TV and film star Goldie Hawn. She introduced herself, and I politely said there was no need to tell me who she was. When she asked if I was Jerry Lewis' manager, and I said

I was, she asked, "Rick, is there any chance I could get to meet Jerry?"

Rick Saphire and Goldie Hawn

I assured her Jerry Lewis would be pleased to meet her and offered to introduce her to him before the show. We then discussed sitting together at the banquet following the awards program. All the 2005 Golden Camera Awards participants got together the following evening, and I introduced Goldie Hawn to Jerry Lewis. Goldie and Jerry were seen together on and off camera during the show, having fun. Jerry was clowning, and Goldie was laughing. After the awards ceremony, I spoke to Jerry and reminded him about the affair later that night. He told me that he would not be going to the banquet and would have to see Goldie another time. Although the other celebrities and the mayor of Berlin were going to be in attendance, Jerry asked me to extend his apologies to everyone. This was not a surprise to me because Jerry always declined events like that.

Jerry had several gratis news interviews in Germany. The first was for a television broadcast, and Jerry's entire entourage traveled with him to the station. As a kid, I rode in limousines with Jerry Lewis from hotels to TV studios. Forty-three years later, I was still riding in limousines with Jerry Lewis from hotels to TV studios. What a fabulous rut to be in.

As we entered the TV studio for the live news broadcast, Jerry's expression became sullen. I knew that look, but what could have upset Jerry so much within the first 15 seconds of our arrival? When the studio representative welcomed us, Jerry's first words were, "Is this studio robotic?" Now I knew what was bothering Jerry. He had an aversion to television cameras operated by remote control. Although Jerry claimed he was upset because he felt robotic cameras put people out of work, his angst went deeper. From his earliest days on television, Jerry would play to the cameras, often interacting directly with the camera operator. And Jerry was not comfortable with change.

During the commercial break, Jerry, who attempted to be pleasant, was escorted onto the set. He sat down for his interview, promoted his appearance on the Golden Camera Awards, and discussed his upcoming live interview at the American Academy in Berlin. On our way out, Jerry growled, "If I would have known this was a

Co-authors Sheila and Rick Saphire with Jerry Lewis during a personal appearance tour

fuckin' robotic studio, I wouldn't have agreed to the interview." And then he added, "Check in advance anytime you schedule a television appearance for me."

One magazine interview was for a fee, and Jerry insisted on being paid in cash. The payoff made me feel as if I was in a spy movie. There was a knock at the door of Jerry's suite. A man with an attaché case entered. With a heavy German accent, he introduced himself. He walked toward the desk, opened his briefcase, and counted the money in stacks of newly minted U.S. one hundred dollar bills. The courier returned the money to his attaché case, which he handed to me, and left. I entered the room where Jerry was, opened the briefcase, and presented the cash to Jerry, who peeled off my commission and handed it to me. Waiting in a separate room, the interviewer was invited to join us and conducted his Q&A.

The purpose of our trip to Germany was for Jerry Lewis to appear at the Golden Camera Awards to receive their coveted gold statuette on February 8, 2005. Upon entering the beautiful auditorium where this televised extravaganza was to take place, we were escorted into a private room where Jerry met the person who, after a good deal of negotiation, was selected to be the presenter of the award. Jerry had always spoken with respect and admiration for one of his heroes, Charlie Chaplin, also known as Sir Charles Chaplin. Although Sir Charles was no longer with us, his beautiful and talented daughter, Geraldine Chaplin, was, and she had been selected to present the award to Jerry. Our meeting with Geraldine was extremely gratifying as she and Jerry expressed sincere admiration for each other.

While they were getting acquainted, I strolled back into the theater, where the staff were setting the stage for the show. I wondered if the program was being broadcast live or recorded for future broadcasts on the various networks across Europe. As I looked around the auditorium, I noticed something that sent a shot of adrenaline coursing through my veins. Looking around the room, I realized the show was being televised... robotically. There were no television cameras in sight. Times and technology had changed. My mind flashed back to the 1956 Muscular Dystrophy Telethon I attended, starring Dean Martin and Jerry Lewis.

Broadcast from New York's Carnegie Hall, TV cameras, boom microphones, TV monitors, and cables filled the stage, obstructing the audience's view. The 2005 Golden Camera Awards was run using the most up-to-date technology. Tiny cameras were installed around the room and attached to the balconies' façades. I hoped Jerry's mood would be so euphoric that he would overlook that this was television in the 21st century.

I took a deep breath and rejoined Jerry and Geraldine Chaplin in the other room. Before the 2005 Golden Camera Awards broadcast began, there was an official walk-through on stage, and then I went up to the "green room" to be with the others. The green room, which is not green, is a term for any room in a theater or a television station where participants in a performance can gather to relax, catch up on news, or sit nervously awaiting the show. In this case, the green room was a comfortable classic library a few floors above the theater. I found Jerry and Geraldine chatting with some of the other attendees. Goldie Hawn and I talked briefly and took a few pictures together.

Then came the big surprise for the viewers at home and in the studio audience. Dustin Hoffman entered the green room. The first thing that crossed my mind was how envious my wife at home would be of my position in show business for the first time. She had been a fan of his since she saw his popular film, *The Graduate*. Jerry formally introduced me to Dustin Hoffman, who was reserved and pleasant. He and Jerry had a few good laughs, and then I chatted with Dustin, and he posed for a few pictures. Under the watchful eye of Beate

Jerry Lewis - Dustin Hoffman - Rick Saphire

Wedekind, the 2005 Golden Camera Awards was a well-produced program. Her positive, professional attitude was so infectious that everyone was relaxed and excited about the show.

A few clips from several Jerry Lewis films preceded a fantastic introduction, and then Jerry came on stage to a rousing ovation. Hanging on to his every word, the audience appreciated seeing one of the biggest stars in Hollywood. Many were sitting on the edge of their seats, some teary-eyed at this opportunity to listen to Jerry Lewis talk to them in person. When Geraldine Chaplin presented the award to Jerry, she had some beautiful words regarding her admiration for him. She also spoke about the times that her father watched Jerry Lewis movies on television. When the show was over, all the stars mingled for a while, congratulating one another. Our group returned to the hotel to prepare for the banquet that night. Most of us attended, but Jerry opted out. People thought this was because 78-year-old Jerry Lewis was tired and recovering from health issues, but it was more than that. Jerry disliked these types of functions. So, as his emissary, I attended the banquet to excuse his absence and to eat.

Our itinerary included an appearance at the American Academy, where German film producer Eckhart Schmidt interviewed Jerry in front of a sizable crowd. Eckhard had recently filmed a documentary in the United States featuring Jerry Lewis, Stella Stevens, Anna Maria Alberghetti, and what's his name…Rick Saphire. Jerry's talk to the audience was bright, cheerful, and filled with compliments about German audiences. Then, Jerry dropped a giant bomb when asked, "Why do you feel you are so popular in France?" and "What is it in your films and performance that the French adore?" That's when Jerry began disparaging not only one of France's most respected film directors but also his French fans. I recorded it all. Jerry Lewis systematically took the French to task. At first, the audience laughed, thinking this was one of the "King of Comedy's" attempts at humor, but the smiles quickly turned upside down when they realized that Jerry was dead serious.

Jerry Lewis began his talk by recalling a dinner with his dear friend, French filmmaker François Truffaut. Mocking Truffaut's accent, which lapsed into pigeon Japanese, Jerry quoted his friend, "You know, Jerry, I know why the fat lady in *The Geisha Boy* walk past camera and spilt the groceries."

Jerry responded, "Well, that's very interesting, François. Can you tell ME what it was?" The audience laughed, and Jerry scoffed, "I'm the writer. I don't want to appear stupid, but I'd appreciate it if you'd tell me what I had in mind."

Truffaut commented that it had something to do with Jerry's background and the fact that his mother was obese. Jerry sneered, "My mother? Oh, just eat your goddamn dinner, for Christ's sake." The audience laughed.

Jerry continued, "And they're all like that. They (the French) just love you. They clung to Jerry Lewis because he represents a multifaceted amount of questions, of statements. 'He (Jerry) did that because… or he will maybe…' He's a dart board for them. 'Hit that mark. Hit that one.' And they (the French) are that way and have always been that way. They must get into it. They can't go to a film and see it, walk out, have dinner, and say, 'It was a marvelous film,' and then get on with their lives. They have to take the film apart. They have to make sure everyone knows that they know better than they actually know. And that's the nature of the Frenchmen." The audience was silent.

Jerry added, "Well, you would be amazed at the difference between a German fan and a French fan. I've looked at it for a long time. A German fan is literally that. And because I sit in Berlin, I'm not making the German fan any better than the French fan. I'm only giving you facts. The German fan is just that, for no reasons other than they like it, period. It's that simple. The French fan wants you to know that they thought this out. They want you to know that you should thank your…blessings, for they are recognizing you. And they believe that only they know what's behind every piece of material that has some kind of back story. They know that story, and they want you to know they know. And they're really all full of shit."

At this stage of Jerry's career, he habitually said things to make headlines and gain media attention, and he was well aware of what he said about the French. In February 2006, despite previously criticizing the French at the American Academy in Berlin, the French Culture Minister presented Jerry Lewis with France's highest civilian honor, inducting him into the Legion of Honor as Legion Commander.

We had one more scheduled stop to make in Germany before heading home, the Berlin International Film Festival. In February 2005, Jerry Lewis was supposed to be honored with the Golden Bear Lifetime Achievement Award for directing. When I met with the Berlin International Film Festival officials the day before the event to discuss Jerry's participation in their program, they explained there was a mix-up. Jerry Lewis would not receive a Golden Bear award, although he would be part of the official presentation as a guest of honor at the opening ceremonies. When I asked about returning the following year, I was told they already had their recipient scheduled.

Jerry addresses the German audience about his French fans

The Golden Bear Awards was as opulent as the Academy Awards red carpet celebration. Hundreds of photographers and fans lined the street and the entranceway to the theater where the program took place. Jerry Lewis and I were ushered to our seats near the front of the first balcony. By this time, Jerry was exhausted and looking forward to the trip home, so he was not upset about not going on stage as an award recipient.

As showtime approached, the house lights dimmed. Fifteen minutes later, the house lights were still dim as the audience waited for the show to start. The crowd became antsy. Although there was movement on the stage, no announcement addressed the delay. After 30 minutes, the tension in the audience was mounting. The room was dead silent, and the audience seemed puzzled, concerned, and annoyed. At that point, Jerry got the biggest laugh since he arrived in Germany. Many knew Jerry Lewis was in the house, but most people could not see him, especially those on the main floor. Jerry poked me with his elbow and whispered, "Watch this." In the loudest Jerry Lewis voice he could muster, he broke the silence by yelling, "I'm going to have to shave again." The audience broke into hysterical laughter and applause. Shortly afterward, the show began as the master of ceremonies introduced the first film to be screened at the festival. Jerry turned to me and said, "Rick, let's get the fuck out of here."

Borrowing a line made popular by Stan Ross, a busy comedian on early TV, I pointed at Jerry and said, "I'm with you." Jerry got my joke, and we ducked out of the theatre.

At breakfast the next morning, Jerry was in a good mood, and out of the blue, he asked me, "Did you ever cheat on your wife?"

I told him, "Nope, I never cheated on either of them."

"You mean you were married before Sheila?"

"Yes," I told Jerry, "Terri Gordon was a college graduate from New Jersey. Sheila, a college graduate from Pennsylvania, became my 'step-wife.'"

Jerry was puzzled and asked, "What's a 'step-wife'?"

"Oh, when Terri stepped out, Sheila stepped in. Sometimes things just work out for the best."

Jerry enjoyed my humor, but he became serious when he asked me if I ever speak to Terri.

"No, when it was over, it was over," I replied. "After 18 months of trying, Terri and I realized it was a very trying marriage." I reminded Jerry that I'd met Sheila a decade earlier at Brown's Hotel in the Catskills in 1963 when he arranged for me to work there. At the time, Sheila was only 14 and I was 16. I continued, "Nine years later, single once again, I called Sheila. We rekindled our romance and got married. Terri went on to marry into a family of successful funeral directors."

Jerry could not resist. "See, Ricky, Terri Gordon didn't love you; she was really in love with your tuxedo."

I laughed and asked, "Do you ever speak with Patti?"

His response to my question about his first wife seemed peculiar. "It's a shame about Patti. She's still in love with me."

During this conversation, I noticed a faraway look in Jerry's eyes. I believe he was thinking about his own breakup, but I wasn't quite sure if he was thinking about Patti or Dean.

Jerry continued, "It's great that you never cheated. I gave it up years ago." With that admission, he began lecturing on how important our spouses are. Having confronted the indiscretions of his past, he could now resist temptations. He was pleased with his choice and at peace with himself. Of course, since he was close to 80 and facing many health issues, those "temptations" might have no longer presented themselves. In any event, he seemed content.

It was Jerry who brought up the subject of his extramarital affairs, and I was curious about them. Actress Stella Stevens told me that she and Jerry had a love affair while filming *The Nutty Professor*. Jerry also told me that every time there was a break in the film production, he and Stella would disappear and have sex, and that's how he knew he was in love with her. Stella told me she ended their affair at the end of the filming because she would not continue it as long as he was still married to Patti. When their romance ended, Jerry once again returned to his wife. In the post-production of *The Nutty Professor*, Jerry Lewis selected the opening theme song as a tribute to the actress with whom he had fallen in love.

I then broached the subject of the motion picture sex symbol Marilyn Monroe. In an interview long after her death, Jerry remarked, "After having sex with Marilyn, I was crippled for a week." His joke was funny, and I asked, "Well, what about you and Marilyn Monroe?"

All he said was, "Ricky, sometimes you have to give the media what they want to hear." Jerry's response suggested he never had an affair with Marilyn Monroe, but the media had an orgasm, fantasizing about Jerry and Marilyn.

Throughout our week in Germany, Jerry and I spent lots of time together, and our conversations were fun and varied. The Golden Camera Awards and everything connected to our trip were highly successful. Beate was an excellent hostess, and it was no secret that she loved and admired Jerry Lewis. It was also no secret that I, too, admired Jerry Lewis, who was in rare form, feeling good after a long battle with illness.

Before leaving Germany, Beate Wedekind told me that Jerry would be invited back for the following year because it was customary for the previous year's Golden Camera Lifetime Achievement recipient to present the award to the next recipient. We both knew there would be negotiations and planning, but things would work out. Having been homebound for an extended period, Jerry felt great about the entire week in Berlin. His health was better; he was traveling and making appearances again.

When we returned to the United States, I called the Academy of Motion Picture Arts and Sciences to inquire about a possible Lifetime Achievement Award for Jerry Lewis, who had often joked with me that at this stage of his life, he was beginning to receive awards for being old. Since I was not a member of the Academy, I could not make an official nomination; however, actress Goldie

Hawn was a member. When I contacted her to ask if she would write a letter nominating Jerry Lewis for some type of honor, Goldie agreed to do it. Months passed, and I received a call from the Academy. The representative read Goldie Hawn's heartfelt letter to me and explained that Academy Award candidates for special tributes are chosen well in advance, sometimes years. Three years later, in 2009, the Motion Picture Academy presented Jerry Lewis with the Jean Hersholt Humanitarian Award in honor of his dedication to the Muscular Dystrophy Association and his telethons. This was a bittersweet victory for Jerry. I believe he would have been much happier and more deserving of recognition from the Motion Picture Academy for his filmmaking, but Jerry Lewis graciously accepted his Oscar.

The REAL Jerry Lewis Story

A Capitol Idea

Even the most informed Jerry Lewis fans may be unaware of his business ventures outside of show business, which is quite a common practice for celebrities. Singer Carol Richards made a name for herself in Bing Crosby movies and with skin products. Basketball star Earvin "Magic" Johnson founded an investment conglomerate. Supermodel Cindy Crawford co-founded Meaningful Beauty's anti-aging skincare line. Award-winning actor Paul Newman sold salad dressing.

On April 20, 1950, Jerry Lewis, an ardent photography fan, both of stills and motion pictures, opened a camera shop on Vine Street in Los Angeles. Amid the Hollywood-style fanfare, well-known actors and actresses and the press surrounded the store to promote the opening of Jerry Lewis' Camera Exchange. As a publicity stunt to attract shoppers, Dean Martin added to the festivities by manning a hot dog and popcorn stand on the sidewalk outside the store. Jerry expected this to be the first in a chain of camera shops, but it never panned out.

In 1969, Jerry Lewis formed the Network Cinema Corporation, devoted to developing a chain of automated mini-theatres. Jerry Lewis was "a principal and one of the key figures in the Network Cinema Corporation," reported the *Atlanta Journal*. For a small investment, franchisees could open a Jerry Lewis Cinema and operate a theatre with as few as two employees at the push of an automated button. The policy of the Jerry Lewis Cinemas was to show only G-rated movies. However, several franchise problems soon surfaced, including the malfunction of the automated button, marketing strategies, and the lack of support inexperienced owners needed on how to run a movie theatre. A main concern was that Hollywood was not producing enough family-friendly films to keep the theatres in business. Filmmakers focused on getting adult ratings to increase viewership. Even family-oriented movies might contain an adult-oriented scene to up the rating. Franchisees brought lawsuits against Jerry Lewis Cinemas, and what started as a good idea did not end well. After that, Jerry's popularity hit a slump. He wasn't young enough to come off as a crazy kid, and he wasn't old enough to be a legend.

Jerry Lewis' need for financial solvency led him into other areas of interest. In the 1980s, Dr. Michael DeBakey, Jerry's world-renowned heart surgeon, recommended that Jerry have a spinal stimulator implanted for the star's debilitating back pain. Manufactured by the Medtronic Company, the device had a handheld remote control. Jerry pushed a button and sent a signal to his spine to block the pain. Often appearing on interview shows like *Larry King Live*, Jerry lamented about his decades-long battle with back pain, a far cry from the funnyman people expected to see. Although this did not advance Jerry's popularity as the "King of Comedy," it did supplement his income. Few people knew that Jerry Lewis was working for Medtronic's Tame the Pain campaign. As their advocate, he explained how this fantastic new technology was an alternative to narcotics. He also put a little humor into his pitch by showing the viewers the remote control and saying, "Not only does it relieve my terrible back pain, but it also opens my garage door."

It was well-known that Jerry suffered back pain during much of his career. Some sources claim he was injured doing a pratfall off of a piano, while others said the condition resulted from a compilation of injuries he sustained over time. Jerry often told different stories on the same subject, especially concerning his personal life. However, on more than one occasion, Jerry said his chronic back pain was so intense that he contemplated suicide. On one of the MDA telethons, Jerry touted the virtues of this device and talked about how it could relieve millions of sufferers and reduce suicide attempts by people who have ongoing intolerable pain.

Famous people often lend their names as endorsements for private companies and large corporations for financial consideration. As a celebrity representative for Medtronic, Jerry Lewis was a paid spokesman. It is probable that when Jerry promoted Tame the Pain on the MDA telethon, Medtronic was a corporate sponsor for MDA.

Although Jerry Lewis denied ever being paid for doing the telethon, Jerry's youngest son, Joseph, described his father's MDA work during the rest of the year. In his 1980s memoirs, Joseph, who predeceased his father by eight years, wrote, "Jerry actually does his annual telethon for public exposure and for the perks. He is away from his home almost half of each year on MDA promotions. However, he will spend one day on promotion and one week on vacation. He is paid for his frequent trips to France, Spain, and Caribbean cruises.

His claims that his devotion to the cause are because of private personal reasons, are completely false." Jerry's biggest problem was that he claimed he did not receive any compensation for doing the telethons, which was likely true, but there is no reason why he would have traveled the world raising awareness and funds for the MDA at his own expense.

On September 13, 2005, I joined Jerry Lewis in Washington, D.C., where he was campaigning to raise awareness for electronic healthcare technology and lobbying the government to provide pain sufferers with financial coverage. Jerry spoke on these topics in Washington and lectured on Tame the Pain at other locations around the country. Our first stop was at Georgetown University Hospital, where Jerry discussed how this device relieved his chronic back pain without narcotics. When I entered the large room that seated at least 200 people, Jerry's presentation was already underway. Although it was advertised in large display ads in the newspapers as a free lecture, few people attended. Perhaps people did not regard Jerry Lewis as a credible medical spokesman, or maybe because the promotional materials neglected to highlight that the lecture was by Jerry Lewis in person. Jerry's discussion was serious and meaningful, but having the "King of Comedy" address the medical profession seemed like a case of miscasting.

At dinner that evening, a woman asked all of us for our government-issued photo IDs. I was surprised at this request and asked Jerry if I should give it to the stranger. Jerry said, "It's okay. Just do it." After collecting the materials, she assured us she would have them back to

The REAL Jerry Lewis Story

us in the morning. At breakfast the next day, our IDs were returned. Once cleared by security, Anthony Lewis and I were permitted to accompany Jerry Lewis to meet with Washington officials.

Throughout the morning, we met with many politicians. Jerry introduced me to members of Congress, Senators, the Surgeon General, and Medtronic executives as his manager and, a few times, as his illegitimate son. He might have been more accurate if he introduced me as his brother.

One of our meetings was with Senator John McCain (R). I found it interesting that McCain instructed his assistant to contact Senator Ted Kennedy (D) and invite him to

I took this photo during Jerry's meeting with Senator John McCain in his Senate office.

© 2024 Rick Saphire

meet Jerry Lewis; however, Kennedy was not in his office. Sitting face to face with Senator McCain, Jerry emphasized the need to provide relief to severe pain sufferers who turn to narcotics or contemplate suicide, explaining how his electronic device had saved his life.

In preparation for our 2005 meeting with one of President George Bush's cabinet members, a woman from the Medtronic Company gave Jerry and the rest of us a quick briefing about the dignitary we were about to meet. Before entering the room at the end of a long corridor, she told Jerry we were meeting with Richard Carmona, the Attorney General of the United States. The chairs in the austere room were arranged in a semi-circle, one for each of us. As the host of this meeting entered, we rose, and Jerry extended his hand to greet the cabinet member, who was dressed in an army uniform. When Jerry Lewis said, "I'm pleased to meet you, Mr. Attorney General," the man smiled at Jerry and corrected him, introducing himself as the Surgeon General. Jerry seemed unphased at the time. Once in the hallway, he exploded. Instead of laughing the matter off as it had done no harm, or reporting the incident to her superior, he verbally lashed out at the lady who had accidentally given him the misinformation. Vehemently scolding her, Jerry brought the woman to tears, and he was still boiling mad as we left the building.

With the United States Capitol Building in the background, Jerry Lewis gave a press conference outside on the steps of the Senate building, sharing the information he disseminated at the day's meetings.

The REAL Jerry Lewis Story

Medtronic scheduled a luncheon for us at an upscale restaurant, where Jerry was seated at the head of a long banquet table. In attendance were influential business executives. From the time he was a kid, Jerry Lewis was a jokester and a prankster, and where he was did not matter. He lost his first job as a soda jerk when, instead of putting a scoop of ice cream into the glass, he flipped his wrist and flung the ball of ice cream into the air.

While everyone was enjoying the meal's first course, Jerry looked at me with a telltale glint in his eye. He spread his cloth napkin in front of him, folded it into a hammock, put a pat of butter in the center, and pulled the ends taut, launching the butter into the air. Like some unguided missile, the projectile became airborne and chose its own trajectory. Instead of traveling upward toward the ceiling, it flew in an arc, landing in the nicely coifed hair of a woman in our group at the far end of the table. Seated around Jerry were the representatives from Medtronic, including the woman he had hotly confronted earlier. As we all stared in stunned silence, one lady did not see the object traveling toward her but felt something land on her head. As she grabbed for it, the butter squished into her hair. Another woman from Medtronic attempted to remove the yellowy goo, but this only served to spread it. Could Jerry have been aiming at the woman he had brought to tears earlier in the day? Justifiably upset, the woman was escorted to the restroom by her co-worker. When she returned to the banquet table several minutes later, she had a greasy new hairdo. Jerry remained seated, stoic, offering no apology or compensation. Jerry might have been the only person at the table who found this incident humorous, but it did not matter to him. Jerry was never concerned about the consequences of his impractical jokes as long as they amused him.

Due to his health, Jerry traversed the grounds in a wheelchair. As I pushed him, he suddenly asked me to stop and stand in front of him because he wanted to tell me something. This was one of the moments that defined my relationship with Jerry Lewis. He wanted to know if I heard him tearing that woman apart verbally outside the Surgeon General's office. When I told him I did, he explained, "When somebody makes a mistake that could be embarrassing to me, I get so angry that I just have to rip the person to shreds. If I don't do that, I feel like I will die." This was the first time Jerry shared feelings like this with me. Before I could respond, he continued, "You know, Ricky, this seems to get worse as I get older. After I'm finished venting, I feel so much better, but I know it isn't right." When I asked Jerry if he had ever discussed anger management with his doctors, his short answer was an insight into the disturbed thinking of someone I still admired, and he replied, "I hate psychologists. I hate psychiatrists. All they want to do is change who I am. And I don't want that to happen."

I countered, "They can't change you unless you want to be changed." What he was really saying is that he didn't want to be forced to look into the mirror.

The day after I returned to my office, I focused on the positive impact Jerry had on so many people. Having met Senator McCain, I wrote to him and thanked him for his kindness. Then I suggested he petition Congress to award Jerry Lewis with the Presidential Medal of Freedom "by virtue of his untiring work to improve the human condition not only by raising the Country's awareness of Muscular Dystrophy but also for raising more than two billion dollars to combat this killer of children and young adults."

The following year, three U.S. Senators introduced a resolution stating that Jerry Lewis was born Joseph Levitch in Newark, New Jersey. The resolution was never passed. At least Congress got his place of birth correct.

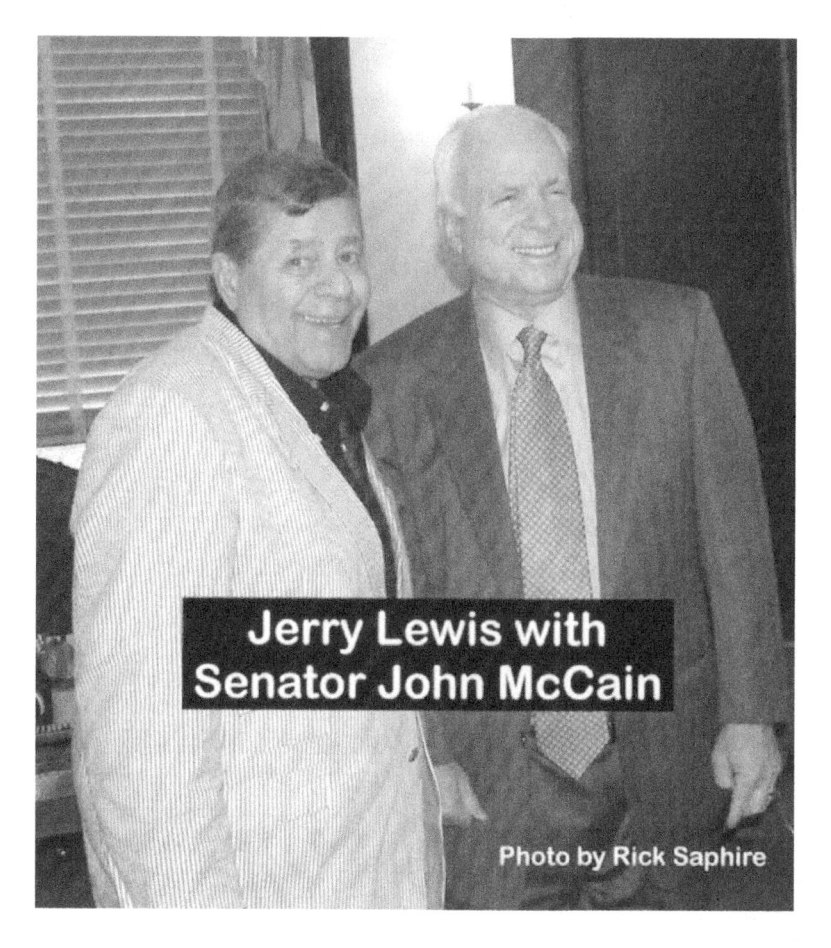

Jerry Lewis with Senator John McCain

Photo by Rick Saphire

Germany Revisited

After returning from Germany in 2005, the days that followed were filled with exciting and profitable projects. Jerry invited me to California for the MDA telethon, and I was genuinely looking forward to it. Jerry's son Gary, who was also my client, was performing in the show with his band, Gary Lewis & the Playboys. This would be the first time I attended the telethon in 46 years, and as usual, there was controversy surrounding the event. Although Jerry was displeased because the telethon was moved to the Beverly Hilton, a smaller venue than in years past, he was pleased because the MDA agreed to donate one million dollars from their proceeds to victims of Hurricane Katrina, which devastated parts of the southeastern United States in August 2005.

Plans for our return trip to Germany were in progress, but negotiations grew increasingly uncertain. As the recipient of the 2005 Golden Camera Lifetime Achievement Award, Jerry Lewis was expected to give the 2006 Award to someone he admired. The producers wanted to pay tribute to the American television interviewer Larry King, whose popular news and interview programs were broadcast in Germany via CNN International. This was a good match because Larry King and Jerry Lewis knew and respected each other.

Getting Larry King on the phone was challenging until I mentioned I was Jerry Lewis' personal manager and had an invitation for Mr. King. In a matter of moments, I found myself speaking to the familiar voice of Larry King. I explained that Jerry had been honored with the Lifetime Achievement Award the year before and that the German audience would be thrilled to see Jerry Lewis present the same award to him. Enthusiastically, Larry King accepted the booking and told me he would make arrangements to travel to Berlin. It was all set…or so we thought.

A few days later, Larry called me, sounding quite upset. "Rick," he said, "you have no idea how badly I feel about this, but I can't do Germany. The powers that be at CNN will not permit me to travel to Berlin to receive the award." There were no hard feelings, only regrets on both sides. When I informed Jerry about Larry's situation, he offered to contact CNN and create a fuss. However, he backed down when he realized it might harm Larry's position within the network.

When the German producers requested another suggestion, Jerry and I thought Stella Stevens, his co-star from *The Nutty Professor*, would be a good candidate. After all, *The Nutty Professor* was Jerry's most well-known film in the European market, and Stella was Jerry's love interest both on and off camera. Even though their romantic relationship ended long ago, their friendship endured. The officials of the Golden Camera, however, did not believe Stella Stevens had enough recognition throughout Europe to merit their award. Time was running short. Jerry's appearance on the program could be in jeopardy without a viable celebrity.

Several other names were bandied about, but the celebrities were unavailable, unreachable, or unknown in Europe. While writing to the Golden Camera officials, a name on my own letterhead caught my eye: Mickey Rooney. Mickey was undoubtedly one of the most famous movie stars in entertainment history. When I ran it by Jerry, he agreed with my choice. With a few days left before the show, Mickey confirmed the booking, and it was approved by the Golden Camera officials. However, when Sheila and I arrived at the airport for our flight to Germany, I received a call from the Golden Camera officials withdrawing Mickey Rooney's invitation to appear at their event.

Without a celebrity to receive the Lifetime Achievement Award from Jerry, our entire trip could be reduced to a limousine ride to and from Newark International Airport. I called Jerry, who was understandably upset and angry, but he quickly came up with a proposal. "Ricky," he said, "tell them when I'm introduced at the Golden Camera Awards, I will do something for the German audience they will absolutely love. Something they will long remember, and it would certainly be worth the Golden Camera Awards' inclusion of me in the program." That was all he said about his "big surprise."

When I contacted Beate Wedekind, who was unashamedly one of Jerry Lewis' biggest fans, and told her about his offer, she agreed. "We trust Jerry Lewis, and I trust you. I know we'll have a great show." Now, there was only one matter left to be resolved. Jerry Lewis had to figure out what the hell he was going to do.

While on the flight to Germany, I wondered what Jerry's thoughts and plans were. I couldn't shake off the memory of his 1963 *Jerry Lewis Live!* fiasco and felt I was in the same position my uncle Ernie Glucksman was in when he was the producer of that ABC broadcast. For nearly a year, the media and everybody else questioned Jerry about his plans for this spectacular program, and his reply was, "You'll be surprised when you see the show." Well, everybody was surprised when Jerry came up empty, and the network canceled the show. The Jerry Lewis of the 1940s through the 1960s, who could sometimes ad-lib his way through a sensational show, was no longer available. This Jerry Lewis of the 2000s hoped something in his brain would click, and all would turn out fine. Like my uncle before me, I hoped for the best.

This was a different Jerry Lewis than the year before. In 2005, Jerry was thankful to be alive and working, but this time he was arrogant, cocky, and acting very self-assured. In addition to appearing at the Golden Camera, he was invited back to the American Academy for a 2006 interview. I had been asked to assist in producing an additional television special for the German market, *An 80th Birthday Celebration for Jerry Lewis*. Our trip was set, and focusing on Jerry's birthday celebration got my mind off of my concerns about Jerry's "big surprise."

Arriving in Germany a few hours before Jerry and his entourage, my wife and I were met at the airport by our translator and assistant. From then until we arrived home a week later, we had drivers and security wherever we went. Because we were traveling with someone high profile, we could be targets of kidnappers, so we spent the week under the watchful eye of our protectors. I met Jerry and his traveling companions at the airport. I had arranged for Jerry's son, Anthony, who was a photographer, to keep a photographic diary of our trip. Anthony and I shared numerous photos and videos we took throughout the week. When I greeted Jerry, he was not in the best of moods, complaining that his ear was bothering him, likely due to the flight. Then, he asked me if I had heard any news about his heart doctor, Michael DeBakey, who had taken ill. However, I had no news to tell.

At the hotel that evening, I briefed Jerry about the upcoming discussion scheduled for the following day regarding his part of the program and inquired about his plans. Sidestepping my question, Jerry replied, "We'll discuss it with the Golden Camera producers tomorrow." His "big surprise" remained a big secret.

At breakfast, Jerry asked Sheila and me to come with him and his entourage to the hospital to have his ear examined. I told him I had to meet with the producers for *An 80th Birthday Celebration for Jerry Lewis*. By the time it ended, Jerry had left for the hospital, but our personal security guard told us Jerry wanted us to meet him there. A chauffeured car was waiting to rush us to the hospital. A different Jerry Lewis emerged from the examination room than the one I last saw. This Jerry Lewis was happy-go-lucky with a big smile on his face. He looked at me and sarcastically quipped, "Oh, I see you made it."

After we returned from the hospital, Jerry asked again if I had any news about Dr. Michael DeBakey's condition. Jerry was gradually becoming agitated and obsessively concerned about his 97-year-old heart surgeon, who was in the hospital. When I found no updates about DeBakey's health online, Jerry made a long-distance call to Houston, Texas, but received no information. Jerry looked worried. What would he do if something happened to Dr. DeBakey? This was the surgeon who had saved Jerry's life in 1983 when he performed open heart surgery on the "King of Comedy." Although Jerry seemed physically fit in 2006, he was anxious about something. I was also worried about something because each time I broached the topic of the Golden Camera, Jerry would express his concern about his heart surgeon.

Our first meeting with the Golden Camera production staff was scheduled for the day after our arrival. Jerry had yet to mention his "big surprise." That morning, we all went shopping. Despite his wife in California asking me to make sure Jerry did not buy any Louis Vuitton luggage, he ignored both of us. As a kid, I traveled with Jerry and his entourage, and we stopped at stores where Jerry purchased many suitcases. At the age of eight, I did not know what Louis Vuitton was, but as an adult, I did. In an upscale mall in Berlin, I watched as Jerry purchased a large suitcase for $5,000. Oh, did I mention we were in the Louis Vuitton Store?

During the meeting, I spoke with the producers of *An 80th Birthday Celebration for Jerry Lewis*, who asked me to get permission from Jerry to use some of his film clips. When I spoke to him about them, Jerry gazed at the floor for 30 seconds as if in a trance. Looking up at me, he said, "Tell them I'll give them whatever they want for $10,000 per 30-second clip." Knowing that Jerry had sold off the rights to much of his film library, I was uncomfortable with his demand. Nevertheless, I presented it to them. Predictably, they were unhappy with Jerry. The producers did not require the clips from Jerry as they already had the broadcast rights to his movies, dubbed in German with English subtitles, but they preferred the English versions with Jerry's voice.

When I reported back to Jerry, he looked me straight in the eye, but I did not say what I was sure he was thinking. To avoid friction among the producers, Jerry, and me, I told Jerry I knew he sold off his rights to many of these movies. He then listed the films he claimed he still owned and offered to charge for only those clips. The producers would not pay Jerry's fee, and I reminded him that they put a lot of faith in us to provide them with what they need for successful shows, adding that he was overcharging them. Jerry looked at me and said, "Ricky, if we return to Germany next year, I'll handle all of the business myself." Staring silently at Jerry, I am sure he knew what I was thinking. I left the room.

Fifteen minutes later, Jerry called and said, "Ricky, do me a favor. Phone Beate and tell her that because I love her, I will not charge for the use of my films." By instructing me to sell property Jerry did not own, he sought to make me his fence. Realizing he was putting both of us in an untenable position, he managed to finesse his way out of it. Ultimately, the producers of *An 80th Birthday Celebration for Jerry Lewis* used their German film clips.

Something was plaguing Jerry Lewis, and he did not want to discuss it. His extreme concern about his heart surgeon was a distraction from what was really bothering him. We went to the theatre where we had been a year ago for the first talk-over for the Golden Camera Awards. As we entered the auditorium, the stage crew was busy building the beautiful set for the Awards program. Jerry walked onto the stage, his eyes widening as he examined it. I got a shot of adrenaline because I knew what was on his mind. He whispered to me, "Where are the fuckin' cameras?"

When Jerry met the director and the crew members, he politely told them what he needed. Included on his list was a clip from his 1961 film, *The Errand Boy*, showing Jerry doing his "Chairman of the Board" routine. In the movie, Jerry's character is an errand boy who walks into an empty board room, fantasizing he is chairman of the board. Done to music in pantomime, the errand boy picks up a cigar. As he pretends to smoke it, he also uses it as a pointer to emphasize his gestures, laughing in silence and mugging the way he envisions the chairman would do. It was a throwback to his early days as a record mime.

A 50-foot-long runway at the foot of the stage was jutting into the audience. Jerry told the director he needed an A-B switch connected to the podium in front of him on the stage to enable him to switch back and forth from a live scene to film. Then, Jerry insisted on a live television camera with a cameraman facing him. When Jerry was reminded that the cameras were embedded in and around the theatre and not visible to the audience as in the old days, Jerry got angry and became demanding. Nobody anticipated that Jerry's "big surprise" would be this complicated. Tensions mounted quickly. Because the equipment Jerry needed was not available, there was no opportunity for a dress rehearsal. As frustration grew, tempers flared, and I suggested to Beate that we end the meeting and resume it in the morning at the hotel when everyone would be more rested and relaxed. I told her in private that there could be a language problem, although I knew that was not the case. We needed a break.

During this trip, Jerry returned to the American Academy, an organization dedicated to bringing the United States and Germany closer together culturally through the arts. Jerry's appearance at the Academy was therapeutic for him. Everyone was in good spirits, and we had some laughs during lunch. Toward the end of the meal, Jerry gave me his mischievous look as he proceeded to smooth out his cloth napkin on the table. Forming it into that familiar hammock, he placed a pat of soft butter in the center, drew the corners up to create a pouch, then snapped the ends apart, catapulting the yellow projectile upward where it hit its intended target and stuck to the freshly painted ceiling.

Author's note: I hope this book will generate readership but will NOT cause an epidemic of butter-stained ceilings in elegant restaurants.

After German film producer Eckhart Schmidt hosted Jerry's 2005 question-and-answer session at the American Academy, he returned to his home in the United States, where he not only interviewed several celebrities like singer Anna-Maria Alberghetti, co-star of *Cinderfella*, and Stella Stevens, co-star of *The Nutty Professor*, and me, but he was also able to locate and interview some of Jerry's office staff from the old days. Throughout the documentary, there were clips of Jerry speaking over the course of several years. During our 2006 trip to Germany, Eckhart proudly debuted *Jerry Lewis: The King of Comedy* (*König der Komöianten*), at the Sony Theatre in Berlin. Jerry's reaction was ambivalent because films of this type remind him of what he used to be but wasn't anymore. Leaving the theater, Jerry was sullen.

Jerry Lewis is at a preserved German WWII deportation station. Our group was given an educational tour of this sadly historic property, which brought real tears to Jerry Lewis's eyes. In Berlin, Germany, this truly was the day the clown cried.

Photograph © 2006 Rick Saphire

When we were not at the studio, our time was filled with side trips, and one was to an abandoned Nazi deportation station that Jerry and my wife wanted to see. In a quiet, suburban middle-class neighborhood, our driver made a turn onto a short, dead-end road that led to a deportation railroad station where thousands upon thousands of Jews, Italians, and other ethnicities had been forced to board the trains that carried them to the death camps. Everybody was extremely serious. Jerry was emotional as non-theatrical tears rolled down his cheek. This was the day the clown really cried.

Our next Golden Camera production staff meeting was off-site and went exceptionally well. Jerry calmly explained precisely what he had in mind, and everybody fully understood what was happening. The producer assured Jerry that the staff would do their best to find a working classic TV camera to use for Jerry's segment. Everything ran smoothly until we assembled back at the theatre for a run-through of Jerry's segment.

Per Jerry's instructions, a tripod-mounted TV camera on the runway was aimed toward the pedestal where he stood to perform his Chairman of the Board bit. Two large buttons were attached to the desktop of this podium, one on the left and one on the right. While the director ran the movie clip, Jerry tried out the buttons. When they did not operate smoothly, Jerry lost his temper. Slamming his hand down on the podium, both buttons crashed to the floor. Jerry was fired up, and this could have been the rehearsal from hell. However, this time, the staff understood that Jerry's outbursts were part of his make-up, and they were professional, calm, and solicitous. We returned to the hotel confident that any problem would be rectified by showtime.

Back at his hotel suite, Jerry, who was agitated, worried that his blood pressure was high. I suggested Jerry use a blood pressure cuff to check it out. Although Jerry only needed one, he instructed his personal assistant to order three of them. Nervously, Jerry inquired about Dr. DeBakey. "If I find out Michael is in very serious condition, I'll have to leave Berlin immediately," he announced. "I have to be at his side. Should he be in critical condition, and if he died, I have to be there." I listened to his panic escalate and wondered what Jerry thought he could do for this highly respected 97-year-old physician.

When the monitors arrived, I sat on the bed beside Jerry and checked his blood pressure. It was high-normal. I then asked Jerry what was really going on and why he was so edgy. "Something is happening to me, Ricky," Jerry said, "and it's happening more and more often as I'm getting older." Jerry added, "I'm scared to death to do the Golden Camera tonight. I've been scared since we got here. I have terrible stage fright."

I reminded Jerry that the show was being handled by consummate professionals and assured him he would be fine. "The people in the audience love you, Jerry. You just have to be charming to please the crowd."

Before leaving for the Golden Camera Awards, my wife was asked if she would be Jerry Lewis' escort for the program. As soon as she agreed, Sheila got the Hollywood treatment and was escorted to the performers' dressing area, where Lancôme did her hair and make-up. That evening, we were driven to the Awards ceremony for the live broadcast in a luxurious Mercedes-Maybach. When we exited the limousine, Jerry, Sheila, and I walked the red carpet, surrounded by the media and scores of photographers. The night was electric.

Once inside the theatre, Jerry and Sheila were seated in the front row seat while Jerry awaited his introduction. Jerry was called to the stage, and his Chairman of the Board routine went as planned, although many in the audience missed what was happening. Just like in the old days, the TV camera in front of Jerry blocked the audience's view of the legendary comedian. Because Jerry switched back and forth between the film clip and his live performance, the best view was on monitors around the theater. It was all quite entertaining, and to his credit, he predictably overcame his stage fright once he assumed the role of comedian Jerry Lewis.

Jerry's appearance on the televised special celebrating his upcoming 80th birthday wrapped up his visit to Germany. The charming host of this program was Michael Mittermeier, a German-born comedian who idolized Jerry Lewis and occasionally imitated him in his comedy routine. The format of this show was a conversation between these two comedy stars from different countries and generations, so no formal rehearsal was needed. A huge video screen at the back of the stage projected images of the speakers and clips highlighting Jerry Lewis' career. Although Jerry did not mention the invisible television cameras this time, he did complain during the walk-through that the volume needed to be turned up. Jerry wore a hearing aid with sound amplification but not modification. In preparation for one of Jerry's signature pantomime routines, the director played the music to Leroy Anderson's "Typewriter" song. Jerry repeatedly complained that the volume had to be increased. Apparently, Jerry was the only person who could not hear the music, and I said, "Jerry, I believe the music is up pretty loud."

He was not happy with my assessment and sneered, "Ricky, can you hear that music?" When I answered him with a "yes," he answered me in two words, "Fuck you." After that charming bit of byplay, Jerry shouted at an invisible person in the control booth to add more treble to the music. Jerry still could not hear and demanded more treble. When people get older, their eardrums often lose a degree of tension and elasticity. People with Jerry's type of hearing loss may have trouble hearing treble but less trouble hearing base.

I entered the control booth and asked the technician to lower the treble and add more bass. Reluctantly, he violated Jerry's directive and did as I asked. When I got downstairs, the music played again. Jerry listened, smiled, and looked up toward the booth. Thinking the technician had followed his instructions, Jerry crowed, "Now you got it right. I can hear it." He looked at me, satisfied he had won his point.

Before the broadcast, Jerry was relaxed and in a good mood, talking about how much he liked Michael Mittermeier. That was a relief because, throughout his career, Jerry Lewis had little tolerance for those who impersonated him. During his conversation with Michael, Jerry, who was in rare form, prevaricated as he recalled his start in show business. In this version, Jerry retold the old story about singing "Brother, Can You Spare a Dime?" in 1931 when he was five years old, which was

Sheila Saphire and Jerry Lewis enjoying their ride in the Maybach Limousine in Berlin, Germany

quite a feat since the song was not written until 1932. Speaking of feet, he also claimed his foot accidentally hit a footlight, which exploded. In this description, the burst bulb jolted him backward onto the ground, and he had his first fall and his first laugh.

Jerry Lewis first performed the "Typewriter" routine on *The Colgate Comedy Hour* in the early 1950s. Set to Leroy Anderson's light orchestral music, which uses the sounds of an actual typewriter, Jerry pretended to be typing a letter, mugging while hitting the carriage return and gesturing in synchronization to the song. It was a throwback to Jerry's early days as a record mime and was warmly received; however, the audience's reaction was less than Jerry expected.

On the way back to our hotel in the limousine, Jerry asked me why I thought the "Typewriter" bit fell flat. "Jerry," I explained, "nobody in the audience under 45 has likely ever used a typewriter. Although it was a funny routine, nobody knew what you were doing." I told him that it might have been better received had he explained that all offices had typewriters before computers and laser printers, and here's what it looked like when somebody was typing. "A description like that," I added, "could have given the audience a better understanding of what they were about to see." Jerry, who resisted changing with the times, stared at me in silence.

If I hadn't cared so much about my famous client, if he hadn't been such an important part of my childhood, growing up, family, and career, I would have agreed with everything Jerry said and did, and I would have simply taken my money to the bank. If I ignored his faults and kept my suggestions to myself, I would not have been faithful to myself or to someone I admired with such incredible talents.

Our week in Germany seemed like a lifetime filled with entertainment, intrigue, sadness, joy, success, and anxiety. Not only did we all survive the week, but so did Dr. Michael DeBakey, who lived another three years. Learning about Jerry's stage fright helped me to form a better understanding of this complex man. Although his outbursts and fits of anger were certainly unwelcome, I understood why Jerry had built a reputation during his career as a volatile man who would find almost any excuse to walk out on a booking or be so uncooperative that the booking would walk out on him. The "King of Comedy" spent much of his life being scared.

We wrapped up our week

Sheila Saphir
Jerry shoves her away, claiming that he IS happy! More of the REAL Jerry Lewis? Saphire with Jerry Lewis who had been a family friend of the Saphires for decades.

together in Jerry's hotel suite with everyone in our group laughing, shaking hands, and talking about our next adventure in the USA. My wife, Sheila, was the last to bid

Jerry a fond farewell. Just as Dorothy from *The Wizard of Oz* embraced the scarecrow in her last few moments before clicking her heels to return home, Sheila and Jerry gave each other a warm hug and a kiss on the cheek.

As their embrace ended, Sheila looked at Jerry and said, "Thank you for a wonderful week. Be happy." Instantly, Jerry Lewis put his hands on Sheila's shoulders and shoved her away from him. As she stepped backward to maintain her balance, Jerry glared at her and shouted, "What do you mean? I AM happy!"

Bits & Pieces

This is a collection of intriguing tales, each unique in its own way. While captivating, these stories are not lengthy enough to fill entire chapters, so here are the bits and pieces.

Double Standards

In 1941, Jerry Lewis physically assaulted his high school principal for calling him a "Jew." In a 1962 network television interview, Jerry made a controversial joke about the name of a 15-year-old Jewish performer to an audience of over 30 million viewers. Jerry's comment revealed a double standard as he quipped, "With a name like Rick Norman, You know, you could very easily be a 'goy' from Port Chester." [The word "goy" was used as a derogatory term meaning non-Jew.] It was clear Jerry did not have an issue with ethnic slurs as long as he was not the target. I can confirm this because I was the 15-year-old Jewish kid, Jerry's protégé, who appeared on *The Tonight Show* as his guest. This time, in the name of humor, I was on the receiving end when he ridiculed my initial stage name, Rick Norman.

Mouseketeer Sharon Baird and the Driving Force

Before becoming one of the original Mouseketeers on Walt Disney's popular 1955 *Mickey Mouse Club*, my friend Sharon Baird appeared as a singer and dancer on *The Colgate Comedy Hour* with Eddie Cantor. Sharon performed a tap dance solo, showcasing her talents in a skit with Cantor and actor Robert Clary, best known for his role as Corporal Louis LeBeau on TV's *Hogan's Heroes*. Sharon's theatrical resumé would not be complete without mentioning that she was also an actress and dance instructor. Diminutive and animated, Sharon worked in children's programming as a "live" puppet for many years.

Although uncredited, 12-year-old Sharon Baird performed a memorable song-and-dance routine with Dean Martin in a scene from Paramount's romantic musical comedy film *Artists and Models*, starring Martin & Lewis. As a child, Sharon followed instructions, but she soon realized that comedians often do not. On the first take, Dean's song and dance routine with her was going well. Joined by a number of other child performers, Dean and Sharon musically traversed the New York street constructed for this scene. The take was abruptly interrupted when Jerry Lewis purposely whizzed passed the cameras in his own car. Jerry's behavior surprised the young Sharon Baird. However, this was only one of many stunts Jerry pulled that interfered with Dean Martin's scenes.

Sharon shared memories about the studio commissary, where the actors would go for lunch. The performers appearing in Artists and Models had to remain in their costumes, even during their breaks and were told to keep their costumes clean. This was a particularly challenging task because Jerry Lewis was seated at a table nearby, flinging hunks of red Jell-O at people. Now, that was Jerry being Jerry, and Sharon thought he was crazy.

Oh, the humanity!

Jerry Lewis shared many stories with me over the 60 years I knew him. While some of his stories seemed far-fetched, this particular tale was one of the most plausible and captivating. On May 6, 1937, the largest dirigible ever to fly was heading majestically from Frankfurt, Germany, on its 11th voyage to the USA. Radio announcer Herb Morrison was on hand that day to report his description of the arrival of the Zeppelin Hindenburg for broadcast later. Nobody knew that Morrison's recorded description would become one of the most famous news broadcasts of all time. His tearful exclamation, "Oh, the humanity..." brought him instant fame. But Herb Morrison was not the only person at Lakehurst that afternoon known for his deep concern for the human condition.

Early that morning, 11-year-old Jerome Levitch and his mother Rae traveled from their home in northern New Jersey to the naval base at Lakehurst in central New Jersey to witness the arrival of the Hindenburg. Like many kids of that era, Jerry was fascinated by airplanes, dirigibles, and rocket ships. This trip was a belated birthday gift from his parents, and his mother was fulfilling her son's dream.

Standing in the visitors' area, young Jerome watched the huge ship drift close to the mooring mast. But his fascination quickly turned to terror as the Hindenburg burst into flames. Clutching his mother's hand, Jerome witnessed passengers jumping from the ship in an attempt to save their own lives. At the same time, he could feel the heat of the burning hydrogen gas on his face, even though he was quite a distance away from the airship.

Just nine years after the tragic Hindenburg disaster, a young Jerome Levitch catapulted to fame. Throughout his illustrious 70-year career, he helped to raise an impressive two billion dollars to find a cure for neuromuscular diseases. Although he never graduated high school, he is globally recognized as "the nutty professor." Yes, the same Jerome Levitch, who learned the fragility of life that fateful day in Lakehurst, New Jersey, grew up to be a Nobel nominee, filmmaker, Oscar and Emmy recipient, and beloved entertainer, Jerry Lewis.

On Tour with Cousin Brucie

Rick Saphire with everyone's Cousin Brucie through the years

It used to be common for movie stars to make personal appearances at theaters in order to promote their motion pictures. Jerry Lewis' fanbase grew significantly thanks to these appearances, which contributed to his success in the film industry. Jerry would go on a tour, stopping to perform for 15 to 20 minutes with a small musical ensemble. There would also be a master of ceremonies, who was often a local media celebrity, a few personal assistants, and an excessive amount of luggage. During his short program, he might sing, dance, do comedy vignettes, or entertain with a throwback to his original record mime act, mugging and lip-syncing in costume to an operatic recording like "Figaro." Before the applause died down and the Jerry Lewis movie flashed on the big screen, the entire cast and crew were already on the bus on their way to the next venue.

In 1963, Bruce Morrow, the legendary radio rock 'n' roll disc jockey known as Cousin Brucie on 77-WABC AM Radio, was on a one-day bus tour with Jerry Lewis, who was promoting his latest film *The Nutty Professor*. When they first met, Jerry was cordial to Bruce but standoffish. Jerry boarded the bus and took a seat near the front as if he wanted to control how the driver was driving.

Some of the appearances took place on the stage inside the theatre while others were held outside on a flatbed truck that served as a makeshift stage. Seeing Bruce Morrow in person was a major draw, attracting large crowds. Paramount bought time on WABC radio to advertise the local showings of The Nutty Professor and hired Bruce to be the genial host and warm up the crowd. Wherever they performed, inside or out, it was always jam-packed. Bruce, who would introduce Jerry, noticed that Jerry never looked happy until he got to the stage. As soon as he was within the eye of the audience, a transformation occurred, and he became Jerry Lewis, the clown. He smiled, his body language changed, and he made funny faces and silly sounds. There he was, "Jerry Lewis."

This change surprised Cousin Brucie, who realized that this was not the same man whose movies he had enjoyed so much. "Where was Jerry Lewis?" Bruce wondered. "This wasn't the guy that I knew." As soon as Jerry stepped off the stage, away from the public eye, he transformed back into that sullen, irritable person. Everything was running smoothly. The accommodating crew efficiently set up for the show and dismantled it afterward, all right on schedule, yet Jerry was always cross at someone.

Throughout his career, Bruce studied entertainers and observed that Jerry Lewis was two completely different people. There were 10 to 12 stops that day, and each time, the pattern was the same. After a successful appearance, Jerry consistently sought out someone to reprimand. Bruce, who was a veteran of many personal and promotional appearances, remarked, "I know the business, and there was never anything wrong. Jerry just wanted to be angry and felt he had to yell at somebody."

Cousin Brucie shared an interesting, albeit somewhat disturbing, story about an incident he witnessed while on this tour with Jerry Lewis. They would make a stop and then head to their next appearance. While on the way to a theater in Newark, New Jersey, Bruce noticed Jerry gazing out of the window and could tell Jerry was irritated and depressed. All of a sudden, Jerry shouted, "Pull over! Pull over!" When the bus driver stopped at the curb, Jerry got off the bus alone, unaccompanied by a security guard or companion, and approached a man standing on the sidewalk. From his window, Bruce watched as Jerry walked up to this unhappy, disheveled man. Jerry placed his arms on the man's shoulders as if to comfort him. After speaking with the stranger for a while, Jerry reached into his pocket and pulled out a substantial wad of money, which he gave to the man. Jerry said a few words to him, then gently placed both hands on his shoulders at arm's length before making his way back to the bus. As Jerry settled into his seat, he openly cried, tears streaming down his face. Then, Jerry motioned to the driver to go. Everyone watched intently as the scene unfolded, but no one dared to speak and sat in stunned silence.

What really took place between Jerry and the stranger that day is a mystery. Bruce Morrow encountered various facets of Jerry Lewis in that single day. He observed the versatile entertainer captivating both children and adults with his live performance. He also witnessed a darker side of Jerry Lewis on the bus: an unhappy, irritable, angry man, which made Bruce feel sad and disheartened. When Jerry got off the bus to interact with the man on the street, was he being empathetic and tender, or was Jerry Lewis making a purchase from a vendor?

Walking and Stalking

In the early 1960s, I spent much of my time in New York City, appearing on local TV shows and visiting agents' offices. On this particular day, I had gone to Manhattan to do a morning children's TV show. It was early in the summer, and my friends Billy Imperial and Valerie Benson came with me. After lunch at the famous Stage Deli, we walked over to Joe Franklin's TV show. I always stopped in to see my friend Joe who was kind enough to have me as his on-air guest at least four times a year. As I approached the set, I saw Joe with…guess who? I had no idea Jerry Lewis would be there. It had not been a full year since Jerry slighted me at Brown's Hotel, and I had no desire to talk to him. When *The Joe Franklin Show* was over, I chatted with Joe as Jerry watched from a distance. Jerry must have thought I planned this visit to see him because he looked at me and walked by in silence.

En route to our next stop, the Little Theatre Off Times Square, where *The Merv Griffin Show* was being broadcast, we saw the media with their notepads in hand gathered in front of the Mayor's office. Valerie, Billy, and I started up the steps of Gracie Mansion to investigate the action. When we got to the top of the steps, we turned around and guess who was right behind us. It was Jerry Lewis and his entourage. Hey, who was stalking whom? As Jerry and his group went into the building, my small group and I retreated and went about our business. We were off to *The Merv Griffin Show*.

Because I was still in my tuxedo, looking far more important than I was, and I knew Pops the Doorman, my friends and I got front-row seats for the Griffin afternoon taping. As the show began, Arthur Treacher, the announcer, said, "…and Merv's special guest, Jerry Lewis." Well, you could have knocked me over with a feather. This Broadway theatre, which had been converted into a TV studio, was small and intimate. Our seats were on the same level as the stage and cameras. When Jerry noticed me in the audience, he seemed stunned. He had just seen me at the *Joe Franklin* studio, at City Hall, and here I was in the front row at the *Griffin Show*. Jerry Lewis must have thought I was stalking him. Each time Jerry would do or say something funny, he would look directly at me. If he was funny, I would laugh, and if he wasn't, I didn't.

As part of his bit on the show, Jerry grabbed a handheld microphone and came into the audience. Passing directly in front of Valerie, Billy, and me, he avoided making eye contact with any of us. As he made his way back to the stage, he stopped directly in front of me, took the mike away from his mouth, got real close, glanced at my entourage, and whispered in my ear, "What is this? The fuckin' Nuremberg jury?"

On Holiday

In 2021, *Vanity Fair* magazine published a report that portended to be a salacious exposé of Jerry Lewis, who, if you believe the headlines, sexually abused some of his female co-stars. Actress Hope Holiday gave a dramatic account of what happened behind closed doors in Jerry's dressing room in 1961 during the filming of *The Ladies Man*. Jerry Lewis was notorious for his predictably unpredictable mood swings, explosive temper, and erratic behavior, and he liked to be in control. As a top money-maker for Paramount, he reveled in using his position to exercise power over others.

The REAL Jerry Lewis Story

Despite his personal flaws, some people in the movie industry consider Jerry Lewis an exceptional motion picture director; however, he only directed Jerry Lewis films. During a casual conversation, Jerry surprised me by revealing director Otto Preminger was his role model and hero. Due to Preminger's tough and dictatorial style, he earned the nickname "Otto the Terrible."

Produced by Preminger, the 1953 classic American film noir *Angel Face* stars Jean Simmons and Robert Mitchum. When Howard Hughes, who owned Simmons' contract, was told by her husband, "Keep your hands off of my wife," Hughes instructed Preminger to punish her. In a revised script, Mitchum's character had to slap Jean Simmons' character in the face. Preminger insisted on reshooting the scene many times, each time with increased intensity and emotion, until Jean Simmons' face was sore, and she was in tears. Reportedly fed up with this mistreatment, Mitchum struck Preminger in the face and asked if that's how he wanted it.

There was a scene in *The Ladies Man* in which Hope had to "act" as if she hated Herbert H. Heebert, Jerry's character. Because Jerry was a family friend, I believe he felt it would be challenging for Hope's character to angrily scream and violently slap him in the face, which may explain why Jerry asked her to meet him in his dressing room to discuss the part where she had to "beat him up."

Representing former child actors such as Hayley Mills, Beverly Washburn, Spanky McFarland, Cathy Garver, Jerry Mathers, Darla Hood, and others, I asked what strategies directors might use to motivate a child to act in a scene. While some children instinctively understand their roles, others need inspiration, and directors could be harsh. For instance, to get a child to cry, a director might make up a story and tell the child that her dog was hit by a car, but before heading home, she had to shoot the scene. The tears would flow as the director wanted. It was a mean means to an end.

Once alone with Hope, Jerry apparently found himself in an awkward situation. He wanted to anger her so that she could hate him enough to play the scene convincingly, but at the same time, he wanted to seduce her. When she rejected his sexual advances, Jerry took matters into his own hands. His behavior was inappropriate and, like Preminger, misogynistic and offensive.

Dynamic layers complicated this situation because Jerry was not only an actor playing opposite Hope but also the film's director. As the director, he wanted Hope's character to hate Herbert Heebert enough so that when the audience viewed the scene, they could feel the venom seeping out of her pores, and when she slapped him in the face, they could feel the sting in the third balcony.

Ms. Holiday, who was about 30 years old at the time the incident occurred, and in her early 90s at the time of her exposé, claimed that Jerry locked the door and complimented her on her figure, focusing on her bust line and legs. Then, in her words, he began talking sexually. At some point, he exposed himself to her and began masturbating. Ms. Holiday did not discuss how this uncomfortable meeting with Jerry Lewis ended. Moreover, she went on to describe a totally unrelated encounter she had with another man, a nameless predator, who entered her home and raped her. Why this totally unrelated story was included in a piece about Jerry Lewis is unfair.

If what happened between Jerry and Hope in his dressing room that day was exactly as she described it, then Jerry was certainly guilty of highly reprehensible behavior. Shame on Jerry Lewis. If Hope Holiday waited 60 years to make Jerry's behavior known to others, then shame on her for not reporting it earlier to protect other actresses from being similar victims. Although Jerry was known for his womanizing ways, shamelessly betraying his wife to satisfy his ego and sexual desires, I do not recall hearing any stories of him forcing his intentions on women.

I am aware that during the 1950s, the actress we know as Hope Holiday was originally known as Hope Zee. She began her career as a chorus girl turned stage singer. By the time she appeared in The Ladies Man with Jerry Lewis, she was already an experienced stage performer.

The day after Hope Holiday's disconcerting encounter with Jerry in his dressing room, she was in a pivotal scene that required her to slap him in the face several times. Because Hope had known Jerry Lewis since she was 13 and considered him a family friend, it might have been challenging for her to act violently toward someone she had admired for so long. Is it possible that Jerry Lewis, following Otto Preminger's example, used an inappropriate technique to provoke a strong emotion in hopes that she would deliver a believable, angry slap during the scene? It is a possibility I wouldn't discount.

In the words of Peter Falk from TV's *Columbo*, "Oh, just one more thing." In December of 1960, during the filming of *The Ladies Man*, Sidney Skolsky, a Los Angeles columnist, quoted Hope Holiday: "She can't understand why Jerry Lewis tells her she's a boy."

Go figure!

Planning Ahead?

The day NBC pulled a fast one on me and Jerry Lewis

You won't believe what happened in 2007 when I got a call from the National Broadcasting Company about Jerry Lewis. When they told me they wanted to interview me about him for the *Today* program, I thought, "Wow, I'm moving up in the world." Plus, they wanted to record the interview at my place. I mean, I was ready to strut through the doors at 30 Rockefeller Plaza, but instead, they were coming to me.

I got the green light from Jerry himself, and on the day of the recording, the NBC crew showed up at my doorstep ready to roll. They set up the camera, the lights, and my microphone, and then they phoned the interview director, who called the shots from his office in New York City.

Because I was led to believe my spot would be aired the next week, I watched the show nonstop for five days. When I did not see my interview, I called the *Today* office for some answers. It was then that I learned I was duped. They were only interviewing me for an "obit piece" on Jerry Lewis. Can you believe it? In plain English, they tricked me into making a recording that was only to be used in the event of Jerry's death. I had no idea. Imagine how stupid I would have looked, laughing and joking about my pal Jerry Lewis, while the *Today* show journalists sat in front of the nation crying and moaning about his death.

In the end, my interview was never aired, and Jerry went on to live an additional 10 years until he passed away on August 20, 2017, at the age of 91.

Epilog: Jerry Lewis in a Nutshell

After all that has been written in these many pages, the question remains: "Who is the REAL Jerry Lewis?

Based on my personal interactions with Jerry Lewis, ranging from my early childhood throughout the years I represented him theatrically, I wondered, "Is there a REAL Jerry Lewis?" That was the man's lifelong dilemma. When on stage or in the movies, being the crazy, lovable "kid" wreaking havoc with the world at large, he was acting. When he turned on the serious mode while discussing how he essentially "taught" Dean Martin how to be a good straight man or how he invented the video assist, he was acting. When he wrote letters to his wife Patti in the 1950s about how much he loved her, fearing that if she left him, he would die, he was acting. In the 1960s, when he began lamenting about wanting a daughter because he only had sons, he was acting. Jerry Lewis was always acting.

Jerry Lewis circa 1944

There was only one time I saw Jerry being real...being himself. We were together in Berlin, Germany, on a personal appearance tour. As usual, Jerry wanted to go shopping, so our hosts took us to a local mall where we all spent a few hours. Jerry and I were sitting in a couple of comfortable chairs at the rear of a store when a woman came along pushing a baby stroller. The woman parked the infant's stroller in front of Jerry and me while she looked at a nearby display. She obviously had no idea who Jerry Lewis was, and the infant in the stroller didn't know what day it was.

Jerry stared at the baby, who was about six months old. The child blankly stared back into Jerry's eyes. Under his breath, Jerry asked the baby, "Do you know who I am?" In those few words, I heard a man in search of his soul asking an infant to assure him that he was somebody.

This time, Jerome Levitch was not acting. This was the REAL Jerry Lewis.

© 2024 Rick Saphire

Acknowledgments

Staff
Author and President of York Publications: Rick Saphire
Co-Author and Editor-in-Chief: Sheila Saphire, M.Ed.
Editor and Copywriter: Linda M. Pierce
Editor: Wendy Klarman Weiss
Proofreader: Joyce Ehrlich Avrach
Legal Advisor: Donald D. Davis, Esq.
Media Spokesperson: Jennifer Lauren Wilson

Consultants
Joellyn L. Ross, Ph.D., Psychologist in Cherry Hill, New Jersey
Daniel M. Rosenberg, Esq., Attorney at Law in Mt. Holly, New Jersey

Special Thanks
I am grateful to my sister, Joan Saphire Ruback Tushinsky, for her unwavering support. Her recollections about her friendship with Jerry and Patti Lewis contributed to the content and accuracy of this book.

Thank you, Gary and Donna Lewis, for always being there for me. Your sound advice, candid stories, and good humor kept me focused and smiling.

Many thanks to François Minoret and his son Jerry for openly sharing their emotional experiences and personal observations, greatly enriching the readers' experience.

© 2024 Rick Saphire

I want to express my sincere gratitude to Kimberlee Marshall Lewis Degen, the former wife of Jerry Lewis' youngest son, Joseph, for her significant contributions and for sharing Joseph's memoirs. I also want to express my gratitude to her sons, Bobby and Dan, Jerry Lewis' grandsons, for sharing their lives with me. Their input has been incredibly valuable.

Last but not least, I am forever thankful for my caring, wise, and talented uncle and mentor, Ernest D. Glucksman, without whom this book would never have been written.

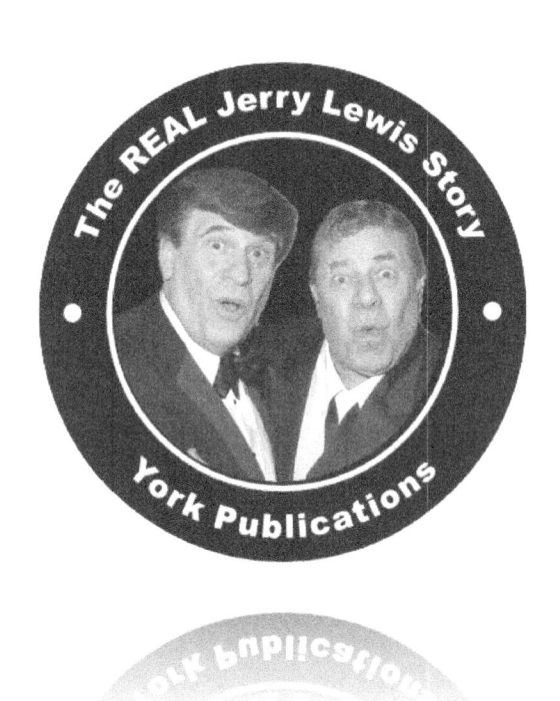